O 1—

D0976254

French
Vocabulary

HANDBOOK

Kate Dobson

French Vocabulary Handbook

The Author:
Kate Dobson is an experienced teacher at primary school, high school and adult level.

The Series Editor:
Christopher Wightwick is a former UK representative on the Council of Europe Modern Languages Project and principal Inspector of Modern Languages for England.

Other titles in the Berlitz Language Handbook Series:

French Grammar Handbook
German Grammar Handbook
Spanish Grammar Handbook
Italian Grammar Handbook
French Verb Handbook
German Verb Handbook
Spanish Verb Handbook
Italian Verb Handbook

German Vocabulary Handbook
Spanish Vocabulary Handbook
Italian Vocabulary Handbook

Published by Berlitz Publishing Co., Ltd.,
Peterley Road, Oxford OX4 2TX

1st printing 1994

Printed in England by Clays Ltd, St Ives plc

CONTENTS

C   Appendices

D   Subject index

How to use this Handbook

This Handbook is a carefully ordered work of reference covering all areas of French vocabulary and phrasing. It is based on the thesaurus structure of the Council of Europe's Threshold Level, expanded to include other major topics, especially in the fields of business, information technology and education. Unlike a dictionary, it brings together words and phrases in related groups. It also illustrates their usage with contextualized example sentences, often in dialogue form. This enables learners and users of the language to:

• refresh and expand their general knowledge of vocabulary;
• revise systematically for public examinations, using the word-groups to test their knowledge from French to English and *vice versa*;
• extend their knowledge of authentically French ways of saying things by studying the example sentences;
• support their speaking and writing on a given topic, when the logical arrangement of the sections will often prompt new ideas as well as supplying the means of expressing them.

THE STRUCTURE OF THE HANDBOOK

After the List of Contents, the Handbook is divided into four parts:

A   Introduction: The vocabulary of the French language

A concise account of the ways in which French creates compound words and phrases in order to express more complex ideas, together with a brief survey of nouns, adjectives and verbs in French. (For a more extensive treatment of these topics, see the *Berlitz French Grammar Handbook*.)

B   The Topic Vocabularies

96 Vocabularies, grouped under 27 major areas of experience. Many Vocabularies are divided into a number of sections, so that words and phrases are gathered together into closely related groups. Almost all sections contain example sentences showing the vocabulary in use. Wherever it makes sense to do so, these sentences are linked together to form short narratives or dialogues which help to fix them in the memory.

In some Vocabularies the lists of words and phrases are both extensive and more independent of context, so that the role of the example sentences is reduced.

C The Appendices

Lists of specific terms such as the names of countries or musical instruments. These would simply clutter up the main Vocabularies, but they are linked to them by clear cross-references.

D The Subject Index

An alphabetical index of topics and themes, enabling you to locate quickly the area you are interested in.

LOCATING THE RIGHT SECTION

The Handbook can be approached in two main ways.

• If you are not sure which topic will be best suited to your needs, start with the *List of Contents* on page iii. This will give you a general picture of the areas covered. You can then browse through the sections until you find the one you want.

• Alternatively, if you have a specific topic in mind, look it up in the *Subject Index* at the end of the book. This will take you directly to the relevant Vocabulary or Appendix. To help you find what you are looking for, topics are often listed more than once, under different headings. Within most sections there are cross-references to other, related areas.

A
INTRODUCTION

The vocabulary of the French language

Conventions used in this Handbook

The vocabulary of the French language

1 Similar features of French and English

Within the very large group of Indo-European languages, French and English could be regarded as second cousins. Although some of the structures of French are different from English patterns, because of the overriding influence of its Latin origin, a very large number of individual words are easily recognizable from the one language to the other.

1a Related words

The Norman Conquest brought a number of Norman French words into English, and the Renaissance and the Modern Age have created a large number of scientific, abstract and technical words common to many European languages. In addition, culinary and artistic terms have been borrowed from French into English. Some English words have been borrowed, somewhat uncomfortably, into French. It is useful for the learner of French to identify this common ground and exploit it. Some words are spelled as in English, some are not quite the same, and of course, adjectives and verbs undergo pronunciation and spelling changes in use.

These are some examples – many more could be cited.

English	*French*
Nouns	
Television; telephone;	**Télévision; téléphone;**
feast, beast, forest; tempest; crest	**fête; bête; forêt; tempête; crête**

[The circumflex accent in French often shows that an 's' has been lost along the way.]

liberty; beauty; quality; variety	**liberté; beauté; qualité; varieté**
doctor; professor; actor	**docteur; professeur; acteur**
interpreter; minister	**interprète; ministre**
racism; communism; Buddhism	**racisme; communisme; Bouddisme**
mystery; ministry	**mystère; ministère**
glory; victory; memory	**gloire; victoire; mémoire**
harmony; (political) party	**harmonie; parti (politique)**
movement; government	**mouvement; gouvernement**
soufflé; flambé; café	**soufflé; flambé; café**

Adjectives

rare; imprudent	**rare; imprudent**
dramatic; comic (adj); domestic	**dramatique; comique; domestique**
socialist; racist;	**socialiste; raciste**
realistic; simplistic	**réaliste; simpliste**
social; national;	**social; national ;**
official; individual	**officiel; individuel**
possible; impossible	**possible; impossible**
capable; probable	**capable; probable**
popular; military	**populaire; militaire**
glorious; precious; pretentious	**glorieux; précieux; prétentieux**

Verbs

to respect; to interpret; to cede	**respecter; interpréter; céder**
to contemplate; to cultivate	**contempler; cultiver**
to film; to sponsor	**filmer; sponsoriser**

1b   False friends

The learner also needs to be aware that there exist a number of words which look similar but have different meanings. These are often called 'false friends' or **faux-amis**.

French	*English*
actuel	contemporary/of the present time
assister (à)	to attend, be present at
contrôler	to check, test
une fabrique	factory
une intoxication	poisoning
large	wide
la métropole	France (as opposed to its overseas territories)
malicieux	mischievous
sensible	sensitive
un stage	short course, period of training
un store	(window)blind

There are also words which have the meaning you anticipate, but which, in certain contexts, may have a different sense:

une action	action; also a share (finance)
une chaîne	chain; also TV channel
l'édition	edition; also publishing
un parent	parent; also any relative
ignorer	to ignore; also (originally) not to know

1c   Recent borrowings from English

Finally, we should mention the many words in French which have been borrowed from English, and still persist despite the attempts of *Académiciens* and others to eradicate them.

le bulldozer, le bungalow, le weekend, le meeting, le parking, le living (living room), **le shopping, le jogging, le basket** (training shoe), **le sweat-shirt** (often abbreviated to **le sweat**), **le hit-parade, le hamburger, la star** (in entertainment), **le hovercraft, le car-ferry**

and many more!

For a good number of such words, a French equivalent exists, but fails to suppress the use of the English word. Hence the term 'Franglais', to describe these hybrids.

2   Using the language correctly: a few notes on French structures

2a   Nouns

(i)   Gender

All nouns in French are masculine or feminine in gender. The gender needs to be learnt with the word itself, as it affects the use of articles, adjectives, pronouns and some verb forms.

It is not generally possible to predict the gender of a noun from its meaning – if in doubt, check in a dictionary. However:

• Most nouns for male persons are masculine, female persons are feminine.

le père; le frère;   la mère; la soeur;

Confusion arises where women exercise professions where previously only men were found.

un docteur; un ministre; un ingénieur; un professeur (all masculine words, even if applied to women)

Nowadays forms such as **une professeur, une ministre** are also increasingly found. Otherwise, the feminine form is **une femme ingénieur.**

Some words can be either masculine or feminine:

le/la dentiste; le/la collègue

Jobs done by men and women often have a masculine and a feminine form:

le boulanger/la boulangère   **le fermier/la fermière**
le coiffeur/la coiffeuse   **l'instituteur/l'institutrice**
l'infirmier/l'infirmière

A few words are always feminine, even when they refer to men:

une personne, une victime, une star/vedette (de cinéma)

• All languages, days of the week, months, seasons and colours are masculine; as are most trees and shrubs, and those fruits and flowers not ending in **-e.**

The majority of abstract nouns, most countries, all the continents, and all fruits and flowers ending in **-e** are feminine.

Almost all nouns adopted into French from English are masculine (**le club; le bungalow**, but **la star**). Nouns taken from other languages tend to keep their original gender (**la vodka; la pizza**).

• Some noun endings denote gender, and it may be helpful to memorize the more common of these. (There are occasional exceptions)

-et; -eau ; -isme; -oir; -al; -ail; -ent are masculine endings

-ise; -té; -tion; -ance; -ence; -oire are feminine endings.

• In this Handbook the definite or indefinite article is given before the noun, to show the gender:

Masculine: **le béton**   **un téléphone**
Feminine: **la fabrication**   **une taxe**

Where a noun is preceded by the articles **l'** or **les/des**, the gender is given after the noun:

l'échafaudage (*m*)   **les affaires** (*f*)

(ii)   *Plural of nouns*

• Most French nouns form the plural by adding **-s.**

une voiture   **deux voitures**   **un croissant**   **des croissants**

However, this **-s** is not pronounced. The listener understands the plural from the expression which precedes the noun: **les... des... deux... quelques... beaucoup de...** etc

• Some nouns have irregular plurals. For instance, those ending in **-al** form the plural in **-aux;** this also applies to some nouns ending in **-ail.**

un cheval   **des chevaux**   **le travail**   **les travaux**
                                                     (road works)

Other plurals in **-x** include:

un bijou	**des bijoux**
un œil	**les yeux**
le ciel	**les cieux**

(iii)   Compound Nouns

Compound nouns in French are formed in a variety of ways. There are noun/noun and verb/noun combinations, linked with a hyphen; various combinations linked by prepositions **à, de** or **en**; and noun/adjective phrases (without hyphenation). It is not possible to predict with accuracy; each compound noun needs to be learnt or checked. (See Berlitz *French Grammar Handbook*, chapter 3.)

noun-noun	**un timbre-poste**
verb-noun	**un lave-vaisselle**
noun + **à** +noun	**un verre à vin** (denotes usage)
noun + **à** + verb	**une machine à écrire** (denotes usage)
noun+ **de** + noun	**une auberge de jeunesse**
noun + adjective	**une année scolaire**
preposition + noun	**un hors d'oeuvre**

Verb-noun and preposition + noun compounds are generally invariable, though some of the former add **-s**.

un hors d'oeuvre	**des hors d'oeuvre**
un porte-monnaie	**des porte-monnaie**

BUT

un tire-bouchon	**des tire-bouchons**

Plurals of other compound nouns vary according to the elements in the compound.

une timbre-poste	**des timbres-poste**
un lave-vaisselle	**des lave-vaisselle**
un verre à vin	**des verres à vin**
une machine à écrire	**des machines à écrire**
une auberge de jeunesse	**des auberges de jeunesse**
une année scolaire	**deux années scolaires**

Consult the Berlitz *French Grammar Handbook* (paragraph 18e), or a dictionary for further information on all these forms.

2b   Adjectives

(i)   Agreement

Adjectives alter their form according to what or who is being described. There may be as many as four forms: masculine singular, masculine plural; feminine singular and feminine plural.

Possessives (**mon, ma, mes,** etc.) and demonstratives (**ce, cet, cette, ces**) and their usages need to be learned by heart.

• The majority of adjectives make their agreements with the noun as follows:

Masculine singular	as in the dictionary
Feminine singular	add **-e** (unless the masculine already ends in **-e**)
Masculine plural	add **-s** to singular (unless it already ends in **-s**)
Feminine plural	

un chapeau noir et jaune	**deux chapeaux noirs et jaunes**
une robe noire et jaune	**des robes noires et jaunes**

It should be noted that these added letters are frequently unheard, as in the example above, where all forms of **noir** and **jaune** have the same pronunciation.

When an adjective ends in a silent consonant in the masculine singular, the feminine agreement will cause the consonant to be pronounced, but the **-s** of the plural will still be unheard.

un chat gris	**une souris grise** /z/

• Some adjectives have other slight changes from masculine to feminine. The most common are:

Doubling final consonant + **-e**

gentil, cruel	**gentille, cruelle**
parisien, italien	**parisienne, italienne**
gras, gros	**grasse, grosse**

-eux/euse, oux/-ouse
heureux, paresseux	**heureuse, paresseuse**
jaloux	**jalouse**

-er/-ère
cher, premier	**chère, première**

• Some common adjectives have an irregular feminine form :

blanc	**blanche**	**doux**	**douce**
frais	**fraîche**	**long**	**longue**
public	**publique**		

• Most adjectives ending in **-al** in the masculine singular end in **-aux** in the masculine plural:

un problème social   **des problèmes sociaux**

(ii)   Position of Adjectives

• Most adjectives follow the noun in French.
• A few very common adjectives precede the noun:

bon, mauvais, beau, grand, gros, petit, vieux, jeune, nouveau, joli, premier

• A number of adjectives change their meaning according to the position:

une maison *ancienne* 'old'   **un *ancien* élève 'former'**

Consult the Berlitz *French Grammar Handbook* for a full treatment.

2c   Verbs

In this Handbook, most verbs are entered in the first person singular of the present tense.

(i) Verbs ending in **-e** in the Vocabulary lists belong to the **-ER** conjugation, the largest group in French.

j'accuse	Infinitive:	**accuser**	accuse

The infinitive is included alongside the entry for otherwise regular **-ER** verbs which undergo minor spelling changes.

il aboie	Infinitive:	**aboyer**	bark
je jette	infinitive:	**jeter**	throw
je me lève	Infinitive:	**se lever**	get up

(ii) Verbs ending in **-is** (except irregular verbs, whose infinitives are given) belong to the **-IR** conjugation.

j'établis	Infinitive:	**établir**	establish'
je finis	Infinitive:	**finir**	finish

(iii) Verbs ending in **-ds** belong to the **-RE** conjugation
je réponds	Infinitive:	**répondre**	answer
je vends	Infinitive:	**vendre**	sell

(iv) All irregular verbs apart from **être, avoir, aller** and **faire** have the infinitive shown alongside the entry.

je dis *(dire)*   **j'éteins *(éteindre)***

Conventions used in this book

a) Nouns

Nouns are given in the singular form, generally preceded by the definite article. The plural form is included if irregular.

le/un indicates masculine gender
la/une indicates feminine gender
l' could apply to either gender for nouns beginning wth a vowel, so the correct gender is given in brackets.

b) Verbs
Verbs are entered in the first person singular, of the present tense. Where this is inappropriate, the entry is in the third person singular – for convenience, **il** is employed.

The infinitive of irregular verbs and verbs which undergo spelling changes follow the entry. Conjugations of all regular and regular verbs are found in the Berlitz French Verb Handbook, under the infinitive heading, along with explanations of usage and tenses.

c) Adjectives

Adjectives are in the masculine singular form. Irregular feminine forms are indicated in brackets.

Abbreviations

acc	accusative	inf	infinitive
adj	adjective	intr	intransitive
adv	adverb	invar	invariable
conj	conjunction	m	masculine
dat	dative	pl	plural
f	feminine	subj	subjunctive
fam	familiar usage	tr	transitive

Symbols

( )	a part of a translation which is optional: **le repas (léger)**
/	alternative word: **la chambre double/pour deux personnes** – **la chambre double** or **la chambre pour deux personnes.**
,	an alternative translation
[ ]	feminine adjectival ending, included when it is not **-** or **-e**

( )   the infinitive of an irregular verb, or verb with a minor spelling change

➤   a cross-reference to a Vocabulary or chapter

B

VOCABULARY TOPICS

Functional words

Articles

a	**un/une**
the	**le/la/les**
some	**des**

Demonstrative adjectives/pronouns

this/that	**ce/cet/cette**
these	**ces**
this one	**celui-ci/celle-ci**
that one	**celui-là/celle-là**
those (ones)	**ceux-là/celles-là**
the red one	**le/la rouge**

Personal pronouns (subject)

I	**je**
you	**tu /vous/on**
he	**il**
she	**elle**
it	**il/elle**
we	**nous/on**
they	**ils/elles**
one	**on**
them	**ils/elles**

Personal pronouns (accusative & dative)

me	**me**
you	**te/vous**
him	**le** *(acc)*, **lui** *(dat)*
her	**la** *(acc)*, **lui** *(dat)*
it	**le/la**
us	**nous**
them	**les** *(acc)*, **leur** *(dat)*
one	**vous**

Reflexive pronouns

myself	**me**
yourself	**te/vous**
himself	**se**
herself	**se**

itself	**se**
ourselves	**nous**
themselves	**se**
oneself	**se**
each other	**se**

Stressed pronouns

it's me	**c'est moi**
me	**moi**
you	**toi/vous**
him	**lui**
her	**elle**
it	**(ça)**
us	**nous**
them	**eux/elles**

Possessive adjectives

my	**mon/ma/mes**
your	**ton/ta/tes, votre/vos**
his	**son/sa/ses**
her	**son/sa/ses**
its	**son/sa/ses**
our	**notre/nos**
their	**leur/leurs**
one's	**son/sa/ses**

Possessive pronouns

mine	**le mien/la mienne/les miens/les miennes**
your	**le tien/etc., le/la vôtre, les vôtres**
his/hers	**le sien/etc.**
ours	**le nôtre/la nôtre/les nôtres**
theirs	**le leur/la leur/les leurs**
this is mine!	**celui-ci est à moi!**

Relative pronouns

who	**qui/que**
which	**qui/que**
that	**qui/que**
of which/whose	**dont**

what   **ce qui/ce que/ce dont**

Indefinite pronouns

somebody/one   **on, quelqu'un**
no one   **personne (ne...)**
anybody   **n'importe qui**
not ... anybody   **ne ... personne**
anyone   **n'importe qui**
not ... anyone   **ne ... personne**
nobody   **personne ...**
each (one)   **chacun/chacune**
everybody/one   **tout le monde**
something   **quelque chose**
anything   **n'importe quoi**
not ... anything   **ne ... rien**
nothing   **rien/ne ... rien**
everything   **tout**
all (of them)   **tous/toutes**
both (of them)   **tous les
   deux/toutes les deux**
some (of them)   **quelques-uns**

Questions

when   **quand?**
where   **où?**
how   **comment?**
how far   **à quelle distance?**
how much   **combien?**
how long   **pendant combien de
   temps?**
how hot   **à quelle température?**
why   **pourquoi?**
who   **qui?**
whom   **qui?**
to whom   **à qui?**
whose   **à qui?**
what   **que?, qu'est-ce que?**
which bus/car?   **quel bus?/quelle
   voiture?**
which buses/cars?   **quels bus?/
   quelles voitures?**
which one   **lequel/laquelle?**
which ones   **lesquels/lesquelles?**

*Common prepositions &
   conjunctions*

after he had bought sth.   **après
   qu'il eut acheté quelque chose**
after lunch   **après le déjeuner**
also   **aussi**
although   **bien que/quoique**
   (+ subj)
and   **et**
as (since)   **comme**
as if   **comme si**
as well as   **aussi bien que**
because   **parce que**
before he reads it   **avant qu'il le
   lise** (+ subj)
both ... and   **et ... et**
but   **mais**
even though/if   **même si**
except   **sauf**
however   **cependant**
if   **si**
(in order) to   **pour, afin de** (+ inf)
not ... either   **ni ... ni**
on condition that   **à condition que**
   (+ subj)
only   **seulement/ne...que**
or   **ou**
provided that   **pourvu que** (+ subj)
since *(causal)*   **puisque**
since   **(time) depuis**
so   **donc**
so that   **afin que/pour que** (+ subj)
then   **puis, ensuite**
therefore, consequently   **par
   conséquent**
too   **aussi**
unless   **à moins que ... ne** (+ subj)
until he arrives   **jusqu'à son
   arrivée**
until she writes   **jusqu'à ce qu'elle
   écrive** (+ subj)
when   **quand, lorsque**
while *(time)*   **pendant que**
while/whereas   **tandis que**
with   **avec**
without   **sans**

Where? – position & movement

2a Position

about **environ**	beside **à côté de**
above **au-dessus de**	between **entre**
above *(adv)* **au-dessus**	beyond **au-delà de**
across **à travers**	bottom **du fond**
after **après**	at the bottom (of) **au fond (de)**
against **contre**	centre/center **le centre**
ahead **en avant**	in the centre/center **au centre**
ahead of **à l'avance**	direction **la direction, le sens**
along **le long de**	in the direction of Dijon **en**
among **parmi**	**direction de Dijon**
anywhere **quelque part**	distance **la distance**
around *(adv)* **autour**	in the distance **au loin**
around the house **autour de la**	distant **distant**
maison	down here/there **ici/là en bas**
as far as **jusqu'à**	downstairs **en bas**
at **à**	edge **le bord**
at home **à la maison**	at the edge **au bord**
at school **à l'école**	end **le bout**
at work **au travail**	at the end of **au bout de**
back **en arrière**	everywhere **partout**
at the back of **à l'arrière de**	far **loin**
to the back **à l'arrière**	far away (from) **loin (de)**
backwards **en arrière**	first **le premier**
behind **derrière**	first (of all) **(tout) d'abord**
behind *(adv)* **en arrière**	I am first **je suis le premier**
below **sous, au-dessous de**	forward(s) **en avant**
below *(adv)* **en bas, en-**	from **à partir de**
dessous	front **le devant**

Over there in the distance is the river. It's not far away – about 1 km from our house.

Opposite the houses is the church and nearby are the shops/stores.

Là-bas, au loin, se trouve la rivière. Ce n'est pas loin d'ici – à environ 1 km de notre maison.

En face des maisons, il y a l'église et tout près d'ici, les magasins.

I am in front   **je mène**
in front of   **devant**
to the front   **à l'avant**
here   **ici**
   here and there   **çà et là**
in   **dans**
   in there   **là-dedans**
inside   **à l'intérieur de**
   inside *(adv)*   **dedans**
into   **dans**
last   **le dernier**
   last of all   **le tout dernier**
   last of all *(adv)*   **en tout dernier**
   I am last   **je suis le dernier**
left   **gauche**
   on the left   **à gauche**
   to the left   **sur la gauche**
middle   **le milieu**
   in the middle (of)   **au milieu (de)**
I move   **je bouge**
movement   **le mouvement**
near   **près de**
near(by)   **près d'ici, tout près**
neighbourhood/neigborhood   **les alentours**
   in the neighbourhood/
   neigborhood of   **aux alentours**
next   **prochain**
   next *(adv)*   **après**
   next to   **auprès de**
nowhere   **nulle part**
on the way   **en route**
onto   **sur**
opposite   **en face de**
out of   **en dehors de**

   out there   **là-bas**
outside   **devant**
   outside *(adv)*   **dehors, à l'extérieur**
over   **(par-)dessus**
   over there   **là-bas**
past   **plus loin que**
position   **la position**
right   **droite**
   on the right   **à droite**
   to the right   **sur la droite**
round/around   **autour**
   round/around the tree   **autour de l'arbre**
side   **le côté**
   at the side   **au côté**
   at both sides of   **des deux côtés de**
somewhere   **quelque part**
there   **là**
to   **à**
top   **le haut**
   top (of mountain)   **le sommet (de la montagne)**
   at the top   **en haut/au sommet**
   on top   **dessus**
towards   **vers**
under   **sous**
up   **haut**
   up here/there   **ici/là en haut**
upstairs   **en haut**
where?   **où?**
where from?   **d'où?**
where to?   **vers où?**
with   **avec**

At the top of the hill is a farm and in the middle of the village is the post office.

En haut de la colline, il y a une ferme et au milieu du village se trouve la poste.

The first house in the high street is near the river. Our house is the last. The next village is about five kilometres/kilometers away.

La première maison de la rue principale est près de la rivière. Notre maison est la dernière. Le prochain village est à environ cinq kilomètres.

2b Directions & location

Points of the compass

atlas   **l'atlas** *(m)*
east   **l'est** *(m)*
   in the east   **dans l'est**
   to the east (of)   **à l'est (de)**
   east wind   **le vent d'est**
   on the east side   **du côté est**
   eastern France   **l'est de la France**
compass   **la boussole**
latitude   **la latitude**
location   **l'emplacement** *(m)*
longitude   **la longitude**

map   **la carte**
north   **le nord**
   in the north   **dans le nord**
   to the north (of)   **au nord (de)**
   north wind   **le vent du nord**
   north coast   **la côté nord**
   in northern France   **dans le nord de la France**
northeast   **le nord-est**
northnortheast   **le nord-nord-est**
northwest   **le nord-ouest**
northnorthwest   **le nord-nord-ouest**

Nantes is north of La Rochelle. Right in the north is Lille. I prefer the north of France to the south.

Nantes est au nord de la Rochelle. Dans le nord, se trouve Lille. Je préfère le nord de la France au sud.

Look on the map. You go north(wards).

Regarde sur la carte. Tu vas vers le nord.

To the south of the wood you can see the church spire.

Au sud du bois, tu peux voir le clocher de l'église.

The town lies at a longitude of 32°.

La ville se trouve par 32° de longitude.

– Are you lost?
– Yes. Can you tell me the quickest way to the post office?

– Êtes-vous perdu?
– Oui. Pouvez-vous m'indiquer le chemin le plus court pour aller à la poste?

– It's down there on the left.

– C'est là-bas à gauche.

– How to I get to Antibes?

– Pour aller à Antibes, s'il vous plaît?

– Go straight on to the second crossroads/intersection. Turn right at the lights and take the road to Nice. It's 25 kilometres/kilometers from here.

– Continuez tout droit jusqu'au deuxième carrefour. Tournez à droite aux feux et prenez la route de Nice. C'est à 25 kilomètres d'ici.

point of the compass **le point cardinal**
south **le sud** *(see also* north*)*
   in the south **dans le sud**
   to the south (of) **au sud (de)**
southeast **le sud-est**
southsoutheast **le sud-sud-est**
southwest **le sud-ouest**
southsouthwest **le sud-sud-ouest**
west **l'ouest** *(see also* east*)*
   in the west **dans l'ouest**
   to the west (of) **à l'ouest (de)**

Location & existence

I am **je suis**
   there is **il y a**
   there isn't (any) **il n'y a pas de**
I become **je deviens** *(devenir)*
I exist **j'existe**
existence **l'existence** *(f)*
it lies **il se trouve**
I have got/I have **j'ai**
I possess **je possède** *(posséder)*
possession **la possession**
present **présent**
   I am present **je suis présent**
   I am present at **j'assiste à**
I am situated **je me trouve**

– Is there a bank nearby?
– There is one behind the supermarket.
– Where is the tourist office?

– Opposite the town hall.

– Who's that? – It's me.

– How many children are present?

– There are 25. Five of them are at home.

– Is there any cake? Are there still any biscuits/cookies?
– I am sorry, there is no cake, but there are some sandwiches.

I have been to London. I was present at a concert.

– Y a-t-il une banque près d'ici?
– Il y en a une derrière le supermarché.
– Où se trouve l'office de tourisme?

– En face de la mairie.

– Qui est là? – C'est moi.

– Combien d'enfants sont présents?

– Il y en a 25. Cinq d'entre eux sont à la maison.

– Y a-t-il du gâteau? Est-ce qu'il y a encore des biscuits?
– Je suis désolé, il n'y a pas de gâteau, mais il y a des sandwiches.

Je suis allé à Londres. J'étais présent à un concert.

2c Movement

I arrive **j'arrive**
I bring **j'apporte**
by car **en voiture**
I carry **je porte**
I climb *(intr)* **je monte**
  I climb *(tr)* **je grimpe**
I come **je viens** *(venir)*
  I come back (home) **je rentre à la maison**
  I come down **je descends**
  I come in **j'entre**
  I come out **je sors** *(sortir)*
  I come up **je monte**
I creep **je rampe**
I drive **je conduis** *(conduire)*
  I drive on the right **je roule à droite**
I fall **je tombe**
  I fall down **je tombe par terre**
I follow **je suis**
I get in **j'entre**
  I get out **je sors** *(sortir)*
  I get up **je me lève** *(se lever)*
I go **je vais**
  I go down **je descends**
  I go for a walk **je vais me promener**

I go in **j'entre**
I go out **je sors** *(sortir)*
I go round **je fais le tour**
I go up **je monte**
I go (by vehicle) **je pars** *(partir)* (en véhicule)
I hike **je vais à pied**
I hitch-hike **je fais du stop**
I hurry (up) **je me dépêche**
I jump **je saute**
I leave **je pars** *(partir)*
  I leave *(place, person)* **je quitte**
  I leave *(something)* **je laisse**
I lie down **je m'allonge**
I march **je marche**
I move **je bouge**
on foot **à pied**
I pass **je passe devant**
  I pass (in car) **je double, je dépasse**
I pull **je tire**
I push **je pousse**
I put **je mets** *(mettre)*
I ride **je monte**
  I ride (a horse) **je monte (à cheval)**
I run **je cours** *(courir)*

Put the picnic in the car! Don't forget your umbrella.

Mets le pique-nique dans la voiture! N'oublie pas ton parapluie.

I will take you as far as the river. Then you must get out and walk.

Je t'emmènerai jusqu'à la rivière. Ensuite tu devras sortir et marcher.

Keep to the left. Be careful not to fall into the river.

Tenez la gauche. Fais attention de ne pas tomber dans la rivière.

We go down the hill, along the river, and then turn left towards the woods. We pass a farm.

Nous descendons la colline, le long de la rivière, ensuite, nous tournons à gauche en direction du bois. Nous passons devant une ferme.

I run away   **je pars *(partir)* en courant**
I rush   **je me précipite**
I sit down   **je m'assieds *(s'asseoir)***
I sit up   **je me redresse**
I slip   **je glisse**
I stand   **je me tiens *(se tenir)* debout**
  I stand still   **je reste debout**
  I stand up   **je me mets *(se mettre)* debout**
I step   **je marche**
I stop   **je m'arrête**
straight   **droit**
  straight ahead   **tout droit**
I stroll   **je me promène *(se promener)***
I take   **je prends**
I turn   **je tourne**
  I turn left   **je tourne à gauche**
walk   **la promenade, la marche**
I walk   **je marche, je me promène *(se promener)***
I wander   **j'erre**
way   **le chemin**

Here and there

Come here!   **Viens *(venir)* ici!**

I go there   **je vais là-bas**
I rush there   **je me précipite là-bas**
I travel there   **je voyage là-bas**

Up and down

I climb the mountain   **je fais l'ascension de la montagne**
I climb up the mountain   **j'escalade la montagne**
I climb the stairs   **je monte les escaliers**
I climb the wall   **j'escalade le mur**
I fall down   **je tombe (par terre)**
I go down the path   **je descends le chemin**
I lie down   **je m'allonge**
Do sit down!   **Mais assieds-toi!**
Stand up!   **Mets-toi *(se mettre)* debout!**

Round

I go round the town   **je fais le tour de la ville**
I run round the tree   **je cours *(courir)* autour de l'arbre**
I run around   **je cours *(courir)* çà et là**
I turn round   **je fais demi-tour, je me retourne**

– Where are you going? – To town. Are you coming?
– No, I am going to my mother's.
– Which direction is that?
– I take the first road on the left, then straight ahead up to the market place, then I turn right.

– I will follow you as far as the market.
– I am going by car but some of us will go on foot. John is going by bike.

– **Où vas-tu? – En ville. Tu viens?**
– **Non, je vais chez ma mère.**
– **C'est dans quelle direction?**
– **Je prends la première rue à gauche, puis je vais tout droit jusqu'à la place du marché et je tourne à droite.**

– **Je vous suivrai jusqu'au marché.**
– **Je vais en voiture mais certains d'entre nous iront à pied. John va en vélo.**

▶ POSITION 2a; DIRECTIONS 2b

19

When? – expressions of time

3a Past, present & future

about **environ**
after **après**
   after *(conj)* **après (que)**
   afterwards **après, ensuite**
again **encore**
   again and again **à plusieurs reprises**
ago **il y a**
   a short time ago **il y a peu de temps**
already **déjà**
always **toujours**
anniversary **l'anniversaire** *(m)*
annual **annuel[le]**
as long as *(conj)* **tant que**
as soon as *(conj)* **dès que**
at once **immédiatement , tout de suite**
before **avant**
   before *(conj)* **avant que**
   before leaving **avant de partir**
   before, beforehand **auparavant**
I begin **je commence**
beginning **le début**
birthday **l'anniversaire** *(m)*
brief **bref [-ève]**
briefly **brièvement**

by (next month) **avant (le mois prochain)**
calendar **le calendrier**
centenary **le centenaire**
century **le siècle**
   in the twentieth century **au vingtième siècle**
continuous **continuel[le]**
daily **quotidien[ne], tous les jours**
date **la date**
dawn **l'aube** *(f)*
   at dawn **à l'aube**
day **le jour, la journée**
   by day **pendant la journée**
   every day **tous les jours**
   one day (when) **un jour (où)**
   the days of the week **les jours de la semaine**
decade **la décennie**
delay **le retard**
   delayed **retardé**
during **pendant**
early **tôt**
   I am early **je suis en avance**
end **la fin**
   I end *(something)* **je termine**

– Hello Peter, John Brown here/speaking. I have been working on the project for a few days. Have you finished yours yet? Call me this afternoon. We must meet sometime, what about the first of March?

– Allô Peter, c'est John Brown à l'appareil. Ça fait plusieurs jours que je travaille sur ce projet. Avez-vous terminé le vôtre? Appelez-moi cet après-midi. On devrait se retrouver un de ces jours, est-ce que le premier mars vous irait?

---

it ends   **il se termine**
ever   **jamais**
every   **chaque**
   every time   **chaque fois**
exactly   **exactement**
fast   **rapide**
   my watch is fast   **ma montre avance**
finally   **finalement**
I finish (reading)   **je finis (ma lecture)**
first   **premier [-ère]**
   at first   **au début, d'abord**
firstly   **pour commencer**
for   **pour, pendant, depuis**
for a day *(duration)*   **pendant une journée**
   (future)   **pour une journée**
for good/ever   **pour toujours, à jamais**
formerly   **autrefois, jadis**
fortnight/two weeks   **quinze jours**
frequent   **fréquent**
frequently   **fréquemment**
from   **de**
   as from today   **à partir d'aujourd'hui, dorénavant**

from now on   **désormais**
I go on (reading)   **je continue à (lire)**
half   **la moitié, un demi**
   half   **demi**
   one and a half hours   **une heure et demie**
it happens   **ce sont des choses qui arrivent, c'est la vie**
holiday/vacation   **les vacances** *(f)*
hurry   **la hâte**
   I am in a hurry   **je suis pressé**
I hurry up   **je me dépêche**
instant   **instantané**
just   **juste, justement**
   just now   **à l'instant**
last/final   **dernier [-ère], final**
   last night   **hier soir**
last/previous   **dernier [-ère]**
late   **tard, en retard**
   I am late   **je suis en retard**
   it's late   **il est tard**
   lately   **ces derniers temps**
   later (on)   **plus tard**
long   **long[ue]**
   long term   **à long terme**
   in the long term   **à long terme**

– Hello, John, Peter here/ speaking. Thank you for yesterday's call. Sorry I couldn't call back sooner. I only got back from London a quarter of an hour ago.

After getting back I spent a long time with Anna; she thinks the project will take all month. We should start on the work at the beginning of June, before the summer holidays/vacations start. We can then get it done in good time.

– **Allô, John, c'est Peter à l'appareil. Merci pour votre appel d'hier, désolé de ne pas y avoir répondu plus tôt. Je viens de rentrer de Londres il y a un quart d'heure.**

Après mon retour j'ai passé un long moment avec Anna, elle pense que le projet prendra tout le mois. On devrait commencer le travail début juin, juste avant les grandes vacances. On aura alors amplement le temps pour le terminer.

a long time **longtemps**
many **plusieurs, de nombreux [-ses]**
    many times **plusieurs fois**
meanwhile **pendant ce temps**
    in the meanwhile **en attendant**
middle **le milieu**
moment **le moment**
    at the moment **en ce moment**
    at this moment *(right now)* **à l'instant**
    at this moment **en ce moment**
    at that moment **à ce moment**
    in a moment **dans un instant**
month **le mois**
    monthly **par mois, mensuel[le]**
much **beaucoup**
never **ne ... jamais**
next **suivant**
    next *(adv)* **puis, ensuite**
not till/until **pas avant**
now **maintenant**
nowadays **de nos jours, actuellement**
occasionally **de temps en temps**
it occurs **il arrive (que)**
often **souvent**

on and off **parfois**
once **une fois**
    once upon a time **il était une fois**
    once in a while **une fois de temps en temps**
    once a day **une fois par jour**
one day (when) **un jour (où)**
only **seulement**
past **le passé**
per (day) **par (jour)**
present **le présent**
    present *(adj)* **présent**
    presently **tout de suite**
    at present **en ce moment**
previous **précédent**
prompt **à l'heure**
    promptly at (two) **(à deux heures) pile**
rare(ly) **rare(ment)**
recent **récent**
recently **récemment**
regular **régulier [-ère]**
I remain **je reste**
right away **tout de suite**
season **la saison**
seldom **rarement**
several **plusieurs**

– Last Friday the train was late and you didn't arrive till a quarter to/before three.
– I'll make it by three at the latest. How long does your bus take?

– Half an hour.
– If I'm late you can have a coffee till I get there.

– I don't want to spend all afternoon drinking coffee. Then there will be no time left for shopping.

– Vendredi dernier le train avait du retard et tu n'es pas arrivé avant trois heures moins le quart.
– J'arriverai avant trois heures au plus tard. Combien de temps met le bus?

– Une demi-heure.
– Si je suis en retard, vous pouvez prendre un café en m'attendant.

– Je ne veux pas passer toute l'après-midi à boire du café. Il ne me restera plus assez de temps pour faire les courses.

several times **plusieurs fois**
short **court**
  (in the) short term **à court terme**
  shortly **bientôt**
since **depuis**
slow **lent, qui retarde**
  my watch is slow **ma montre retarde**
sometimes **parfois, quelquefois**
soon **bientôt**
  sooner or later **un jour ou l'autre**
  the sooner the better **le plus tôt sera le mieux**
I stay **je reste**
still **encore, toujours**
I stop (doing) **j'arrête (de faire)**
suddenly **soudain, tout à coup**
sunrise **le lever du soleil**
sunset **le coucher du soleil**
I take (an hour) **je mets** *(mettre)* **(une heure)**
  it takes (an hour) **ça prend (une heure)**
then *(next)* **puis**
  then *(at that time)* **alors**
till **jusqu'à ce que**

time *(in general)* **le temps**
time *(occasion)* **une fois**
  at any time **n'importe quand**
  at that time **en ce temps-là, à ce moment-là**
  at the same time **au même moment**
  from time to time **de temps en temps**
  the whole time **tout le temps**
time zone **le fuseau horaire**
twice **deux fois**
until **jusqu'à ce que**
usually **d'habitude**
I wait **j'attends**
week **la semaine**
  weekly **hebdomadaire**
  weekday **le jour ouvrable**
  weekend **le week-end**
when **quand**
whenever **chaque fois que**
while *(conj)* **pendant que**
year **l'an** *(m)*, **l'année** *(f)*
  yearly **par an**
yet **encore**
  not yet **pas encore**

– You're sometimes late too.

– **Vous êtes parfois en retard vous aussi.**

– Only in winter or in bad weather.

– **Uniquement en hiver ou quand il fait mauvais.**

– Last month I had to wait for twenty minutes.

– **Le mois dernier j'ai dû attendre vingt minutes.**

– Oh dear, what a pity! I've just remembered that I haven't yet finished painting the kitchen.

– **Oh la la, quel dommage! Je viens de me souvenir que je n'ai pas encore fini de peindre la cuisine.**

– Perhaps it would be better to meet another time. I'll call next week.

– **Peut-être vaudrait-il mieux se rencontrer une autre fois. Je rappellerai la semaine prochaine.**

3b The time, days & date

The time of day

a.m.   **du matin**
morning   **le matin, la matinée**
   in the morning   **le matin, dans la matinée**
   in the mornings   **le matin**
   early in the morning   **tôt le matin**
noon   **midi**
at noon   **à midi**
afternoon   **l'après-midi** *(m/f)*
   in the afternoon   **dans l'après-midi**
   in the afternoons   **l'après-midi**
p.m.   **de l'après-midi**
evening   **le soir, la soirée**
   in the evening(s)   **le soir, dans la soirée**
night   **la nuit**
   at night   **le soir, la nuit**
midnight   **minuit**
   at midnight   **à minuit**
today   **aujourd'hui**
   today week   **dans une semaine**
tomorrow   **demain**
   tomorrow morning/evening   **demain matin/soir**
   the day after tomorrow   **après-demain**
tonight   **ce soir**
yesterday   **hier**
   yesterday morning   **hier matin**
   yesterday evening   **hier soir**

the day before yesterday   **avant-hier**

Telling the time

second   **la seconde**
minute   **la minute**
hour   **une heure**
   half an hour   **une demi-heure**
   in an hour's time   **dans une heure**
   hourly   **toutes les heures**
quarter   **un quart**
   quarter of an hour   **un quart d'heure**
   three quarters of an hour   **trois-quarts d'heure**
   quarter past/after (two)   **(deux) heures et quart**
   quarter to/of (two)   **(deux) heures moins le quart**
half past (two)   **(deux) heures et demie**
half past twelve   **midi/minuit et demi**
17:45   **dix-sept heures quarante-cinq**
five past/after six   **six heures cinq**
two a.m.   **deux heures du matin**
two p.m.   **deux heures de l'après-midi**
eight p.m.   **huit heures du soir**
12:00 noon   **midi**
12:00 midnight   **minuit**

– What's the date today?
   – **On est le combien aujourd'hui?**

– The twenty-first of January.
   – **Nous sommes le vingt et un janvier.**

– And what's the time, please?
   – **Et quelle heure est-il s'il vous plaît?**

– Ten past/after ten.
   – **Dix heures dix.**

The days of the week*

Monday	**lundi**
Tuesday	**mardi**
Wednesday	**mercredi**
Thursday	**jeudi**
Friday	**vendredi**
Saturday	**samedi**
Sunday	**dimanche**

The months*

January	**janvier**
February	**février**
March	**mars**
April	**avril**
May	**mai**
June	**juin**
July	**juillet**
August	**août**
September	**septembre**
October	**octobre**
November	**novembre**
December	**décembre**

The seasons

spring	**le printemps**
summer	**l'été** (m)

autumn/fall   **l'automne** (m)
winter   **l'hiver** (m)
in spring   **au printemps**
in summer/autumn(fall)/winter   **en été/automne, hiver**

The date

last Friday   **vendredi dernier**
on Tuesday   **mardi**
on Tuesdays   **le mardi**
by Friday   **avant vendredi**
(on) the first of January   **le premier janvier**
in (the year) 2000   **en (l'an) deux mille**
1st January/January 1st, 1994   **le premier janvier 1994**
at the end of 1999   **à la fin de l'année 1999**
at the beginning (of July)   **au début du mois (de juillet)**
in December   **en décembre**
in mid/the middle of January   **à la mi-janvier**
at the end of March   **à la fin du mois de mars**

– What time does the film/movie start this evening?	**– À quelle heure le film commence-t-il ce soir?**
– 20:00 hours.	**– À vingt heures**
– How long does it last?	**– Combien de temps dure-t-il?**
– One and a half hours. It will be over by 21:30 hours.	**– Une heure et demie. Il sera terminé avant vingt et une heures trente.**
We're going on holiday/vacation nex week. In three days we'll be in Spain.	**Nous partons en vacances la semaine prochaine. Dans trois jours nous serons en Espagne.**
In 1993 we had to wait a long time at the airport. We got there three hours late.	**En 1993 il nous a fallu attendre longtemps à l'aéroport. Nous sommes arrivés avec trois heures de retard.**

* All days and months in French are masculine.

How much? – expressions of quantity

4a Length and shape

angle **l'angle** *(m)*
area **l'aire** *(f)*, **la superficie**
big **grand**
centre/center **le centre**
concave **concave**
convex **convexe**
curved **courbé**
deep **profond**
degree **le degré**
depth **la profondeur**
diagonal **la diagonale**
dimentions **les dimensions** *(f)*
distance **la distance**
I draw **je dessine**
height **la hauteur**
high **haut**
horizontal **l'horizontale** *(f)*
large **gros[se]**
length **la longueur**
line **la ligne**
long **long[ue]**
low **bas[se]**
it measures **il mesure**
narrow **étroit**

parallel **la parallèle**
perpendicular **perpendiculaire**
point **le point**
room *(space)* **la place**
round **rond**
ruler **la règle**
shape **la forme**
short **court**
size **la taille**
small **petit**
space **l'espace** *(m)*
straight **droit**
tall *(person)* **grand**
  tall *(thing)* **haut**
thick **épais[se]**
thin **mince**
wide **large**
width **la largeur**

Shapes

circle **le cercle**
  circular **circulaire**
cube **le cube**
  cubic **cubique**

You need a straight ruler and pencil. Measure the space and then draw a plan.

Don't make the lawn too wide. Leave room for some vegetables. The distance from the house to the fence is 12 metres/meters. The garden is not wide enough for a pool.

– How high is the tree? – About 5 metres/meters.

Tu as besoin d'une règle et d'un crayon. Mesure l'espace et dessine un plan.

Ne fais pas la pelouse trop large. Laisse de la place pour les légumes. La distance entre la maison et la palissade est de 12 mètres. Le jardin n'est pas assez large pour une piscine.

– Quelle est la hauteur de l'arbre? – Environ 5 mètres.

cylinder   **le cylindre**
pyramid   **la pyramide**
rectangle   **le rectangle**
   rectangular   **rectangulaire**
sphere   **la sphère**
   spherical   **sphérique**
square   **le carré**
   square *(adj)*   **carré**
triangle   **le triangle**
triangular   **triangulaire**

Units of length

centimetre/centimeter   **le centimètre**
foot   **le pied**
inch   **le pouce**
kilometre/kilometer   **le kilomètre**
metre/meter   **le mètre**
mile   **le mile**
millimetre/millimeter   **le millimètre**
unit of length   **l'unité** *(f)* **de longueur**
yard   **le yard**

Expressions of quantity

about   **environ**
almost   **presque**
approximate   **approximatif [-ve]**
approximately   **à peu près**
as much as   **autant de**
at least   **au moins**

capacity   **la capacité**
it contains   **il contient** *(contenir)*
cubic capacity   **le volume**
it decreases   **il diminue**
difference   **la différence**
empty   **vide**
I empty   **je vide**
enough   **assez**
I fill   **je remplis**
full (of)   **rempli, plein (de)**
growth   **la croissance, la pousse**
hardly   **à peine**
increase   **l'augmentation** *(f)*
it increases   **il augmente**
little   **peu**
   a little   **un peu**
a lot (of)   **beaucoup (de)**
I measure   **je mesure**
measuring tape   **le mètre ruban**
   folding metre/meter measure   **le mètre pliant**
more   **plus**
nearly   **presque**
number   **le nombre**
part   **la partie**
quantity   **la quantité**
sufficient   **suffisant**
too much   **trop**
volume   **le volume**
whole   **l'ensemble** *(m)*
   whole *(adj)*   **tout, entier [-ère]**

The shed will be at an angle of about 40 degrees to the house, diagonally across from the gate.

L'abri sera à un angle d'environ 40 degrés de la maison, en diagonale depuis la porte.

The area of our garden is 100 square metres/meters. It is 10 metres/meters long and 10 wide, so it is a square.

La surface de notre jardin est de 100 mètres carrés. Il fait 10 mètres de long et 10 mètres de large, donc c'est un carré.

We put a round pond in, only 80-100 centimetres/centimeters deep.

Nous avons creusé un bassin rond, de 80-100 centimètres de profondeur seulement.

➤ CALCULATIONS 4d

4b Measuring

Expressions of volume

bag   **le sac**
bar   **la barre**
bottle   **la bouteille**
box   **la boîte**
container   **le conteneur, le récipient**
cup   **la tasse**
gallon   **le gallon**
glass   **le verre**
hectare   **l'hectare** *(m)*
litre/liter   **le litre**
   centilitre/centiliter   **le centilitre**
   millilitre/centiliter   **le millilitre**

pack   **le paquet**
pair   **la paire**
piece   **le morceau**
   a piece of cake   **une part de gâteau**
pint   **la pinte**
portion   **la portion**
pot   **le pot**
sack   **le sac**
tube   **le tube**

Temperature

it boils   **il bout** *(bouillir)*
I chill   **je mets** *(mettre)* **au frais**

– How many centilitres/liters are there in the bottle?
– 75, but you can also get it in litre/liter bottles.

– **Combien y a-t-il de centilitres dans la bouteille?**
– **75, mais tu peux l'avoir aussi en bouteilles d'un litre.**

Could I have two packets of tissues and a bottle of aspirin please?

Pourrais-je avoir deux paquets de Kleenex® et un tube d'aspirine, s'il vous plaît?

I need a little flour and a lot of sugar.

J'ai besoin d'un peu de farine et de beaucoup de sucre.

– What is the volume of water in the swimming pool?
– 10,000 gallons, that is about 45,000 litres/liters.

– **Quel est le volume d'eau dans la piscine?**
– **10.000 gallons, cela représente environ 45.000 litres.**

– How much wood do you want? – Enough for the whole fence. I must not buy too much. Yes, that should be sufficient. Give me a bag of cement too.

– **Quelle quantité de bois voulez-vous? – Assez pour toute la palissade. Je ne dois pas en acheter de trop. Oui, ça devrait être suffisant. Donnez-moi un sac de ciment aussi.**

– How many cubic metres/meters of concrete do you need? – About two.

– **Combien de mètres cubes de ciment avez-vous besoin? – Environ deux.**

cold   **le froid**
   cold   **froid**
cool   **frais [fraîche]**
   I cool it down   **je le fais**
   refroidir
degree   **le degré**
it's freezing   **il gèle** *(geler)*
heat   **la chaleur**
   I heat   **je fais chauffer**
   I heat (the house)   **je chauffe**
   (la maison)
hot   **chaud**
temperature   **la température**
warm   **(assez) chaud**
   warmth   **la chaleur**
I warm it (up)   **je le fais réchauffer**

Weight & density

dense   **dense**
density   **la densité**
gram   **le gramme**
heavy   **lourd**
kilo   **le kilo**
light   **léger [-ère]**
mass   **la masse**
ounce   **l'once** *(f)*
pound *(lb)*   **la livre**
scales/balance   **la balance**
ton(ne)   **la tonne**
I weigh   **je pèse** *(peser)*
weight   **le poids**

– It's so hot! What's the
temperature? It must be nearly 30
degrees. I am too hot.

– Would you like a cup of tea? –
No, I would prefer a glass of water.

– In winter it's cold here. We all
freeze in this house and have to
put the heating on in September.
When the temperature reaches
zero we have to light two fires.

Can you warm some water? The
vegetables are still frozen. The
water is boiling now. Warm up the
pizza in the oven. Have you chilled
the wine?

– Can you weigh out the
ingredients? – How many
gram(me)s of sugar do we need?
 – I want a pound - that must be
about 500 gram(me)s.

– **Il fait si chaud! Quelle est la
température? Il doit faire environ
30 degrés. J'ai trop chaud.**

– **Aimerais-tu une tasse de thé?**
– **Non, je préférerais un verre
d'eau.**

– **En hiver, il fait froid ici. Nous
tous gelons dans cette maison
et nous devons mettre le
chauffage en septembre. Quand
la température descend à zéro,
nous devons allumer deux feux.**

**Peux-tu faire chauffer de l'eau?
Les légumes sont encore gelés.
L'eau bout maintenant. Fais
réchauffer la pizza dans le four.
As-tu mis le vin au frais?**

– **Peux-tu peser les ingrédients?**
– **De combien de grammes de
sucre avons-nous besoin?** –
**J'en veux une livre. Cela doit
faire environ 500 grammes.**

➤ WEATHER 24d

4c Numbers

Cardinal numbers

zero	**zéro**
one	**un**
two	**deux**
three	**trois**
four	**quatre**
five	**cinq**
six	**six**
seven	**sept**
eight	**huit**
nine	**neuf**
ten	**dix**
eleven	**onze**
twelve	**douze**
thirteen	**treize**
fourteen	**quatorze**
fifteen	**quinze**
sixteen	**seize**
seventeen	**dix-sept**
eighteen	**dix-huit**
nineteen	**dix-neuf**
twenty	**vingt**
twenty-one	**vingt et un**
twenty-two	**vingt-deux**
twenty-nine	**vingt-neuf**

thirty	**trente**
thirty-one	**trente et un**
forty	**quarante**
fifty	**cinquante**
sixty	**soixante**
seventy	**soixante-dix, septante** *(Bel, Switz*)*
seventy-one	**quatre-vingt-onze, huitante-un** *(Bel, Switz)*
eighty	**quatre-vingt, huitante** *(Bel, Switz)*
eighty-one	**quatre-vingt-un, huitante-un** *(Bel, Switz)*
ninety	**quatre-vingt-dix, nonante** *(Bel, Switz)*
ninety-two	**quatre-vingt-douze, nonante-deux** *(Bel, Switz)*
a hundred	**cent**
a hundred and one	**cent un**
two hundred	**deux cents**
a thousand	**mille**
two thousand	**deux mille**
million	**un million**
two million	**deux millions**
billion	**un milliard**

Half of the house belongs to my brother. We divided it between us. However, he only pays a quarter of the costs as I let my half out in summer.	**La moitié de la maison appartient à mon frère. Nous l'avons partagée entre nous. Cependant, il ne paie qu'un quart des dépenses car je loue ma moitié pendant l'été.**

* *Bel, Switz* indicate variants used in Belgium and Switzerland.

Ordinal numbers

first **premier**
second **deuxième**
third **troisième**
fourth **quatrième**
nineteenth **dix-neuvième**
twentieth **vingtième**
twenty-first **vingt-et-unième**
hundredth **centième**

Nouns

one **un**
units **les unités** *(f)*
ten **dix**
tens **les dizaines** *(f)*
dozen **la douzaine**
about twenty **une vingtaine**
hundred **cent**
hundreds of **des centaines de**
about one hundred **une centaine**
thousands of **des milliers de**

Writing numerals

1,000 **1.000**
1,500 **1.500**
1st **1ᵉʳ**
2nd **2ᵉ, 2ᵉᵐᵉ**
1.56 **1,56 (un virgule cinquante-six)**
.05 **0,05 (zéro virgule zéro cinq)**

Fractions

half **la moitié**
a half **la moitié**
one and a half **un et demi**
two and a half **deux et demi**
quarter **le quart**
a quarter **un quart**
three-quarters **trois quarts**
third **le tiers**
fifth **le cinquième**
sixth **le sixième**
five and five sixths **cinq et cinq sixièmes**
tenth **le dixième**
hundredth **le centième**
thousandth **le millième**

– You can not all have half a bar of chocolate.

There is only enough for a quarter each.
And a quarter of a litre/liter of apple juice.
– I don't want a quarter, I want a half.

– Vous ne pouvez pas tous avoir la moitié d'une barre de chocolat.

Il y en a seulement assez pour un quart chacun.
Et un quart de litre de jus de pomme.
– Je n'en veux pas le quart, j'en veux la moitié.

4d Calculations

addition **l'addition** *(f)*
  I add **j'additionne**
average **la moyenne**
  I average out **je fais la**
  moyenne
  on average **en moyenne**
I calculate **je calcule**
  calculation **le calcul**
  calculator **la calculatrice**
correct **juste**
I count **je compte**
data **les données** *(f)*
  piece of data **la donnée**
decimal **la décimale**
  decimal point **la virgule**
diameter **le diamètre**
digit **le chiffre**
  two digits **deux chiffres**
I double **je double**
division **la division**
  I divide by **je divise par**
  six divided by two **six divisé**

  par deux
equal **égal**
  three times four equals twelve
  trois fois quatre font douze
equation **l'équation** *(f)*
it is equivalent to **cela équivaut**
  (équivaloir) **à**
I estimate **j'estime**
even **pair**
figure **le chiffre**
fraction **la fraction**
graph **le graphe, le graphique**
is greater than **est plus grand que**
is less than **est moins grand que**
maximum **le maximum**
  maximum *(adj)* **maximum**
  up to a maximum of **jusqu'à un**
  maximum de
medium **le milieu**
  medium *(adj)* **moyen[ne]**
minimum **le minimum**
  minimum **minimum**

An inch is the same as 2.54 cm, and there are twelve inches in a foot, 36 in a yard. A mile is 1,760 yards. A kilometre is 1,000 metres.

Un pouce est égal à 2,54 cm et il y a douze pouces dans un pied, 36 dans un yard. Un mile représente 1.760 yards. 1.000 mètres font un kilomètre.

What is 14 plus 8? It equals 22. Did you get the right result?

Combien font 14 plus 8? Ça fait 22. Est-ce que tu as répondu juste?

20 minus 5 is 15, 20 divided by 5 equals 4.

20 moins 5 font 15, 20 divisé par 5 font 4.

Work out 12 times 22. That is an easy sum.

Résous 12 fois 22. C'est une somme facile.

2 to the power of 3 is 8. Three squared equals 9.

2 à la puissance 3 égal 8. Trois au carré égal 9.

minus   **moins**
mistake/error   **la faute**
multiplication   **la multiplication**
    I multiply   **je multiplie**
    three times two   **trois fois deux**
negative   **négatif [-ve]**
number   **le nombre**
    cardinal numbers   **les nombres**
    (m) **cardinaux**
    ordinal numbers   **les nombres**
    (m) **ordinaux**
numeral   **le numéral**
odd   **impair**
percent   **pour cent**
    by 10%   **de 10%**
    percentage   **le pourcentage**
plus   **plus**
    two plus two   **deux plus deux**
positive   **positif [-ve]**
power   **la puissance**
    to the power of 5   **puissance 5**
problem   **le problème**
quantity   **la quantité**
ratio   **le rapport**

a ratio of 100:1   **un rapport de**
    100 contre 1
result   **le résultat**
similar   **identique**
solution   **la solution**
    I solve   **je résous** *(résoudre)*
square   **le carré**
square root   **la racine carrée**
    three squared   **trois au carré**
statistic   **la statistique**
statistics   **les statistiques** *(f)*
statistical   **de statistique**
sum   **la somme**
subtraction   **la soustraction**
I subtract/take away   **je soustrais**
    (soustraire)
symbol   **le symbole**
total   **le total**
    in total   **au total**
I treble   **je triple**
triple   **le triple**
I work out   **je résous** *(résoudre)*
wrong   **faux [-se]**

– I estimate that we have some
500 visitors a year.
– What percentage of visitors are
local? – 20% (percent).

A snail travels at an average
speed of 0.041 kilometres/
kilometers per hour.

– In this game you add up your
score over the week.
– What was the total score?
– I have a total of 500 points.
– To calculate the average you
add up the totals and divide by the
number of games

– **J'estime que nous recevons
environ 500 visiteurs par an.**
– **Quel est le pourcentage de
gens du quartier? – 20% (pour
cent).**

**Un escargot se déplace à une
vitesse moyenne de 0,041
kilomètres par heure.**

– **Dans ce jeu, tu additionnes
ton score de la semaine.**
– **Quel était le résultat final?**
– **J'ai un total de 500 points.**
– **Pour calculer la moyenne, tu
additionnes et tu divises par le
nombre de jeux.**

What sort of? – descriptions & judgements

5a Describing people

appearance	**l'apparence** (f)
attractive	**séduisant**
average	**la moyenne**
bald	**chauve**
beard	**la barbe**
bearded	**barbu**
beautiful	**beau [belle]**
beauty	**la beauté**
blond	**blond**
broad	**large**
build	**la carrure**
chic	**chic**
clean-shaven	**rasé de près**
clumsy	**maladroit**
complexion	**le teint**
curly	**bouclé**
dark	**foncé**
I describe	**je décris** (décrire)
description	**la description**
different (from)	**différent (de)**
elegant	**élégant**
energy	**l'énergie** (f)
expression	**l'expression** (f)
fat	**gras[se]**
features	**les traits** (m) **du visage**
female	**la femme**
feminine	**féminin**
figure	**la ligne**

fit	**en forme**
I frown	**je fronce**
glasses	**les lunettes** (f)
good-looking	**beau [belle]**
I grow	**je grandis**
hair	**les cheveux** (m)
hairstyle	**la coupe de cheveux**
handsome	**attrayant**
heavy	**lourd**
height	**la hauteur**
large	**gros[se]**
I laugh	**je ris** (rire)
laugh	**le rire**
I am left/right-handed	**je suis gaucher [-ère]/droitier [-ère]**
light	**léger [-ère]**
long-sighted	**presbyte**
I look like	**je ressemble à**
I look well	**j'ai bonne mine**
male	**l'homme** (m)
masculine	**masculin**
moustache	**la moustache**
neat	**soigné**
neatness	**la propreté, l'ordre** (m)
obese	**obèse**
overweight	**trop gros[se]**
part of body	**la partie du corps**
paunch	**le ventre**

adolescence	**l'adolescence** (f)
adolescent/teenager	**un adolescent, une adolescente**
age	**l'âge** (m)
elderly	**une personne âgée**
grown up	**adulte**
grown up	**un/une adulte**
middle-aged	**d'un certain âge**

old	**vieux [vieille]**
older/elder	**aîné**
young	**jeune**
young person	**un/une jeune**
young people	**les jeunes** (m/f)
youth	**la jeunesse**
youthful	**jeune**

physical **physique**
plump **grassouillet[te]**
pretty **joli**
red-haired **roux [rousse]**
I scowl **je fronce les sourcils**
sex/gender **le sexe**
short **petit**
short-sighted **myope**
similar (to) **pareil[le] (à)**
similarity **la ressemblance**
size **la taille**
slim/slender **mince**
small **petit**
I smile **je souris** *(sourire)*
smile **le sourire**
spot **le bouton**

spotty **boutonneux [-se]**
stocky **trapu**
strength **la force**
striking **frappant**
strong **fort**
tall **grand**
thin **maigre**
tiny **minuscule**
trendy **dans le vent**
ugliness **la laideur**
ugly **laid**
walk **la marche**
wavy **ondulé**
I weigh **je pèse** *(peser)*
weight **le poids**

I get fat **je grossis**
I get fit **je me mets** *(se mettre)* **en forme**
I get thin **je maigris**

I lose weight **je perds du poids**
I make up **je me maquille**
I put on weight **je grossis**
I slim **je maigris**

– What a wonderful family photo! What's your uncle like? Can you describe him?
– He looks very like my father, but he wears glasses.
– Look, who's that tall fellow with the beard? – That's my brother. He's mad on keeping fit.

– What a pretty girl! Is that your cousin? – Yes, she's blond with blue eyes. She's very slim, with a good figure and a beautiful smile.

– Little Ben now has dark hair and is about 1 metre/meter tall. – He looks very well, but he's very thin.

– Yes, he only weighs 16 kilos.

– Quelle merveilleuse photo de famille! À quoi ressemble ton oncle? Peux-tu me le décrire?
– Il ressemble beaucoup à mon père, mais il a des lunettes.
– Regarde, qui est ce grand type à barbe? – C'est mon frère. Il est obsédé par son maintien en forme.

– Quelle jolie fille! C'est ta cousine? – Oui, elle est blonde aux yeux bleus. Elle est très mince, bien faite et elle a un beau sourire.

– Le petit Ben a maintenant les cheveux noirs et il mesure environ 1 mètre. – Il a bonne mine, mais il est très maigre.
– Oui, il ne pèse que 16 kilos.

➤ PHYSICAL STATE 11d

5b The senses

bitter **amer [-ère]**
bright **clair**
bright (harsh) **criard, vif [-ve]**
cold **le froid**
   cold **froid**
dark **foncé**
dark blue **bleu foncé** *(inv)*
darkness **la teinte foncée**
delicious **délicieux [-se]**
disgusting **dégoûtant**
dull **terne**
I feel ... **je sens** *(sentir)*
   it feels **il semble**
I hear **j'entends**
heat **la chaleur**
hot **chaud**
light *(colour/color)* **clair**
   light grey **gris clair** *(inv)*
I listen **j'écoute**
I look (at) **je regarde**
loud **fort**
noise **le bruit**
noisy **bruyant**
odour/odor **l'odeur** *(f)*
opaque **opaque**
perfume **le parfum**

perfumed **parfumé**
quiet **calme**
rough **dur**
salty **salé**
I see **je vois** *(voir)*
sense **le sens**
shade *(colour/color)* **la nuance, le ton**
shadow/shade **l'ombre** *(f)*
silence **le silence**
silent **silencieux [-se]**
smell **l'odeur** *(f)*, **la senteur**
I smell **je sens** *(sentir)*
   it smells (of onion) **il sent (l'oignon)**
   smelly **malodorant**
soft *(texture)* **soyeux [-se], lisse**
   soft *(sound)* **doux [-ce]**
sound **le son**
it sounds **il semble**
   it sounds like **il ressemble à**
sour **acide**
sticky **collant**
   it is sticky **il colle**
sweet **sucré**
taste **le goût**

– What colour/color is your new coat? – Well, it's sort of red.
– Dark or light red? – It is more mauve.

– **Quelle est la couleur de ton nouveau manteau? – Eh bien, c'est une sorte de rouge.**
– **Rouge clair ou foncé? – Un rouge qui tire sur le mauve.**

– What a beautiful smell! – Yes, that's the flowers.

– **Que ça sent bon! – Oui, ce sont les fleurs.**

The jam tastes of fruit but is very bitter.

La confiture a un goût de fruits mais elle est très amère.

Don't touch that book, your hands are all sticky.

Ne touche pas à ce livre, tes mains sont toutes collantes.

I taste **je goûte**
it tastes (of) **il a un goût (de)**
tepid **tiède**
I touch **je touche**
transparent **transparent**
visible (in-) **(in)visible**
warm **chaud**
warmth **la chaleur**

Common parts of the body

arm **le bras**
back **le dos**
body **le corps**
   part of the body **la partie du**
   corps
chest **la poitrine**
ear **l'oreille** (f)
eye **l'œil** (m) (pl **yeux**)
face **le visage**
hand **la main**
head **la tête**
leg **la jambe**
mouth **la bouche**
neck **le cou**
nose **le nez**
shoulder **l'épaule** (m)
stomach **l'estomac** (m)
tooth **la dent**

Colours/Colors	
beige **beige**	mauve **mauve**
black **noir**	orange **orange**
blue **bleu**	pink **rose**
brown **brun, marron**	purple **pourpre, violet**
brownish **brunâtre**	red **rouge**
colour/color **la couleur**	scarlet **écarlate**
cream **crème**	silver **argent**
gold **or**	turquoise **turquoise**
green **vert**	violet **violet**
grey/gray **gris**	white **blanc**
	yellow **jaune**

– What's in that bag? It feels hard.

– Let me feel ... It's a bottle. What's in it?

– I don't know. It looks like orange juice. I'll taste it ... It's disgusting! It tastes of oranges but it's too sweet.

– Have you seen my new perfume?
– What does it look like?
– It's in a small, pink bottle.

– **Qu'est-ce qu'il y a dans ce sac? Ça a l'air dur.**

– **Laisse-moi toucher ... C'est une bouteille. Qu'est-ce qu'il y a dedans?**

– **Je ne sais pas. Cela ressemble à du jus d'orange. Je vais goûter ... C'est dégoûtant! Ça a le goût d'orange mais c'est trop sucré.**

– **As-tu vu mon nouveau parfum?**
– **À quoi ressemble-t-il?**
– **C'est une petite bouteille rose.**

5c Describing things

big **grand**
　something big **quelque chose de grand**
broad **large**
broken **cassé**
appearance **l'apparence** (f)
clean **propre**
closed **fermé**
colour/color **la couleur**
　colourful/colorful **coloré**
　coloured/colored **en couleur, coloré**
damp **humide**
deep **profond**
　depth **la profondeur**
dirt **la saleté**
dirty **sale**
dry **sec [sèche]**
empty **vide**
enormous **énorme**
fashionable **à la mode**
fat **gros[se]**
fatty (food) **gras[se]**
firm **ferme**
flat **plat**
flexible **souple**
fresh **frais [fraîche]**

full (of) **plein (de)**
genuine/real **vrai**
hard **dur**
height **la hauteur**
kind **gentil[le]**
large **gros[se]**
liquid **liquide**
little **petit**
long **long[ue]**
it looks like **il ressemble à**
low **bas[se]**
main **principal**
material **le tissu**
it matches **il va bien ensemble**
matter **la matière**
moist **moite**
mouldy/moldy **moisi**
narrow **étroit**
natural **naturel[le]**
new **nouveau, neuf [-ve]**
open **ouvert**
out of date **démodé**
painted **peint**
pale **pâle**
pattern **le motif**
　patterned **à motifs**
plump **rembourré**

– What's that over there?
– That thing there? It's a new kind of bottle opener.
– Does it work? – Yes indeed. It's the best there is.

– I'm looking for something big to stand on.
– Will anything do?

– Well, it must be something solid.

– What about this?
– Is there nothing bigger?

– Qu'est-ce qu'il y a là-bas?
– Cette chose-là? Une nouvelle sorte d'ouvre-bouteille.
– Ça marche? – Bien sûr. C'est le meilleur qui soit.

– Je cherche quelque chose de grand pour me mettre dessus.
– Est-ce que n'importe quoi fera l'affaire?
– Et bien, il faut que ce soit solide.

– Que dis-tu de cela?
– Il n'y a rien de plus grand?

resistant **résistant**
rotten **pourri**
shade **la nuance**
shallow **peu profond**
shiny **brillant**
short **court**
shut **fermé**
small **petit**
smooth **lisse, soyeux [-se]**
soft (texture) **doux [-ce]**
solid **solide**
soluble **soluble**
sort **la sorte**
spot **le pois**
spotted **à pois**
stain **la tache**

stained **taché**
stripe **la rayure**
striped **à rayures**
subsidiary **subsidiaire**
substance **la substance**
such **tel[le]**
synthetic **synthétique**
thick **épais[se]**
thing **la chose**
thingummyjig **le truc**
tint **la teinte**
varied **varié**
water-proof **imperméable**
wet **mouillé**
wide **large**

Ten questions

What's that thingummyjig?
Qu'est-ce que c'est que ce truc?
What's it for? **Ça sert à quoi?**
What do you use it for? **Tu l'utilises pour quoi faire?**
Can you see it? **Tu peux le voir?**
What's it like? **C'est comment?**

What does it look like? **À quoi ça ressemble?**
What does it sound like? **De quoi ça a l'air?**
What does it smell of? **Ça sent quoi?**
What colour is it? **C'est de quelle couleur?**
What kind of thing is it? **C'est quoi, exactement?**

– Stand on the chair.
– It's too soft.
– All the other chairs are too low.

– Fetch a ladder. Which one? This one?
– No, that one there.

– I am looking for a striped material, something to match my coat.

The fridge/refrigerator is empty and the sink full of water.

– **Monte sur la chaise.**
– **C'est trop mou.**
– **Toutes les autres chaises sont trop basses.**

– **Va me chercher une échelle. Laquelle? Celle-ci?**
– **Non, celle-là là-bas.**

– **Je cherche un tissu à rayures, quelque chose qui va avec mon manteau.**

Le frigo est vide et l'évier est plein d'eau.

5d Evaluating things

abnormal **anormal**	I enjoy **j'aime**
I adore **j'adore**	easy **facile**
all right **d'accord, bon**	essential **essentiel[le]**
it is all right **c'est d'accord/bon**	excellent **excellent**
appalling **effroyable**	expensive **cher [-ère]**
bad **mauvais**	I fail **j'échoue**
beautiful **beau [belle]**	failure **l'échec** *(m)*
better/best **meilleur/le meilleur**	false **faux [-sse]**
cheap **bon marché** *(invar)*	fine **bon[ne]**
correct **exact**	good **bon[ne]**
it costs **il coûte**	good value **un bon rapport**
delicious **délicieux [-se]**	**qualité-prix**
I detest **je déteste**	great/terrific **génial, terrible**
difficulty **la difficulté**	I hate **je déteste**
difficult/hard **difficile**	high **haut**
disgusting **dégoûtant**	important (un-) **(pas) important**
I dislike **je n'aime pas**	incorrect **inexact**

a bit **un peu**	much (better) **bien mieux**
enough **assez**	not at all **pas du tout**
extremely **extrêmement**	particularly **surtout**
fairly **plutôt**	quite **assez**
hardly ... at all **presque pas du**	rather **plutôt**
tout	really **vraiment**
litte **peu**	so **tellement, si**
a little **un peu de**	too (good) **trop (bon[ne])**
a lot **beaucoup**	very **très**

I tried to ring/call you yesterday, but the telephones were out of order.	– J'ai essayé de t'appeler hier, mais les téléphones étaient en panne.
– Would you like to try this wine?	– Voudriez-vous goûter ce vin?
– Thank you, it is quite delicious.	– Merci, il est vraiment délicieux.
– Do you enjoy going to the cinema/movies?	– Vous aimez aller au cinéma?
– Yes, I particularly enjoyed last week's film/movie.	– Oui, j'ai surtout aimé le film de la semaine dernière.

inessential **superflu**
interesting (un-) **(in)intéressant**
I like **j'aime**
mediocre **médiocre**
necessary (un-) **(pas) nécessaire, (in)utile**
normal **normal**
order **l'ordre** *(m)*
  in order **en ordre**
  out of order **en panne**
out of date **démodé**
ordinary **ordinaire**
pleasant **agréable**
poor **pauvre**
practical (im-) **(pas) pratique**
I prefer **je préfère** *(préférer)*
quality **la qualité**
  top quality **de haute qualité**
  poor quality **de mauvaise**

qualité
right **juste**
strange **étrange, bizarre**
I succeed **je réussis**
success **le succès**
successful **qui réussit**
true **vrai**
I try **j'essaie** *(essayer)*
ugly **laid**
unpleasant **désagréable**
unsuccessful **qui est un échec**
I use **j'utilise**
use **l'emploi** *(m)*
useful **utile**
well **bien**
worse **plus mauvais, pire**
I would rather **je préférerais** *(préférer)*
wrong **mauvais, faux [-sse]**

How do you like our neighbour's garden/neighbor's yard? We do not like it at all.

Que pensez-vous de jardin de notre voisin? Nous ne l'aimons pas du tout.

I wish he would throw away that broken seat. It is only plastic anyway. We always buy the best!

Si seulement il jetait ce siège cassé. Ce n'est que du plastique de toute façon. Nous n'achetons que le meilleur!

And his lawn mower is out of order. He never puts it away, and now he'll have to get it mended/ fixed.

Et sa tondeuse à gazon est en panne. Il ne la range jamais et maintenant, il doit la faire réparer.

I fear he's not a very successful gardener. His vegetables are a complete failure.

Je crains qu'il ne soit pas un jardinier très accompli. Ses légumes sont un échec total.

I do like to keep the garden tidy/neat. I always put everything away.

J'aime garder le jardin en ordre. Je range toujours tout.

People always says our garden is the best in the road.

Les gens disent toujours que notre jardin est le plus beau de la rue.

➤ EXPRESSING VIEWS 5b

5e Comparisons

*Regular comparatives &
superlatives*

small   **petit**
  smaller   **plus petit**
  smallest   **le plus petit**

*Irregular comparatives and
superlatives*

bad   **mauvais**
  worse   **pire, plus mauvais**

  worst   **le pire, le plus mauvais**
good   **bon[ne]**
  better   **meilleur**
  best   **le meilleur**
well   **bien**
  better   **mieux**
  best   **le mieux**
much   **beaucoup**
  more   **plus**
  most   **le plus**

– Look at the children! Peter, our eldest son, is now the tallest. He's best at football, too. That's what he enjoys best.

– **Regarde les enfants! Peter, notre fils aîné est maintenant le plus grand. Il est aussi le meilleur en football. C'est ce qu'il aime le mieux.**

John is now fairly large, almost as tall as Peter, and he really is too fat. He prefers to swim.

John est maintenant assez gros, presque aussi grand que Peter, mais il est vraiment trop gros. Il préfère la natation.

The smallish boy over there is Alan. He is quite small compared with the others, but on the other hand very confident. He behaves less well than his brother.

Le garçon plutôt petit là-bas, c'est Alan. Il est assez petit comparé aux autres, mais d'un autre côté, il est très confiant. Il se comporte moins bien que son frère.

John has eaten the largest cake. He gets larger and larger.

John a mangé le plus gros gâteau. Il devient de plus en plus gros.

– Have you seen our latest products? They are just as cheap as the competition.
We can not ask a higher price, as the greatest demand is for the cheaper product.

– **Avez-vous vu nos derniers produits? Ils sont aussi bon marché que la concurrence. Nous ne pouvons pas demander un prix plus élevé, car la demande plus forte est pour le produit le moins cher.**

5f Materials

acrylic	**l'acrylique** *(m)*
brick	**la brique**
cambric	**la batiste**
cardboard	**le carton**
cashmere	**le cachemire**
cement	**le ciment**
chiffon	**la mousseline**
china	**la porcelaine**
concrete	**le béton**
corduroy	**le velours côtelé**
cotton	**le coton**
crêpe	**le crêpe**
denim	**la toile de coton/jean**
felt	**le feutre**
flannel	**la flanelle**
gas	**le gaz**
glass	**le verre**
gold	**l'or** *(m)*
iron	**le fer**
lace	**la dentelle**
leather	**le cuir**
linen	**le lin**

man-made fibre/fiber	**les fibres** *(f)* **artificielles**
metal	**le métal**
mineral	**le minéral**
nylon	**le nylon**
oil	**le pétrole**
paper	**le papier**
plastic	**le plastique**
polyester	**le polyester**
pottery	**la poterie**
satin	**le satin**
silk	**la soie**
silver	**l'argent** *(m)*
steel	**l'acier** *(m)*
stone	**la pierre**
suede	**le daim**
terylene	**le tergal**
towelling	**le tissu éponge**
velvet	**le velours**
viscose	**le viscose**
wood	**le bois**
wool	**la laine**

– Which dress would you like? Silk is softer than wool, but it costs a lot.

The most beautiful dress is the one made of cotton. The colours/colors are brighter and I think the cut is better, although it is not as warm as the woollen/woolen dress.

It is not at all expensive. I prefer it to the others.

– All the same I would rather have the other.

– Did you succeed in finding something less expensive?

– Yes, this coat is particularly good value. And it's better quality.

– **Quelle robe voulez-vous? La soie est plus douce que la laine, mais elle coûte cher.**

La robe la plus belle est celle en coton. Les couleurs sont plus vives et je pense qu'elle est mieux coupée, bien qu'elle ne soit pas aussi chaude que la robe en laine. Elle n'est pas chère du tout. Je la préfère aux autres.

– **Mais je voudrais quand même prendre l'autre.**

– **Avez-vous réussi à trouver quelque chose de moins cher?**

– **Oui, ce manteau est d'un bon rapport qualité-prix et de meilleure qualité.**

➤ CLOTHING 9c; COMPOUNDS & ALLOYS, CHEMICAL ELEMENTS App.23b

The human mind & character

6a Human character

active **actif [-ive]**
I adapt **je m'adapte**
amusing **amusant**
I annoy **j'agace, j'irrite**
bad **mauvais**
bad-tempered **qui a mauvais caractère**
I behave **je me conduis**
behaviour/behavior **la conduite**
I boast **je me vante**
calm **calme**
care **le soin**
careful **soigneux [-se], prudent**
careless **peu soigneux [-se], inattentif [-ive]**
character **le caractère, le tempérament**
characteristic **la caractéristique**
characteristic *(adj)* **caractéristique**
charming **charmant**
cheerful **joyeux [-se], heureux [-se]**
clever **intelligent**
confident **confiant**

discipline **la discipline**
I disobey **je désobéis à**
dreadful **horrible**
evil **mauvais**
foolish **bête**
forgetful **étourdi**
friendly (un-) **(peu) aimable**
fussy **difficile, grincheux [-se]**
generous **généreux [-se]**
I get on with **je m'entends avec**
gifted **doué**
good **bon[ne]**
good-tempered **de bonne composition**
guilty **coupable**
habit **une habitude**
hard-working **travailleur [-se]**
I help **j'aide**
helpful **serviable**
honest (dis-) **(mal)honnête**
humour/humor **l'humeur** *(f)*
humorous **qui a de l'humour**
immorality **l'immoralité** *(f)*
innocent **innocent**
intelligence **l'intelligence** *(f)*

Our neighbour/neighbor is a lazy fellow, but very gifted.
He has a good sense of humour but is always boasting.

Notre voisin est un type paresseux mais très doué.
Il a le sens de l'humour, mais il est tout le temps en train de se vanter.

The pupils here are hard-working and well-behaved. We encourage self-confidence and discipline. Bad behaviour/behavior and laziness are punished.

Les élèves ici sont travailleurs et bien élevés. Nous encourageons la confiance en soi et l'auto-discipline. Les mauvaises manières et la paresse sont punies.

intelligent **intelligent**
kind (un-) **gentil[le]**
kindness **la gentillesse, la bonté**
lazy **paresseux [-se]**
laziness **la paresse**
lively **vivant**
mad **fou [folle]**
manners **les manières** (f)
memory **la mémoire**
mental(ly) **mental(ement)**
moral (im-) **(im)moral**
morality/morals **la moralité**
nervous **nerveux [-se]**
nice **bien, gentil[le], agréable, sympathique**
I obey **j'obéis à**
optimistic **optimiste**
patient (im-) **(im)patient**
personality **la personnalité**
pessimistic **pessimiste**
pleasant **plaisant**
polite (im-) **(im)poli**
popular **populaire**
quality **la qualité**
reasonable (un-) **(peu) raisonnable**
respect **le respect**
I respect **je respecte**
rude **grossier [-ère]**
sad **triste**
self-confidence **la confiance en soi**

self-esteem **l'amour-propre** (m)
sense **le sens**
    common sense **le bon sens**
    good sense **le bon sens**
sensible **raisonnable, avisé**
serious **sérieux [-se]**
shame **la honte**
shy **timide**
skill **l'habileté** (f), **le talent, l'aptitude** (f)
skilful **habile, adroit, apte**
sociable (un-) **(peu) sociable**
strange **étrange**
stupid **stupide, idiot**
stupidity **la bêtise, la stupidité**
suspicious **soupçonneux [-se], louche, suspect**
sympathetic **compatissant**
sympathy **la sympathie, la compassion**
talented **doué**
temperament **le tempérament**
temperamental **instable**
I trust **je fais confiance à**
trusting **confiant**
unkind **mesquin**
warm **chaleureux [-se]**
well-known **bien connu**
wise **sage, prudent**
wit **l'esprit** (m)
witty **spirituel[le], amusant**

Don't be so suspicious. Please trust me.

Ne soyez pas si soupçonneux. Faites-moi donc confiance.

The children have such different personalities. The eldest is very sensible and rather shy. Our daughter is more sociable and witty. The youngest is gifted but rather temperamental.

Les enfants ont des personnalités si différentes. L'aîné est très raisonnable et plutôt timide. Notre fille est plus sociable et amusante. La plus jeune est douée mais elle a son caractère.

➤ THOUGHT PROCESSES 6c; EXPRESSING VIEWS 6d; RELATIONSHIPS 7

6b Feelings & emotions

I am afraid (of/that) **j'ai peur (de/que)**

I am amazed (at) **je suis très surpris/stupéfait/sidéré (par)**

amazement **la surprise, la stupéfaction, l'étonnement** *(m)*

I amuse **j'amuse**

I am amused by **je trouve amusant**

amusement **l'amusement** *(m)*

anger **la colère**

angry **en colère, furieux [-se]**

I am annoyed (at/about/with) **je suis furieux [-se] (envers/contre)**

anxiety **l'anxiété** *(f)*

anxious **anxieux [-se]**

I approve (of) **j'approuve**

I am ashamed (of) **j'ai honte (de)**

I am bored (by) **je m'ennuie (par), j'en ai assez (de)**

boredom **l'ennui** *(m)*

content (with) **satisfait (de)**

cross (with) **en colère (contre)**

delighted (about) **ravi (de)**

I dislike **je n'aime pas**

dissatisfaction **le mécontentement**

dissatisfied (with) **peu satisfait (de)**

embarrassed (about) **gêné (par)**

embarrassment **la gêne, l'embarras** *(m)*

emotion **l'émotion** *(f)*

emotional **émotionnel[le]**

I enjoy ... **j'apprécie, j'aime**

envy **l'envie** *(f)*

envious (of) **envieux [-se] (de)**

fear **la crainte**

I feel **je ressens** *(ressentir)*, **je me sens** *(se sentir)*

I forgive **je pardonne**

forgiveness **le pardon**

I am frightened (of) **j'ai peur (de)**

furious (about) **furieux [-se] (envers)**

fussy **difficile, pinailleur [-se]**

grateful (to so) **reconnaissant (de)**

gratitude **la reconnaissance, la gratitude**

grumpy **grincheux [-se]**

happiness **le bonheur**

happy (about) **heureux [-se] (de)**

hate **la haine**

We are very fond of our uncle. He has many good qualities. However, he is often somewhat temperamental.
He hates it when we thank him. It makes him embarrassed.

– I am really ashamed of my behaviour/behavior yesterday. I was so upset and worried.
– It really doesn't matter. I am thankful that you feel better.

– I am so glad you are not angry with me.

Nous aimons beaucoup notre oncle. Il a beaucoup de qualités. Toutefois il a souvent des sautes d'humeur.
Il a horreur qu'on le remercie, ça le gêne.

– J'ai vraiment honte de ma conduite d'hier. J'étais si bouleversée et inquiète.
– Cela n'a vraiment pas d'importance, je suis content que vous vous sentiez mieux.

– Je suis si soulagé que vous ne soyez pas en colère contre moi.

I hate **je hais** *(haïr)*, **je déteste**
I have a grudge against him **je lui en veux** *(vouloir)*
hope **l'espoir** *(m)*
I hope **j'espère** *(espérer)*
hopeful **plein d'espoir**
idealism **l'idéalisme** *(m)*
indifference **l'indifférence** *(f)*
indifferent (to) **indifférent (envers)**
 I am indifferent **ça m'est indifférent/égal**
interest **l'intérêt** *(m)*
I am interested (in) **je m'intéresse (à)**
jealous **jaloux [-se]**
jealousy **la jalousie**
joy **la joie**
joyful **joyeux [-se]**
I like **j'aime bien**
 I would like **je voudrais** *(vouloir)*
love **l'amour** *(m)*
I love **j'aime**
miserable (about) **malheureux [-se] (à cause de)**
misery **la tristesse, la déprime**
mood **l'humeur** *(f)*

in a good/bad mood **de bonne/mauvaise humeur**
I'm pleased/glad that **je suis content/heureux [-se] que**
I prefer **je préfère** *(préférer)*
I regret **je regrette**
satisfaction **la satisfaction**
satisfied (with) **satisfait de**
surprise **la surprise**
I am surprised (at) **je m'étonne (de)**
thankful **reconnaissant**
unhappy **malheureux [-se]**
unhappiness **le malheur, la tristesse**
I am upset (about) **je suis vexé/contrarié/peiné (à cause de)**
I want **je veux** *(vouloir)*
I wonder (at) **je m'étonne de, je suis étonné par**
 I wonder if **je me demande si**
worried (about) **soucieux [-se] (au sujet de)**
worry **le souci**
I worry (about) **je me fais du souci (au sujet de)**
 it worries me **cela m'inquiète** *(inquiéter)*

The boss is in a bad mood. He is cross with his secretary. She is bored with the work and indifferent to his annoyance.

Le patron est de mauvaise humeur. Il est en colère contre sa secrétaire. Elle trouve le travail ennuyeux et son humeur la laisse indifférente.

I like our neighbour/neighbor a lot but I'm worried about his wife. She cares for her old mother, who has not adapted to life in town. She is often in a bad temper and very fussy.

J'aime beaucoup notre voisin mais je me fais du souci pour sa femme. Elle s'occupe de sa mère qui est âgée et ne s'est pas adaptée à la vie en ville. Elle est souvent de mauvaise humeur et très difficile.

6c Thought processes

afterthought   la pensée après coup
I analyze   j'analyse
analysis   l'analyse *(f)*
I assume   je suppose
assuming that ...   à supposer que
attention   l'attention *(f)*
aware of (un-)   (in)conscient (de)
I base ... on   je base ... sur
basic   de base
basically   à la base
basis   la base
belief   la croyance, l'opinion *(f)*
I believe (in)   je crois *(croire)* (à/en)
certainty   la certitude
certain, sure   certain, sûr
coherent (in-)   (in)cohérent
complex   le complexe
   inferiority   le complexe d'infériorité
I comprehend   je comprends *(comprendre)*
comprehensible   compréhensible
I concentrate   je me concentre
   I concentrate (on)   je fixe mon attention (sur)
I conclude (that)   je conclus *(conclure)* (que)
conscious   conscient
conscience   la conscience
consciousness   la conscience
I consider ...   je considère *(considérer)* que ...
consideration   la considération
   I take into consideration   je tiens *(tenir)* compte (de)
   taking everything into consideration   tout compte fait
I contemplate   je contemple
context   le contexte

on the contrary   au contraire
controversial   controversé
I decide   je décide
decision   la décision
I deduce   je déduis *(déduire)*
I delude myself   je me fais des illusions
delusion   l'illusion *(f)*, le fantasme
I determine   je détermine
I disbelieve   je me refuse à croire
I distinguish   je distingue
doubt   le doute
I doubt   je doute
doubtful   douteux [-se]
doubtless/without a doubt   sans aucun doute
exception   l'exception *(f)*
evidence   la preuve
evident   évident
evidently   évidemment
fact   le fait
   in fact   en fait
false   faux [-sse]
fantasy   la fantasie
fiction   la fiction
for   pour
   I am for it   je suis pour
I forbid   j'interdis *(interdire)*
I forget   j'oublie
genius (for)   le génie (de)
I grasp   je saisis
hypothesis   l'hypothèse *(f)*
implication   l'implication *(f)*
interesting   intéressant
I imagine   je me répresente, je m'imagine
imagination   l'imagination
I invent   j'invente
invention   l'invention *(f)*
issue   le problème *(m)*
I judge   je juge

judgement **le jugement**
justice **la justice**
I justify **je justifie**
I know *(place/person)* **je connais**
  (connaître)
I know that **je sais** *(savoir)* **que**
knowledge **la connaissance**
knowledgeable **bien informé**
logic **la logique**
logical **logique**
I go mad **je deviens** *(devenir)* **fou**
  [folle]
madness **la folie**
meaning **le sens**
it means **cela veut** *(vouloir)* **dire**
I meditate (on) **je médite (sur), je**
  réfléchis (à)
memory **la mémoire**
metaphysics **la métaphysique**
mind **l'esprit** *(m)*, **l'intelligence** *(f)*
  a great mind **un grand esprit**
I misunderstand **je comprends**
  (comprendre) mal
misunderstanding **l'erreur** *(f)*, **la**
  méprise, le malentendu
motive **le motif, l'intention** *(f)*
it occurred to me that **il m'est**
  venu à l'esprit que
philosophy **la philosophie**
point of view **le point de vue**
I ponder **je considère**
  (considérer), je pèse *(peser)*
premise **la prémisse**
I presume **je présume**
principle **le principe**
  in/on principle **en/par principe**
problem **le problème**
proof **la preuve**
I prove **je prouve**
psychology **la psychologie**
psychoanalysis **la psychanalyse**
rational (ir-) *(thinking)* **rationnel[le]**
  (déraisonnable)

reality **la réalité**
I realize **je me rends compte de**
I reason *(conclude)* **j'en conclus**
  (conclure)
  I reason **je raisonne**
reason *(faculty of)* **la raison**
I recognize **je reconnais**
  (reconnaître)
I reflect **je réfléchis**
relevant **significatif [-ve]**
I remember **je me rappelle** *(se*
  rappeler), **je me souviens** *(se*
  souvenir) **de**
right **vrai, juste**
  I am right **j'ai raison**
  it is right **il est bon/juste**
I see **je vois** *(voir)*
I solve **je résous** *(résoudre)*
solution **la solution**
I speculate **je spécule**
subconscious **le subconscient**
I suppose **je suppose**
I summarize **je résume**
summary **le résumé**
theoretical **théoriquement**
theory **la théorie**
  in theory **en théorie**
I think (of/about) **je pense (à)**
thought **la pensée**
true **vrai**
truth **la vérité**
I understand **je comprends**
understanding **la compréhension**
valid (in-) **(non) valable**
view **l'avis** *(m)*, **l'opinion** *(f)*
  in my view **d'après moi, à mon**
  avis
wrong **faux [-sse]**
  I am wrong **j'ai tort**
  it is wrong **on a tort, c'est faux**

THE HUMAN MIND & CHARACTER

6d Expressing views

I accept **j'accepte**
I agree (with/about) **je suis d'accord (avec/au sujet de)**
I answer **je réponds**
answer **la réponse**
I argue **je (me) dispute**
argument **la discussion,**
I ask **je demande**
I ask (a question) **je pose (une question)**
in brief **bref**
I contradict **je contredis (contredire)**
I criticize **je critique**
I define **je définis**
definition **la définition**
I deny **je nie**
I describe **je décris (décrire)**
description **la description**
I disagree (with/about) **je ne suis pas d'accord (avec/sur)**
I discuss **je discute (de)**

discussion **la discussion**
I maintain **je maintiens (maintenir)**
I mean **je veux (vouloir) dire**
opinion **l'opinion (f)**
in my opinion **à mon avis**
question **la question**
I question **je mets (mettre) en question**
a thorny question **une question épineuse**
I suggest **je suggère (suggérer)**
it is a question of **c'est une question de**
I say **je dis (dire)**
I state **je déclare**
statement **la déclaration**
suggestion **la suggestion**

Giving examples
as is known **tel que nous le connaissons**

– What do you think of the speaker?

– In my opinion he did not consider the basic problem.

In principle I agree with his views. On the one hand he proved the need for new housing. On the other hand he discussed the problems of finding a site.

– I suggest we try to analyze the problem carefully. Then we shall be able to judge the situation and come to a sound conclusion.

– **Que pensez-vous de la personne qui parle?**

– **À mon avis, il n'a pas abordé le problème essentiel.**

Je suis d'accord sur le principe. D'une part il a démontré que l'on avait besoin de nouveaux logements, et de l'autre il a discuté des problèmes pour trouver des sites.

– **Je propose que nous essayions d'analyser le problème avec soin. Nous serons alors en mesure de parvenir à une conclusion mesurée.**

etc./and so on   **etc/ainsi de suite**
example/instance   **un exemple**
for example   **par exemple**
i.e.   **c.a.d. (c'est à dire)**
namely   **voire**
I quote   **je cite**
such as   **tel[le] que**

Comparing and contrasting

advantage   **l'avantage** *(m)*
I compare   **je compare**
comparison   **la comparaison**
  in comparison with   **comparé avec/à, en comparaison avec**
it contrasts with   **il contraste avec**
contrast   **le contraste**
  in contrast   **par contraste**
I differ   **je diffère**
difference   **la différence**
different (from)   **différent (de)**
disadvantage   **l'inconvénient** *(m)*
dissimilar   **dissemblable, différent de**
I distinguish   **je distingue**
pros and cons   **le pour et le contre**

relatively   **relativement**
same   **le/la même**
similar   **qui ressemble, semblable**

Expressing reservations

even if   **même si**
even so   **malgré tout**
to some extent   **jusqu'à un certain point**
at first sight   **à première vue**
hardly   **à peine**
in general   **en général**
in the main   **dans l'ensemble**
in part/partly   **en partie**
perhaps/maybe   **peut-être**
presumably   **probablement, sans doute**
probably   **probablement**
relatively   **relativement**
reservation   **la réserve**
unfortunately   **malheureusement**
unusual(ly)   **inaccoutumé**
virtually   **pratiquement**
in a way   **dans un sens**

---

conclusion   **la conclusion**
  in conclusion   **en conclusion**
finally   **finalement**
first   **premier**
firstly   **premièrement**
  for one thing …, for another …
  d'abord …, ensuite …
furthermore   **de plus, en outre**
on the one hand   **d'une part**
  on the other hand   **d'autre**
initially   **pour commencer**

last   **dernier**
lastly   **pour finir**
  at last   **enfin, finalement**
next   **suivant**
place   **la place**
  in the first place   **pour commencer, d'abord**
  in the second place   **ensuite**
secondly   **ensuite**
in short   **en résumé**

– He is partly right about the reasons for our difficulties, but there is probably much more behind it.

– Il a raison en partie en ce qui concerne la source de nos problèmes, mais cette histoire cache sans doute beaucoup de choses.

Arguing a point

admittedly   **il faut le reconnaître**
all the same   **néanmoins,**
   toutefois, quand même
although   **bien que**
anyway   **de toute façon**
apart from   **à part**
as for....   **quant à**
as I see it   **comme je le perçois**
as well   **également**
despite this   **en dépit de cela**
in effect   **en fait**
however   **cependant, toutefois**
incidentally   **à propos**
instead   **à la place**
instead of   **au lieu de**
just as important   **tout aussi**
   important
likewise   **de même**
no matter whether   **quoi qu'il en**
   soit
that may be so   **cela est peut-être**
   vrai
nevertheless   **néanmoins**
otherwise   **autrement**

in reality   **en réalité**
in many respects   **à plusieurs**
   égards
in return   **en revanche**
as a rule   **en règle générale**
so to speak   **pour ainsi dire**
in spite of   **en dépit de**
still,....   **et pourtant, …**
to tell the truth   **à vrai dire**
whereas   **tandis que, alors que**
on the whole   **dans l'ensemble**

Cause & effect

all the more (because)   **d'autant**
   plus que
as   **comme**
because   **parce que**
because of   **à cause de**
cause   **la cause**
consequence   **la conséquence**
consequently   **en conséquence**
effect   **un effet**
it follows that   **il en résulte que**
how?   **comment?**
if   **si**

In many respects things are not too bad. As a rule people try to obey the law. However, crime is still common, in spite of the efforts of the police. All the same, we are not discouraged.

Honestly I'm extremely angry with him. Thanks to his carelessness we missed the plane.
Fortunately there was another, but we got to Chicago completely exhausted.

Vraiment je suis très en colère contre lui. En raison de sa négligence nous avons manqué l'avion. Heureusement il y en avait un autre, mais nous sommes arrivés à Chicago complètement épuisés.

À plusieurs égards les choses ne vont pas trop mal. En règle générale les gens essaient d'obéir à la loi. Toutefois les crimes sont encore fréquents, en dépit des efforts de la police. Malgré tout, nous ne perdons pas l'espoir.

reason **la raison**
  for this reason **pour cette raison**
result **le résultat**
  as a result **en conséquence**
provided that **à condition que**
since **puisque**
so long as **tant que**
therefore, so **ainsi, c'est pourquoi**
thus **ainsi**
whether **si**
why? **pourquoi?**

Emphasizing

above all **par-dessus tout**
in addition **en outre**
all the more **d'autant plus**
also **aussi**
both ... and **à la fois/et ... et**
certainly **certainement**
clearly **clairement**
under no circumstances **en aucun cas**
completely **complètement**
especially **surtout, spécialement**

even (more) **encore (plus)**
without exception **sans exception**
I emphasize **je souligne**
extremely **extrêmement**
far and away **de loin**
fortunately **heureusement**
honestly **honnêtement**
just when **au moment précis où**
mainly **pour l'essentiel**
moreover **de plus**
naturally **naturellement**
not at all **pas du tout**
not in the least **pas le moins du monde**
obviously **de toute évidence**
in particular **en particulier**
particularly **particulièrement**
in every respect **à tous les niveaux**
I stress **je souligne**
thanks to **grâce à**
undeniably **sans aucun doute**
very **très**
and what is more **et qui plus est**

And what is more, he clearly didn't care at all. Obviously I shall tell his firm exactly what I think of him. Under no circumstances will I employ him again.

Et qui plus est, de toute évidence ça lui était complètement égal. Bien évidemment je dirai à son entreprise ce que je pense de lui. En aucun cas je ne le réemploierai.

– How did he break his leg?

– Comment s'est-il cassé la jambe?

– When he fetched the ladder he did not notice it was broken. So he fell off it.

– Lorsqu'il est allé chercher l'échelle il n'a pas remarqué qu'elle était cassée, alors il en est tombé.

– Why did he want the ladder?

– Pourquoi avait-il besoin de l'échelle?

– Because he wanted to paint the house.

– Parce qu'il voulait peindre la maison.

Human life & relationships

7a Family & friends

Friendship

acquaintance **la connaissance**
boyfriend **le petit ami**
chum/pal **le copain, la copine**
classmate **le/la camarade de classe**
companion **le compagnon, la compagne**
friend (close) **un ami/une amie (proche)**
friendship **l'amitié** *(f)*
gang **la bande**
we get on well together **nous nous entendons bien**
I get on with **je m'entends avec**
we get together **nous nous retrouvons**
I get to know **j'apprends à connaître**
girl friend **la petite amie**
I introduce **je présente**
mate/buddy **le/la pote**
penfriend/pen pal **le/la correspondant[e]**
quarrel **la querelle**
I quarrel with **je me querelle avec**
relationship **les liens** *(m)* **de parenté**

school-friend/pal **un ami/une amie d'école**

The family and relatives

adopted **adopté**
ancestor **un/une ancêtre**
ancestry **l'ascendance** *(f)*
aunt **la tante**
baby **le bébé**
brother **le frère**
brother-in-law **le beau-frère**
brothers and sisters **les frères et sœurs**
child **l'enfant** *(m)*
close relative **le parent proche**
closely related **proche parent**
common-law husband **l'époux de droit coutumier, le concubin**
common-law wife **l'épouse** *(f)* **de droit coutumier, la concubine**
cousin **le cousin, la cousine**
dad/pa **le papa**
daughter **la fille**
daughter-in-law **la bru, la belle-fille**
distant relative **le parent éloigné**
distantly related **parent éloigné**
elder **aîné**

We are good friends. I get on well with him. We have a good relationship.	**Nous sommes de bons amis. Je m'entends bien avec lui. Nous avons une bonne relation.**
No hard feelings!	**Sans rancune!**
We are more open with one another. We settle conflicts.	**Nous sommes plus francs l'un envers l'autre. Nous réglons les différents.**

elder/-est daughter **l'aînée** *(f)*
elder/-est son **l'aîné** *(m)*
family **la famille**
family-tree **l'arbre** *(m)* **généalogique**
father **le père**
father-in-law **le beau-père**
fiancé(e) **le fiancé, la fiancée**
forbear **un aïeul, une aïeule**
foster **adoptif [-ve]**
genealogy **la généalogie**
goddaughter **la filleule**
godfather **le parrain**
godmother **la marraine**
godson **le filleul**
grandad/grandpa **le papy, le pépé**
grandchildren **les petits-enfants** *(m)*
granddaughter **la petite-fille**
grandfather **le grand-père**
grandmother **la grand-mère**
grandparents **les grands-parents** *(m)*
grandson **le petit-fils**
granny/grandma **la mamie, la mémé**
great-aunt **la grand-tante**
great grandchild **l'arrière petit-fils** *(m)*, **l'arrière petite-fille** *(f)*
great-grandfather **l'arrière grand-père** *(m)*
great-grandmother **l'arrière grand-mère** *(f)*
great-nephew **le petit-neveu**

great-niece **la petite-nièce**
great-uncle **le grand-oncle**
guardian **le tuteur, la tutrice**
half-brother **le demi-frère**
half-sister **la demi-sœur**
husband **le mari, l'époux** *(m)*
maiden aunt **la tante vieille fille**
mother **la mère**
mother-in-law **la belle-mère**
mum/mom **la maman**
nephew **le neveu**
niece **la nièce**
only child **l'enfant** *(m)* **unique**
parents **les parents** *(m)*
partner **le conjoint, la conjointe**
related **apparenté**
relation **le parent, la parente**
relative **le parent, la parente**
second cousin **le petit-cousin**
sister **la sœur**
son **le fils**
son-in-law **le gendre**
spouse **l'épouse** *(f)*, **l'époux** *(m)*
stepbrother **le beau-frère**
stepdaughter **la belle-fille**
stepfather **le beau-père**
stepmother **la belle-mère**
stepsister **la belle-sœur**
stepson **le beau-fils**
twin brother **le frère jumeau**
twin sister **la sœur jumelle**
uncle **l'oncle** *(f)*
wife **la femme, l'épouse** *(f)*
younger/-est **cadet[te]**

– Have you any family?
– I come from a large family. I have four brothers and sisters. We have family problems.

– I have no close family. I am an only child.

We are distantly related.

– **As-tu de la famille?**
– **Je viens d'une famille nombreuse. J'ai quatre frères et sœurs. On a des problèmes familiaux.**

– **Je n'ai aucune famille proche. Je suis enfant unique.**

Nous sommes parents éloignés.

➤ LOVE, MARRIAGE & CHILDREN 7b; GROWING UP 7c

7b Love & children

Love & marriage

adultery **l'adultère**
affair **la liaison**
alimony **la pension alimentaire**
bachelor **le célibataire**
betrothal **les fiançailles** *(f)*
betrothed **fiancé**
breakdown *(marriage)* **la rupture**
bride **la mariée**
bridegroom **le marié**
bridesmaids **les demoiselles** *(f)* **d'honneur**
couple **le couple**
I court **je fais la cour à**
courtship **la cour**
divorce **le divorce**
divorced **divorcé**
I get divorced (from) **je divorce (de)**
divorcee **le/la divorecé[e]**
engaged **fiancé**
I get engaged (to) **je me fiance (avec)**
engagement **les fiançailles** *(f)*
I fall for/in love (with) **je tombe amoureux [-se] de**

I go out with **je sors** *(sortir)* **avec**
we are incompatible **nous ne sommes pas compatibles**
lover **l'amant** *(m)*
marriage **le mariage**
married **marié**
I get married (to) **je me marie (avec)**
married couple **le ménage**
I marry **j'épouse**
matrimony **le mariage**
mistress **la maîtresse**
newly-married couple **les jeunes** *(m)* **mariés**
promiscuity **la promiscuité**
he is promiscuous **il est de mœurs faciles**
I separate from **je me sépare de**
separated **séparé**
separation **la séparation**
unmarried/single **célibataire**
unmarried/single mother **la mère célibataire**
wedding **les noces** *(f)*
widower/widow **le veuf/la veuve**

– We are madly in love. It was love at first sight.

– Nous sommes follement amoureux. Ca a été le coup de foudre.

– Are you married?
– We are getting engaged.

– Vous êtes mariés?
– Nous nous fiançons.

– She doesn't understand me. She is always nagging. She gets me worked up.
– He shouts at me. He drives me mad.
– All that's in the past now. Let's kiss and make up.

– Elle ne me comprend pas. Elle est toujours après moi. Elle m'énerve.
– Il crie après moi. Il me rend folle.
– Tout ça, c'est du passé maintenant. Faisons la paix.

Our relationship is breaking up.

Notre relation est en train de se briser.

Birth & children

baby **le bébé**

babysitter **la gardienne d'enfants, le/la babysitter**

baptism **le baptême**

bib **le bavoir**

birth control **la régulation des naissances, la contraception**

birth-rate **le taux de natalité**

birthday **l'anniversaire** *(m)*

I was born **je suis né[e]**

boy **le garçon**

I bring up/raise a child **j'élève** *(élever)* **un enfant**

I breast feed **j'allaite, je donne le sein à**

child **l'enfant** *(m)*

child-minder/babysitter **la gardienne d'enfants**

childhood **l'enfance** *(f)*

christening **le baptême**

coil **le stérilet**

condom **le préservatif**

contraception **la contraception**

contractions **les contractions** *(f)*

cot/crib **le petit lit, le lit d'enfant**

I deliver **j'accouche**

dummy/teat **la tétine**

I am expecting a baby **j'attends un bébé**

family planning **le planning familial**

fertile (in-) **fécond (stérile)**

fertility **la fertilité**

fertiltity drug **le médicament contre la stérilité**

I give birth (to) **j'accouche (de)**

girl **la fille**

I go into labour/labor **je commence à accoucher**

incubator **la couveuse**

infancy **la petite enfance**

infant **le nouveau-né**

infantile **infantile**

kid **le/la gosse**

lad **le gars**

lass **la jeune fille**

live birth **la naissance viable**

I look like **je ressemble à**

I have a miscarriage **je fais une fausse couche**

midwife **la sage-femme**

nanny **la nounou**

nappy/napkin **la couche**

new-born child **le nouveau-né**

orphan **un orphelin, une orpheline**

period **les règles** *(f)*

pill **la pilule**

pram/perambulator **la voiture d'enfant, la poussette**

pregnant **enceinte**

I remind of **je rappelle** *(rappeler)*

saint's-day **la fête**

sibling *(adj)* **fraternel[le]**

sibling rivalry **la rivalité fraternelle**

stillborn **mort-né**

teenaged **adolescent**

teenager **un adolescent, une adolescente**

teething **le pousse des dents**

toddler **le tout petit, la toute petite**

toys **le jouet**

triplets **les triplés** *(m)*

twin **le jumeau, la jumelle**

I'm on the pill.	**Je prends la pilule.**
I'm six months pregnant.	**Je suis enceinte de 6 mois.**
I spoil my child.	**Je gâte mon enfant.**
He looks like his mother.	**Il ressemble à sa mère.**

7c Life & death

Growing

adolescent	**un adolescent, une adolescente**
adult	**un/une adulte**
adult	**adulte**
age	**l'âge** *(m)*
I age (well)	**je vieillis (bien)**
aged	**âgé (de)**
centenarian	**le/la centenaire**
child	**l'enfant** *(m)*
he comes from	**il vient de**
elder/-est	**un aîné, une aînée**
elderly	**les personnes** *(f)* **âgées**
elderly *(adj)*	**vieux [vieille]**
female	**la femme**
female	**femelle**
foreigner	**un étranger, une étrangère**
generation	**la génération**
generation gap	**le conflit des générations**
I grow old	**je vieillis**

grown-up	**l'adulte** *(m/f)*
grown-up	**adulte**
I grow up	**je deviens** *(devenir)* **adulte**
housewife	**la femme au foyer**
life	**la vie**
life assurance	**l'assurance-vie** *(f)*
male	**l'homme** *(m)*
male *(adj)*	**mâle**
man	**l'homme** *(m)*
mature	**mûr**
maturity	**la maturité**
menopause	**la ménopause**
middle age	**la cinquantaine**
new	**nouveau [nouvelle]**
nickname	**le surnom**
octogenarian	**un/une octogénaire**
old	**vieux [vieille]**
old age	**la vieillesse**
old man, woman	**le vieux, la vieille**
old people's home	**l'hospice** *(m)* **de vieillards**

When I grow up, I want to be an astronaut.	**Quand je serai grand, je serai astronaute.**
He respects his elders.	**Il respecte ses aînés.**
Next door, the couple are getting divorced. The children are suffering as the parents have separated.	**Le couple à côté de chez nous est en train de divorcer. Les enfants souffrent car les parents se sont séparés.**
– What about the elderly? – Most try to stay on in their own homes rather than go into an old people's home.	**– Et les personnes âgées?** **– La plupart des gens essaient de rester dans leur propre maison au lieu d'entrer dans une maison de retraite.**
Their pensions are barely adequate. However, the community looks after them well.	**Leurs pensions sont à peine suffisantes. Cependant, la communauté s'occupe bien d'eux.**

pension **la pension**
pensioner **le retraité, la retraitée**
people **les gens** *(m)*
permissive society **la société permissive**
person **la personne**
present **présent**
in the prime of life **dans la fleur de l'âge**
responsible **responsable**
I retire **je prends ma retraite**
retired **en retraite**
retirement **la retraite**
  early retirement **la retraite anticipée**
septuagenarian **le/la septuagénaire**
single **célibataire**
spinster **la vieille fille**
stranger **un étranger, une étrangère**
surname **le nom de famille**
I take after **je tiens** *(tenir)* **de**
visit **la visite**
I visit **je rends visite**
woman **la femme**
year **l'année** *(f)*
young **jeune**
young person **le/la jeune**
younger **plus jeune**
youngest **le/la plus jeune**
youth **la jeunesse**
youth *(persons)* **les jeunes** *(m/f)*

Death

afterlife **la vie future/eternelle**
angel **l'ange** *(m)*
ashes **les cendres** *(f)*
autopsy **l'autopsie** *(f)*
body **le corps**
burial **l'enterrement** *(m)*
I bury **j'enterre**
corpse **le cadavre, le corps**
he is cremated **il est incinéré**

cremation **la crémation**
crematorium/crematory **le crématorium**
dead **mort**
death **la mort**
death rate **le taux de mortalité**
death certificate **l'acte** *(m)* **de décès**
he dies **il meurt** *(mourir)*
epitaph **l'épitaphe** *(f)*
eulogy **le panégyrique**
funeral **l'enterrement** *(m)*, **les obsèques** *(f)*
grave **la tombe**
gravestone/tombstone **la pierre tombale**
graveyard/cemetery **la cimetière**
heaven **le ciel, le paradis**
hell **l'enfer** *(m)*
I inherit **j'hérite**
inheritance **la succession**
last rites **les derniers sacrements** *(mpl)*
he lies in state **il est exposé solennellement**
mortuary **la morgue**
I mourn **je pleure**
mourning **le deuil**
I am in mourning for **je porte le deuil de**
obituary **la notice nécrologique**
he passes away **il s'éteint** *(s'éteindre)*, **il disparaît** *(disparaître)*
remains **les restes** *(m)*
he goes to heaven **il va au ciel/paradis**
tomb **le tombeau**
undertaker **l'entrepreneur** *(m)* **de pompes funèbres**
will **le testament**
  the last will and testament of **les dernières volontés** *(f)* **de**

Daily life

8a The house

amenities **les aménagements** (m)
apartment **l'appartement** (m)
boarding house **la pension (de famille)**
block of flat/apartment house **l'immeuble** (m)
of brick **en brique**
I build **je construis** (construire)
building **le bâtiment**
building plot **le terrain à bâtir**
building site **le chantier de construction**
bungalow **le pavillon**
caretaker **le gardien, la gardienne**
chalet **le chalet**
council flat/apartment **l'appartement** (m) **loué à la municipalité, le/la H.L.M.**
council house **le/la H.L.M. (Habitation à Loyer Modéré)**
detached house **la maison individuelle**
flat/apartment **l'appartement** (m)
furnished flat/apartment house **l'appartement** (m) **meublé**
furnished house **la maison meublée**
freehold **la propriété foncière libre**
I have an extension built **je fais agrandir la maison**
house **la maison**
housing **le logement**
landlord/landlady **le/la propriétaire**
leasehold/lease **le bail**
leasehold property **la propriété louée à bail**
lodger/roomer **le/la locataire**
I modernize **je modernise**
mortgage **l'emprunt-logement** (m)
mortgage rate **le taux de**

– Are you hoping to buy your own home soon?
– Yes, we are trying to get a mortgage. We have found an older property which we will modernize.

We are renting a flat/an apartment at the moment. The rent is very high, and the landlord is slow to make improvements

We are having a house built.

– Espérez-vous acheter votre propre maison bientôt?
– Oui, nous essayons d'obtenir un emprunt-logement. Nous avons trouvé une propriété plus vieille que nous allons moderniser.

Nous louons un appartement en ce moment. Le loyer est très cher et le propriétaire est lent à faire des améliorations.

Nous faisons construire.

l'emprunt-logement
I move (house) **je déménage**
I move in **j'emménage**
I occupy **j'occupe**
I own **je possède**
owner-occupied **occupé par son/sa propriétaire**
penthouse **l'appartement** (m) **de grand standing**
partly furnished **en partie meublé**
prefabricated house **la maison en préfabriqué**
premises **les locaux** (m)
refuse/garbage collection le **ramassage d'ordures**
removal van **le camion de déménagement**
rent **le loyer**
I rent **je loue**
sewage disposal **l'évacuation** (f) **des eaux usées**
(of) stone **de/en pierre**
street lighting **l'éclairage** (m) **des rues**
I take out a mortgage **je fais un emprunt-logement**
tenancy **la location**
tenant **le/la locataire**

terraced houses **des maisons** (f) **mitoyennes**
unfurnished flat/apartment **l'appartement** (m) **non-meublé**

Rooms

attic **la mansarde**
basement **le sous-sol**
bathroom **la salle de bains**
bedroom **la chambre à coucher**
cellar **la cave**
corridor **le couloir**
dining-room **la salle à manger**
hall(way) **l'entrée** (f)
kitchen **la cuisine**
landing **le palier**
lavatory/bathroom **les toilettes** (f)
living room **la salle de séjour**
loft **le grenier**
lounge **le salon**
shower room **la douche**
sitting-room/living room **le salon/la salle de séjour**
study **le bureau**
utility room **la buanderie**
verandah **la véranda**
W.C. **les W.C.** (m)

Her penthouse is to let/for rent.

Son appartement de grand standing est à louer.

My tenancy has two weeks to run.

Ma location se termine dans deux semaines.

We moved house two years ago.

Nous avons déménagé il y a deux ans.

The house has a fairly pleasant view: it grows on you after a while!

La vue depuis la maison est assez agréable. On s'y fait au bout de quelque temps!

The whole house needs painting before we sell it.

Toute la maison a besoin d'être repeinte avant d'être vendue.

8b The household

aerial **l'antenne** (f)
back-door **la porte de derrière**
balcony **le balcon**
big **grand**
blind **le store**
boiler **la chaudière**
breakfast room **la petite salle à manger**
built-in **encastré**
burglar alarm **la sonnerie d'alarme**
button **le bouton**
carpet **la moquette**
ceiling **le plafond**
central **central**
chimney/smokestack **la cheminée**
clean **propre**
comfortable (un-) **(in)confortable**
cosy **douillet[te]**
cupboard **le placard**
wall-cupboard **le placard mural**
curtain **le rideau**
desk **le bureau**
dirty **sale**
door **la porte**
door-handle **la poignée de la porte**
door-knob **le bouton de la porte**
doorbell **la sonnette**
door-mat **le paillasson**
downstairs **en bas**
dustbin/trash can **la poubelle**
electric **électrique**
electric plug **la prise électrique**
electric socket **la prise électrique**
electricity **l'électricité** (f)
en-suite **attenant**
fireplace **la cheminée**
flex/extension cord **la rallonge**
floor **le sol**
floor/storey **l'étage** (m)
floor board **la planche**

front door **la porte d'entrée**
functional **fonctionnel**
furnished **meublé**
furniture **les meubles** (m)
item of furniture **le meuble**
garage **le garage**
gas **le gaz**
glass (material) **le verre**
ground floor **le premier étage**
gutter **la gouttière**
handle (on drawer, door) **la poignée**
handle (on basket, jug) **l'anse** (f)
hearth **le foyer**
heating **le chauffage**
central heating **le chauffage central**
included **inclus**
key **la clé**
keyhole **le trou de serrure**
lamp **la lampe**
lampshade **l'abat-jour** (m)
letterbox **la boîte aux lettres**
lever **le levier**
lift **l'ascenseur** (m)
light bulb **l'ampoule** (f)
light **la lumière**
light-switch **l'interrupteur** (m)
lighting **l'éclairage**
lock **la serrure**
it looks onto **il donne sur**
mantelpiece **le dessus de cheminée**
mat **le tapis**
mezzanine floor **la mezzanine**
modern **moderne**
new **nouveau, neuf [neuve]**
nice **joli**
off (switches, electrical apparatus) **éteint**
off (tap) **fermé**
old **vieux [vieille]**

on *(switches, electrical apparatus)*
 allumé
 on *(tap)* **ouvert**
on the first floor **au premier étage**
own **propre**
passage **le passage**
pipe **le tuyau, le conduit**
plaster **le plâtre**
plumbing **la plomberie, la tuyauterie**
price **le prix**
radiator **le radiateur**
rent **le loyer**
roof **le toit**
roof tile **la tuile**
room **la pièce**
safety chain **la chaîne de sûreté**
sale **la vente**
shelf **l'étagère** *(f)*
shutters **les volets** *(m)*
situation **la situation**
skirting board/baseboard **la plinthe**
skylight **la lucarne**
small **petit**
spacious **spacieux [-se]**
staircase **l'escalier** *(m)*
stairs **les escaliers** *(m)*
step **la marche**
terrace **la terrasse**
tidy **bien rangé, en ordre**
tile **le carreau**
toilet **les toilettes** *(f)*
upper floor **l'étage** *(m)* **supérieur**
upstairs **en haut**
vase **le vase**
view **la vue**
wall **le mur**
 interior wall **la paroi**
 garden wall **le mur (de clôture)**
waste paper basket **la corbeille (à papier)**
water **l'eau** *(f)*
window **la fenêtre**
window-sill **le rebord de la fenêtre**

wire **le fil**
wiring **l'installation** *(f)* **électrique**
wood **le bois**

Electrical goods

answering machine **le répondeur téléphonique**
cassette player **le lecteur de cassettes**
cassette recorder **le magnétophone**
compact-disc player **le lecteur de CD/disques lasers**
deepfreeze **le congélateur**
dishwasher **le lave-vaisselle**
electric appliance **l'appareil** *(m)* **ménager**
electric cooker/stove **la cuisinière électrique**
electric razor/shaver **le rasoir électrique**
food-mixer **le batteur**
freezer **le congélateur**
fridge/refrigerator **le frigo, le réfrigérateur**
hi-fi **la chaîne hi-fi**
iron **le fer (à repasser)**
micro-wave oven **le four à micro-ondes**
personal stereo **le baladeur**
radio **la (poste de) radio**
record player **le tourne-disque**
refrigerator **le réfrigérateur**
spin-drier **l'essoreuse** *(f)*
stereo system **la chaîne stéréo**
tape player **le lecteur de cassettes**
tape recorder **le magnétophone**
trouser/pants press **le presse-pantalons**
tumble-drier **le sèche-linge**
TV set **le poste de télévision**
vacuum cleaner **l'aspirateur** *(m)*
video recorder **le magnétoscope**
washing machine **la machine à laver**

8c Furnishings

Lounge

armchair   **le fauteuil**
ashtray   **le cendrier**
bookshelf   **l'étagère** (f) **(à livres)**
bookcase   **la bibliothèque**
bureau   **le bureau**
coffee table   **la table basse**
cupboard/closet   **le placard**
cushion   **le coussin**
easy chair   **le fauteuil**
ornament   **l'ornement** (m)
picture   **le tableau**
   picture (portrait)   **le portrait**
photo   **la photo**
poster   **le poster**
pouffe   **le pouf**
rocking-chair   **le fauteuil à bascule**
rug   **le tapis**
settee   **le canapé**
sofa   **la banquette**

Kitchen

bottle-opener   **l'ouvre-bouteille(s)**
   (m)
bowl   **le bol**
clothes line   **la corde à linge**
clothes peg   **la pince à linge**
coffee machine   **le percolateur**
coffee pot   **la cafetière**
colander   **la passoire**
cooker/stove   **la cuisinière**
crockery   **la vaisselle**
cup   **la tasse**
cupboard   **le placard**
   wall-cupboard   **le placard**
   mural
cutlery   **les couverts** (m)
dish   **le plat**
dishcloth   **le torchon à vaisselle**
draining-board   **l'égouttoir** (m)
fork   **la fourchette**
frying-pan   **la poêle**
gas cooker/stove   **la cuisinière à**
   gaz

glass   **le verre**
   wine glass   **le verre à vin**
knife   **le couteau**
   carving knife   **le couteau à**
   découper
milk jug   **le pot à lait**
oven   **le four**
plate   **l'assiette** (f)
pepper pot   **le poivrier, la poivrière**
rubbish bin/garbage can   **la**
   poubelle
saltcellar   **la salière**
saucepan   **la casserole**
saucer   **la soucoupe**
scales   **la balance**
sink   **l'évier** (m)
sink unit   **l'évier** (m) **encastré**
spoon   **la cuillère**
tap/faucet   **le robinet**
teapot   **la théière**
tea-towel   **le torchon à vaisselle**
tin/can opener   **l'ouvre-boîte(s)**
   (m)
tray   **le plateau**
washing powder   **la lessive (en**
   poudre)
washing-up/washing liquid   **le**
   produit pour la vaisselle

Dining-room

chair   **la chaise**
candle   **la bougie, la chandelle**
candelabra   **le chandelier**
candlestick   **le bougeoir**
dresser   **le vaisselier**
place setting   **le couvert**
plate warmer   **le chauffe-assiette**
serviette   **la serviette**
sideboard   **le buffet**
table   **la table**
table-clock   **la pendule de table**
table cloth   **la nappe**
table napkin/serviette   **la serviette**
   de table

Bedroom

alarm clock **le réveil**
bed **le lit**
    bunk bed **la couchette**
    double bed **le grand lit, le lit à deux personnes**
bedclothes **les couvertures** *(f)* **et draps** *(m)*
bedding **la literie**
bedside table **la table de nuit**
bedspread **le couvre-lit**
blanket **la couverture**
chest of drawers **la commode**
dressing table **la coiffeuse**
duvet **la couette**
mattress **le matelas**
pillow **l'oreiller** *(m)*
quilt **l'édredon** *(m)*
sheet **le drap**
wardrobe **l'armoire** *(f)*
    hanging wardrobe **la penderie**

Bathroom

basin **le lavabo**
bath **la baignoire**
bath-mat **le tapis de bain**
bidet **le bidet**
clothes brush **la brosse à habits**
flannel/face cloth **le gant de toilette**
handbasin **le lavabo**
laundry basket **le panier à linge sale**
mirror **le miroir**
nail-brush **la brosse à ongles**
plug **la prise**
scales **le pèse-personne**
shower **la douche**
sink **le lavabo**
soap **le savon**
tap **le robinet**
toilet **les toilettes** *(f)*
toilet paper **le papier hygiénique**
toothbrush **la brosse à dents**
towel **la serviette**
towel rail **le porte-serviettes** *(invar)*
washbasin **la cuvette de lavabo**

The washing machine doesn't work. Can you repair it?	**La machine à laver ne marche pas. Pouvez-vous la réparer?**
Come into the dining-room.	**Entrez dans la salle à manger.**
The bed has not been changed. The hot tap/faucet doesn't work!	**Le lit n'a pas été changé. Le robinet d'eau chaude ne marche pas!**
The toilet will not flush! The bathroom mirror is cracked.	**La chasse d'eau ne marche pas! Le miroir de la salle de bains est fendu.**
Can I take a bath? Have you any shampoo? Could we have some clean towels?	**Est-ce que je peux prendre un bain? As-tu du shampooing? Pourrions-nous avoir des serviettes propres?**
I can't find the razor socket.	**Je ne trouve pas la prise du rasoir.**

➤ HOUSEHOLD ITEMS, TOILETRIES 9b; GARDENING 24c; TOOLS App.8b

8d Daily routine

bath **le bain**	washing **le linge, la lessive**
bed **le lit**	washing up/dish washing
breakfast **le petit déjeuner**	**la vaisselle**
daily **journalier [-ère]**	work **le travail**
dinner **le dîner, le repas du soir**	
evening meal **le dîner**	*Actions*
home **la maison**	I break **je casse**
at home **à la maison**	I bring **j'apporte**
housekeeper/maid **la femme de**	I buy **j'achète** *(acheter)*
ménage	I carry **je porte**
housework **le ménage**	I change (clothes) **je me change**
lunch **le déjeuner**	I chat **je bavarde**
routine **la routine**	I clean **je nettoie** *(nettoyer)*
rubbish/garbage **les ordures** *(f)*	I clear (away) **je débarrasse**
school **l'école** *(f)*	I cook **je fais la cuisine**
shopping **les achats** *(m)*	I close **je ferme**
sleep **le sommeil**	I darn **je raccommode**
spare time **le temps libre**	I decorate **je décore**
supper **le souper**	I defrost **je décongèle**
tea **le thé**	I dirty **je salis**
time *(commodity)* **le temps**	I do **je fais**
time *(of day)* **l'heure** *(f)* **de la**	I drink **je bois** *(boire)*
journée	I dry **je sèche**

We usually get up at 7 o'clock. We have breakfast at eight.	**Nous nous levons normalement à 7 heures. Nous prenons le petit déjeuner à 8 heures.**
Lunch is in the dining-room. Dinner will be at nine p.m.	**Le déjeuner est servi dans la salle à manger. Le dîner sera servi à neuf heures.**
The table has not been cleared!	**La table n'a pas été débarrassée!**
My husband cooks on Saturdays.	**Mon mari fait la cuisine le samedi.**
Don't forget to put the rubbish/ garbage out and to switch/turn off the lights.	**N'oublie pas de sortir les ordures et d'éteindre les lumières.**
She does the dusting and cleaning for us on Fridays.	**Elle fait la poussière et le ménage pour nous tous les vendredis.**

I dry up   **j'essuie** *(essuyer)*
I dust   **je fais la poussière**
I eat   **je mange**
I empty   **je vide**
I fasten   **j'attache**
I fill   **je remplis**
I garden/work in the yard   **je fais du jardinage**
I get dressed   **je m'habille**
I get undressed   **je me déshabille**
I get up   **je me lève**
I go to bed   **je vais au lit**
I go to sleep   **je m'endors** *(s'endormir)*
I go to the toilet   **je vais aux toilettes**
I grow *(vegetables)*   **je cultive**
I have breakfast   **je prends le petit déjeuner**
I have lunch   **je déjeune**
I have tea   **je prends le thé**
I heat   **je chauffe**
I iron   **je repasse**
I knit   **je tricote**
I knock   **je frappe**
I lay the table   **je mets** *(mettre)* **la table**
I leave   **je pars** *(partir)*
I let *(allow)*   **je laisse**
I let/rent   **je loue**
I live   **j'habite**
I lock   **je ferme à clé**
I make   **je fais**
I make wet/dampen   **j'humecte**
I mend/fix   **je répare**
I microwave   **je passe au four à micro-ondes**
I move   **je bouge**
I open   **j'ouvre**
I paint   **je peins** *(peindre)*
I polish   **je cire**
I prepare   **je prépare**
I press (the button)   **j'appuie** *(appuyer)* **(sur le bouton)**
I put right   **je remets** *(remettre)* **en place**

I put on *(clothes)*   **je mets** *(mettre)*
I put on *(radio, TV)*   **j'allume**
I repair   **je fais des réparations**
I rest   **je me repose**
I ring *(telephone)*   **j'appelle** *(appeler)*
I ring *(doorbell)*   **je sonne**
I rinse   **je rince**
I scrub   **je frotte**
I sew   **je couds**
I share   **je partage**
I shine   **je fais briller**
I shop   **je fais les courses**
I shower   **je prends une douche**
I shut/close   **je ferme**
I sit (down)   **je m'assieds** *(asseoir)*
I sleep   **je dors** *(dormir)*
I speak   **je parle**
I stand   **je me tiens** *(se tenir)* **debout, je suis debout**
I stand up   **je me mets** *(se mettre)* **debout**
I start   **je commence**
I stop   **j'arrête**
I sweep   **je balaie**
I switch/turn off   **j'éteins** *(éteindre)*, **je ferme**
I switch/turn on   **j'allume, j'ouvre**
I take off   **j'enlève** *(enlever)*
I throw away   **je jette** *(jeter)*
I tie   **je noue**
I tidy/straighten up   **je range**
I unblock   **je débouche**
I undo   **je défais** *(défaire)*
I use   **j'utilise**
I wake up   **je me réveille**
I wallpaper   **je pose du papier peint**
I wash up/wash dishes   **je fais la vaisselle**
I wash (car, clothes)   **je lave**
I wash (myself)   **je me lave**
I watch TV   **je regarde la télévision**
I wear   **je porte**

➤ GARDENING 24c; CLOTHES 9c

Shopping

9a General terms

article l'article *(m)*
automatic door la porte automatique
bargain l'affaire *(f)*
basement le sous-sol
bank-note le billet
discount la réduction
business les affaires *(f)*
cash-card la carte bancaire
cash desk/register la caisse
cash dispenser/auto-teller le distributeur de billets
catalogue/catalog le catalogue
change *(money)* la monnaie
cheap bon marché
check-out la caisse
choice le choix
closed fermé
coin la pièce
costly coûteux [-se]
credit le crédit
credit card la carte de credit
currency la devise
customer information les renseignements *(m)*
customer service le service relation clientèle

day off/closed le jour de congé/ de fermeture
department le rayon
entrance l'entrée *(f)*
escalator l'escalier *(m)* roulant
exit la sortie
expensive/dear cher [-ère]
fashion la mode
fire door la porte de secours
fire exit la sortie de secours
fitting room le salon d'essayage
free gratuit
free gift le cadeau gratuit
it is good value c'est bon marché
handbag le sac à main
instructions for use le mode d'emploi
item l'article *(m)*
label l'étiquette *(f)*
lift/elevator l'ascenseur *(m)*
mail-order la vente par correspondance
manager le gérant
manageress la gérante
market le marché
money l'argent *(m)*
note le billet

Anything else?/Is that all?	**Et avec ça?, Ce sera tout?**
Are you being served?	**On vous sert?, On s'occupe de vous?**
Can I help you?	**Je peux vous aider?**
Do you want anything in particular?	**Vous cherchez quelque chose de précis?**
What would you like?	**Vous désirez?**
Who's next?	**Qui est le suivant/la suivante?**
Whose turn is it?	**C'est à qui le tour?**

open **ouvert**
opening hours **les heures** (f) **d'ouverture**
packet **le paquet**
pocket **la poche**
pound (weight/money) **la livre**
PULL **tirer**
purse **le porte-monnaie**
PUSH **pousser**
quality **la qualité**
real/genuine **véritable**
receipt **le reçu**
reduction **la réduction**
refund **le remboursement**
refundable **remboursable**
sale **les soldes** (f)
security guard **le garde**
self-service **le libre-service**
shop-assistant/sales person **le vendeur, la vendeuse**
shop-keeper **le commerçant**
shop-lifting **le vol à la tire**
shopping **les courses** (f)
shopping basket **le panier**
shop/store **le magasin, la boutique**
shopping list **la liste de courses**
shopping trip **la tournée des magasins**
shopping trolley/cart **le chariot**
shut **fermé**
slice **la tranche**
special offer **l'offre** (f) **spéciale, la promotion**
stairs **les escaliers** (m)

summer sale **les soldes** (f) **d'été**
till **la caisse**
till receipt **le ticket de caisse**
trader **le négociant, le marchand**
traveller's cheque/traveler's check **le chèque de voyage**
wallet **le portefeuille**

Actions

I change **je change**
I choose **je choisis**
I decide **je décide**
I dress **je m'habille**
I exchange **j'échange**
I have on/wear **je porte**
I order **je commande**
I pay **je paie** (payer)
I put on **je mets** (mettre)
I queue/line up **je fais la queue**
I select **je sélectionne, je choisis**
I sell **je vends**
I serve **je sers** (servir)
I shop **je fais les courses**
I shop-lift **je vole**
I show **je montre**
I spend (money) **je dépense**
I steal **je vole**
I take off **j'enlève** (enlever)
I try on **j'essaie** (essayer)
I wait **j'attends**
I wear **je porte**
I weigh **je pèse** (peser)
I wrap up **je fais un paquet cadeau**

How much is it?	**C'est combien?**
I've no change.	**Je n'ai pas de monnaie.**
Can I pay by cheque/check?	**Est-ce que je peux payer par chèque?**
Can you change this note?	**Est-ce que vous pouvez me faire de la monnaie?**
Do you take credit cards?	**Est-ce que vous acceptez les cartes de crédit?**

➤ CURRENCIES App. 9a

9b Household goods & toiletries

Toiletries

after-shave **l'après-rasage** *(m)*
anti-perspirant **le déodorant**
brush **la brosse**
comb **le peigne**
condom **le préservatif**
cosmetics **les produits** *(m)* **de beauté**
cotton wool **le coton hydrophile**
deodorant **le déodorant**
face cream **la crème de soins**
glasses **les lunettes** *(f)*
hairbrush **la brosse à cheveux**
lipstick **le rouge à lèvres**
make-up **le maquillage**
nail-file **la lime à ongles**
paper handkerchief **le mouchoir en papier, le Kleenex®**
perfume **le parfum**
razor **le rasoir**
razor blades **les lames** *(f)* **de rasoir**
sanitary towel **la serviette périodique/hygiénique**
shampoo **le shampooing**
soap **le savon**
spray **le vaporisateur, l'atomiseur** *(m)*
sunglasses **les lunettes** *(f)* **de soleil**
suntan lotion **le lait solaire**
talcum powder **le talc**
tampon **le tampon**
tissues **les Kleenex®**
toilet water **l'eau** *(f)* **de toilette**
toilet-paper **le papier hygiénique**
toiletry **les produits** *(m)* **de toilette**
toothpaste **le dentifrice**
toothbrush **la brosse à dents**
watch **la montre**

Expressions of quantity

a bar of .... **une barre de ...**
a bottle of ... **une bouteille de ...**
a hundred gram(me)s of ... **cent grammes de ...**
a kilo of ... **un kilo de ...**
a litre/liter of **un litre de ...**
a packet of ... **un paquet de ...**
a slice of ... **une tranche de ...**
a tin/can of … **une boîte de ...**
a pound of **une livre de ...**

Household items

bottle **la bouteille**
bowl **l'assiette** *(f)* **creuse, le bol**
cling-film/cellophane wrapping **le Scellofrais®**
clothes-peg **la pince à linge**
cup **la tasse**
dish **le plat**
foil/aluminum foil **le papier d'aluminium**
fork **la fourchette**
glass **le verre**
jar **le pot**
jug **le pichet, la cruche**
kitchen roll **le Sopalin®, l'essuie-tout** *(m)* *(invar)*
knife **le couteau**
matches **les allumettes** *(f)*
paper napkin/serviette **la serviette en papier**
paper towel **le papier Sopalin®**
plate **l'assiette** *(f)*
pot **la marmite, la casserole**
saucer **le soucoupe**
scouring pad **l'éponge** *(f)* **à gratter, le tampon à récurer**
string **la ficelle**
washing-up/dishwashing liquid **le liquide-vaisselle**
washing/wash powder **la lessive, la poudre à laver**

Basic foodstuffs

bacon **le bacon, le lard**
baguette/French stick **la baguette**
baked beans **les haricots** *(m)*
　blancs à la sauce tomate
beer **la bière**
biscuits **les biscuits** *(m)*
bread **le pain**
　rye bread **le pain de seigle**
　sliced bread **le pain coupé en**
　tranches
　white bread **le pain blanc/bis**
　wholemeal/grain bread **le pain**
　complet
butter **le beurre**
cakes **les gâteaux** *(m)*
cereals **les céréales** *(f)*
chips *(UK)*/French fries **les frites**
　(f)
chocolate spread **la pâte à tartiner**
　au chocolat
condiments **les condiments** *(m)*
cola **le coca®**
coffee **le café**
cream **la crème**
crisps/chips *(US)* **les chips** *(f)*
custard **la crème anglaise**
egg **l'œuf** *(m)*
fish **le poisson**
fruit **le fruit**
garlic **l'ail** *(m)*
ham **le jambon**
jam **la confiture**
juice **le jus**
lemonade **la limonade**
loaf **le pain**
　round loaf **la miche**
macaroni **les macaroni** *(m)*
margarine **la margarine**

marmalade **la confiture/**
　marmelade d'oranges
mayonnaise **la mayonnaise**
meat **la viande**
milk **le lait**
mustard **la moutarde**
oil **l'huile** *(f)*
olive-oil **l'huile** *(f)* **d'olive**
pasta **les pâtes** *(f)*
pâté **le pâté**
peanut-butter **le beurre de**
　cacahuète
pepper **le poivre**
pizza **la pizza**
pork **le porc**
pudding **le dessert**
roll *(bread)* **le petit pain**
salt **le sel**
sandwich **le sandwich**
sardines **les sardines** *(f)*
sauce **la sauce**
sausage *(cold, sliced)* **le**
　saucisson
　sausage *(hot)* **la saucisse**
soup **la soupe, le potage**
spaghetti **les spaghetti** *(m)*
spice **l'épice** *(m)*
sugar **le sucre**
sunflower oil **l'huile** *(f)* **de**
　tournesol
sweets/candies **les bonbons** *(m)*
tea bag **le sachet de thé**
toasted sandwich **le croque-**
　monsieur
vegetables **les légumes** *(m)*
vinegar **le vinaigre**
wine **le vin**
yoghourt **le yaourt**

I'd like something for a cough. **Je voudrais quelque chose**
　contre la toux.

Whole or sliced? **Entier ou en tranches?**
Have you anything cheaper? **Est-ce que vous avez quelque**
　chose de moins cher?

▶ FOOD AND DRINK 10

9c Clothing

anorak/parka **l'anorak** *(m)*
beautiful **beau [belle]**
big **grand**
bikini **le bikini**
blouse **le chemisier**
boot **la botte, la chaussure**
bra **le soutien-gorge**
brand new **tout neuf [toute neuve]**
cagoule **la cagoule**
cap **la casquette**
cardigan **le cardigan, le gilet**
checked **à carreaux**
clothes **les habits** *(m)***, les vêtements** *(m)*
clothing **les vêtements** *(m)*
coat **le manteau, la veste**
colour/color-fast **qui ne déteint pas, grand teint**
colourful/colorful **coloré, aux couleurs vives**
cravate **la cravate**
denim **la toile de jean, le jean**
dress **la robe**
elegant **élégant**
embroidered **brodé**
fashionable **à la mode**
glove **le gant**
handkerchief **le mouchoir**
hat **le chapeau**
heel **le talon**
high-heeled **les talons** *(m)* **hauts**
in the latest fashion **à la dernière mode**
jacket **la veste**
jewellery/jewelry **les bijoux** *(m)*
jumper **le pull**
knitted **tricoté**
knitwear **le tricot**
ladies' wear **les vêtements** *(m)* **pour dames**
lingerie **la lingerie**
long **long[ue]**
long-sleeved **à manches longues**
loose **ample**

loud/brash **tape-à-l'œil, voyant**
low-heeled **à talons plats**
matching **coordonné**
men's wear **les vêtements** *(m)* **pour hommes**
non-iron **infroissable**
pair **la paire**
panties **le slip**
pants **le pantalon**
plain **uni**
printed **imprimé**
pyjamas/pajamas **le pyjama**
raincoat **l'imperméable** *(m)*
sandal **la sandale**
scarf **le foulard, l'écharpe** *(f)*
shirt **la chemise**
shoe **la chaussure**
shoe-lace **le lacet**
short-sleeved **à manches courtes**
silky **soyeux [-se]**
size **la taille**
size *(shoes)* **la pointure**
skirt **la jupe**
slip **la combinaison**
small **petit**
smart **élégant, chic**
sneakers **les baskets** *(f)*
sock **la chaussette**
soft **doux [-ce]**
stocking **le bas**
striped **rayé**
suit **le costume**
sweater **le pull**
sweatshirt **le sweat-shirt**
swimsuit/bathing suit/swimming trunks **le maillot de bain**
tie **la cravate**
tight **serré, étroit**
tights **le collant**
too big/small **trop grand/petit**
trainers **les baskets** *(f)*
trousers **le pantalon**
T-shirt **le T-shirt, le ti-shirt**
ugly **affreux [-se], moche**
umbrella **le parapluie**

underpants **le slip, la culotte**
underwear **les sous-vêtements**
    (m)
unfashionable **démodé**
vest **le tricot de peau**

Alterations & repairs

alteration **la retouche**
I alter **je retouche**
belt **la ceinture**
buckle **la boucle**
button **le bouton**
I (dry)clean **je nettoie** *(nettoyer)*
    (à sec)
collar **le col**
cuff *(shirt/blouse)* **le poignet**
dressmaker **la couturière**
dressmaking **la couture**
dry cleaning **la teinturerie**
hat pin **l'épingle** *(f)* **à chapeau**
hem **l'ourlet** *(m)*
I hem **je fais l'ourlet**
hole **le trou**
I iron **je repasse**
knitting machine **la machine à**
    tricoter

knitting needle **l'aiguille** *(f)* **à**
    tricoter
material **le tissu**
needle **l'aiguille** *(f)*
patch **la pièce**
I patch **je rapièce**
pin **l'épingle** *(f)*
pocket **la poche**
I press **je repasse**
press stud/snap fastener **le**
    bouton-pression
I repair **je raccommode**
safety pin **l'épingle** *(f)* **de sûreté**
I sew **je couds**
sewing machine **la machine à**
    coudre
sleeve **la manche**
I shorten **je raccourcis**
I stitch **je recouds**
I take in/let out **je reprends**
    (reprendre), **j'élargis**
tailor **le tailleur**
tailored **bien taillé, bien coupé**
thread **le fil**
turn-up/cuff *(US)* **le revers**
zip(per) **la fermeture-éclair, le zip**

Can I try it on?	**Je peux l'essayer?**
Do you have the same in red?	**Est-ce que vous avez le/la même en rouge?**
I bought it at the sales.	**Je l'ai acheté en solde.**
I like it.	**Il/elle me plaît.**
I prefer ...	**Je préfère ...**
I take/wear size ...	**Je fais du ...**
I would like it in brown.	**Je le/la voudrais en marron.**
I would like to change ...	**Je voudrais changer ...**
I would rather have ...	**Je préférerais prendre ...**
I'll take the big one.	**Je prends le/la grand[e].**
I'd like it two sizes bigger.	**Je voudrais le/la même deux tailles au-dessus.**
It suits me.	**Il/elle me va bien.**
That's is not quite right.	**Ça ne va pas tout à fait.**
They don't go together.	**Ils/elles ne vont pas ensemble.**
What colour/color?	**Quelle couleur?**
Would you like me to wrap it up?	**Voulez-vous que je l'emballe?**

➤ COLOURS/COLORS 5b; LEISURE & SPORTS WEAR 16c

Food & Drink

10a Drinks & meals

Drinks

alcoholic	**alcoolisé**
aperitif	**l'apéritif** *(m)*
beer	**la bière**
black coffee	**le café noir**
brandy	**le cognac**
champagne	**le champagne**
chocolate (drinking)	**le chocolat (chaud)**
cider	**le cidre**
cocktail	**le cocktail**
coffee	**le café**
cola	**le coca®**
draught beer	**la bière pression**
drink	**la boisson**
dry	**sec [sèche]**
fizzy	**gazeux [-se], mousseux [-se]**
fruit-juice	**le jus de fruit**
juice	**le jus**
lemonade	**la limonade**

low-alcohol	**l'alcool** *(m)* **léger**
orange/lemon squash	**l'orangeade** *(f)*/**la citronnade**
milk	**le lait**
milk-shake	**le milk-shake**
mineral water	**l'eau** *(f)* **minérale**
non-alcoholic	**non alcoolisé**
red wine	**le vin rouge**
sherry	**le vin de Xérès**
sparkling	**mousseux [-se]**
spirits	**les alcools** *(m)* **forts**
straight	**sec [sèche], sans eau**
sweet	**sucré**
tea	**le thé**
water	**l'eau** *(f)*
still water	**l'eau non gazeuse**
with ice	**avec de la glace**
whisky	**le whisky**
white/milk coffee	**le café au lait**
white wine	**le vin blanc**
wine	**le vin**

---

cafeteria	**la cafétéria**
canteen	**la cantine**
hot-dog stall	**le stand de hot dogs**
pizza parlour/parlor	**la pizzéria**
restaurant	**le restaurant**
self-service	**le libre-service**
snack-bar	**le snack-bar**
take-away	**à emporter**

Where can we get a drink around here?	**Où peut-on boire un verre par ici?**
Can you tell me where the nearest cafe is, please?	**Pouvez-vous m'indiquer le café le plus proche, s'il vous plaît?**
Can I have a mineral water and two white/milk coffees, please.	**Puis-je avoir une eau minérale et deux cafés au lait, s'il vous plaît?**

Drinking out

bar **le bar**
barman/barmaid **le serveur, la serveuse**
beer hall **la brasserie**
bottle **la bouteille**
cafe **le café**
coffee bar **le café**
cellar **la cave**
coffee-shop **le salon de thé**
counter/bar **le comptoir, le bar**
cup **la tasse**
I drink **je bois**
glass **le verre**
pub(lic-house) **le bar, le pub**
refreshments **les rafraîchissements** *(m)*
saucer **la soucoupe**
sip **la petite gorgée**
straw **la paille**
teaspoon **la petite cuillère**
wine cellar **la cave à vin**
wine glass **le verre de vin**
wine-tasting **la dégustation de vin**

Meals

appetizer/starter **le hors-d'œuvre**
breakfast **le petit déjeuner**
course **le plat**
    first course **l'entrée** *(f)*
dessert **le dessert**
I dine **je dîne**
dinner **le dîner**
I eat **je mange**
I have a snack **je prends un casse-croûte**
I have breakfast **je prends le petit déjeuner**
I have dinner **je dîne**
I have lunch **je déjeune**
lunch **le déjeuner**
main **principal**
meal **le repas**
snack **le casse-croûte**
supper **le souper**

Eating out

I add up the bill **je calcule l'addition** *(f)*
bill/check **l'addition** *(f)*, **la note**
bowl **le bol**
charge **le prix**
cheap **pas cher, bon marché**
children's menu **le menu d'enfant**
I choose **je choisis**
it costs **il coûte**
cover charge **le couvert**
I decide **je décide**
expensive **cher**
first course **l'entrée** *(f)*
fixed price **le prix fixe**
fork **la fourchette**
inclusive **inclus**
inclusive price **prix net**
knife **le couteau**
main course **le plat principal**
menu **le menu**
menu of day **le menu du jour**
napkin **la serviette**
I order **je commande**
order **la commande**
place-setting **le couvert**
plate **l'assiette** *(f)*
portion **la portion**
reservation **la réservation**
I serve **je sers**
service **le service**
set menu **la carte, le menu**
side-dish **le plat d'accompagnement**
spoon **la cuillère**
table **la table**
tablecloth **la nappe**
tip/gratuity **le pourboire**
I tip **je donne un pourboire**
toothpick **le cure-dent**
tourist menu **le menu touriste**
tray **le plateau**
waiter **le serveur**
waitress **la serveuse**
wine list **la liste des vins**

10b Fish & meat

Fish & seafood

anchovy **l'anchois** *(m)*
clam **la palourde**
cockles **les coques** *(f)*
cod **la morue**
crab **le crabe**
crayfish **l'écrevisse** *(f)***, la langouste**
eel **l'anguille** *(f)*
fish **le poisson**
frog's legs **les cuisses** *(f)* **de grenouilles** *(f)*
hake **le colin**
herring **le hareng**
langouste **la langouste**
lobster **le homard**
mullet **le rouget**
mussels **les moules** *(f)*
octopus **la pieuvre**
oyster **l'huître** *(f)*
pike **le brochet**

plaice **le carrelet, la plie**
prawn **la crevette**
salmon **le saumon**
sardine **la sardine**
scampi **la langoustine**
sea bass **le loup**
seafood **les fruits** *(m)* **de mer**
shell **le coquillage**
shellfish **le crustacé**
shrimp **la crevette**
snails **les escargots** *(m)*
sole **la sole**
sprat **le sprat**
squid **le calmar**
swordfish **l'espadon** *(m)*
trout **la truite**
tuna **le thon**
turbot **le turbot**
whitebait **la blanchaille**
whiting **le merlan**

What is there for starters?	**Qu'y a-t-il en hors-d'œuvres?**
Would you prefer cod or sole?	**Vous préféreriez de la morue ou de la sole?**
– Shall we try the chicken? – I'd like a pork chop.	**– On essaie le poulet?** **– J'aimerais une côtelette de porc.**
Can we both have steak, one rare and one well cooked?	**Est-ce qu'on peut prendre tous les deux un bifteck, l'un saignant et l'autre bien cuit?**
Can I have a clean tea-spoon?	**Puis-je avoir une petite cuillère propre, s'il vous plaît?**

Meat

bacon	**le lard, le bacon**
beef	**le bœuf**
beefburger	**le hamburger**
bolognese	**(à la) bolognaise**
brains	**la cervelle**
casserole	**le ragoût en cocotte**
chop	**la côtelette**
cold table	**le buffet froid**
cutlet	**la côtelette**
escalope	**l'escalope** *(f)*
ham	**le jambon**
hamburger	**le hamburger**
hot-dog	**le hot dog**
kidney	**le rognon**
lamb	**l'agneau** *(m)*
liver	**le foie**
marrow	**la moelle**
meat	**la viande**
meat-balls	**les boulettes** *(f)* **de viande**
minced beef	**le bifteck haché**
mixed grill	**le mélange de grillades**
mutton	**le mouton**
offal	**les abats** *(m)*
oxtail	**la queue de bœuf**
pate	**le pâté**

pork	**le porc**
rabbit	**le lapin**
rib	**la côte**
salami	**le salami**
sausage	**la saucisse**
sausage *(cold, sliced)*	**le saucisson**
sirloin	**le faux-filet**
steak	**le steak**
stew	**le ragoût**
tenderloin steak	**le médaillon**
veal	**le veau**

Poultry

capon	**le chapon**
chicken	**le poulet**
chicken breast	**le blanc de poulet**
duck	**le canard**
duckling	**le caneton**
goose	**l'oie** *(f)*
pheasant	**le faisan**
pigeon	**le pigeon**
poultry	**la volaille**
quail	**la caille**
turkey	**la dinde**
woodcock	**la bécasse**

Traditional dishes

bœuf bourguignon rich beef stew with vegetables, braised in red wine

bouillabaisse fish and seafood stew

bourride fish stew (chowder) from Marseilles

canard à l'orange braised duck with oranges and orange liqueur

chateaubriand double fillet steak

coq au vin chicken stewed in red wine

coquilles St-Jacques scallops in a creamy sauce, served on half the shell

entrecôte rib or rib-eye steak

matelote fish stew (generally eel) with wine

quenelles light dumplings made of fish, fowl or meat

quiche a flan with a rich filling of cheese, vegetables, meat or seafood

10c Vegetables, fruit & dessert

Vegetables

artichoke l'artichaut *(m)*
asparagus l'asperge *(f)*
aubergine/eggplant l'aubergine *(f)*
avocado l'avocat *(m)*
beans les haricots *(m)*
beetroot/beets la betterave rouge
broccoli les brocolis *(m)*
Brussels sprout les choux *(m)* de Bruxelles
cabbage le chou
carrot la carotte
cauliflower le chou-fleur
celeriac le céleri-rave
celery le céleri
chick-pea le pois chiche
corn le maïs
corn on the cob l'épi *(m)* de maïs
courgette/zucchini la courgette
cucumber le concombre
endive/chicory l'endive *(f)*
French bean le haricot vert
garlic l'ail *(m)*
gherkin le cornichon
herb l'herbe *(f)* aromatique
leek le poireau
lentil les lentilles *(f)*
lettuce la laitue
marrow la courge
mushroom le champignon
onion l'oignon *(m)*
parsley le persil
parsnip le panais
pea le petit pois

pepper (red/green) le poivron (rouge/vert)
potato la pomme de terre
pumpkin la citrouille, la courge
radish le radis
rice le riz
salad la salade
spinach les épinards *(m)*
sweetcorn le maïs
sweet pea le pois mange-tout
tomato la tomate
turnip le navet
vegetable le légume
vegetable *(adj)* végétal
watercress le cresson

Fruit

apple la pomme
apricot l'abricot *(m)*
banana la banane
berry la baie
bilberry la myrtille
blackberry la mûre
blackcurrant le cassis
Brazil nut la noix du Brésil
bunch of grapes la grappe de raisins
cherry la cerise
chestnut le marron, la châtaigne
coconut la noix de coco
currant la groseille
date la date
fig la figue
fruit le fruit

I want a tomato salad.
Does it have garlic in it?

Je veux une salade de tomates.
Il y a de l'ail dedans?

Two strawberry ice-creams.

Deux glaces à la fraise

Have you got any apple pie?

Avez-vous de la tarte aux pommes?

gooseberry **la groseille à maquereau**
grape **le raisin**
grapefruit **le pamplemousse**
hazelnut **la noisette**
kiwi-fruit **le kiwi**
lemon **le citron**
lime **le citron vert**
melon **le melon**
nectarine **la nectarine, le brugnon**
nut **la noisette**
olive **l'olive** *(f)*
orange **l'orange** *(f)*
passion fruit **le fruit de la passion**
peach **la pêche**
peanut **la cacahuète**
pear **la poire**
piece of fruit **le morceau de fruit**
pineapple **l'ananas** *(m)*
pip **le pépin**
plum **la prune**
pomegranate **la grenade**
prune **le pruneau**
raisin **le raisin**
raspberry **la framboise**
redcurrant **la groseille**
rhubarb **la rhubarbe**
stone **le noyau, le pépin**
strawberry **la fraise**
sultana **les raisins** *(m)* **de Smyrne**
tangerine **la mandarine**
walnut **la noix**

Dessert

biscuit/cookie **le biscuit**
bun **la brioche**
cake **le gâteau**
caramel **le caramel**
chocolate **le chocolat**
chocolates **les chocolats** *(m)*
cake **le gâteau**
cream **la crème**
creme caramel **la crème caramel**
custard **la crème anglaise**
custard tart **le flan**
dessert **le dessert**
doughnut **le beignet**
flan **la tarte**
fresh fruit **le fruit frais**
fruit of the day/season **le fruit du jour/de saison**
fruit salad **la salade/macédoine de fruits**
gateau **le gâteau**
ice cream **la glace**
mousse **la mousse**
pancake **la crêpe**
pastry **la pâtisserie**
pie **la tarte**
pudding/sweet **le pudding, le pouding, le dessert**
tart **la tourte**
trifle **la charlotte russe**
vanilla **la vanille**
whipped cream **la crème Chantilly**
yoghurt **le yaourt**

Traditional dishes

julienne de légumes shredded vegetable soup
soupe à l'oignon French onion soup

crêpe suzette large pancakes simmered in orange juice and flambéd with orange liqueur
mille-feuille cream slice

omelette norvégienne baked Alaska
poire Belle Hélène pear with vanilla ice-cream and chocolate sauce
profiterole puff pastry filled with whipped cream or custard
sorbet water ice/sherbet
velouté de tomates cream of tomato soup

10d Cooking & eating

Food preparation

I bake	**je fais cuire**
baked	**cuit au four**
barbeque	**le barbecue**
I beat	**je bats** *(battre)*
beaten	**battu**
I boil	**je fais bouillir**
boiled	**bouilli**
bone	**l'os** *(m)*
boned	**désossé**
boned *(fish)*	**sans arêtes**
I bone	**je désosse, j'ôte les arêtes de**
I braise	**je braise**
braised	**braisé**
in breadcrumbs	**en miettes**
breast	**le blanc**
I carve	**je découpe**
I chop	**je hache**
I clear the table	**je débarrasse la table**
I cook	**je fais la cuisine**
cooking/cuisine	**la cuisine**

I cut	**je coupe**
I dice	**je coupe en cubes**
dough	**la pâte**
I dry up	**j'essuie** *(essuyer)*
flour	**la farine**
food preparation	**la préparation culinaire**
fried	**frit**
I fry	**je fais frire**
I garnish with	**je garnis de**
I grate	**je rape**
grated	**rapé**
gravy	**le jus, la sauce**
I grill	**je fais griller**
grilled	**grillé**
ingredient	**l'ingrédient** *(m)*
large	**grand**
I lay/set the table	**je mets** *(mettre)* **la table**
leg	**la patte, le gigot**
I marinate	**je fais mariner**
marinated	**mariné**
medium *(rare)*	**à point**

Fruit salad

Ingredients:
2 apples, 2 pears, 2 oranges, 1 banana, 100g cherries, 100g grapes

Peel and slice apples, pears, oranges and the banana. Wash grapes and cherries, add to bowl. Add 100ml of orange juice. Chill before serving.

Salade de fruits

Ingrédients:
2 pommes, 2 poires, 2 oranges, 1 banane, 100g de cerises, 100g de raisin

Pelez et coupez les pommes, les poires, les oranges et la banane. Lavez le raisin et les cerises et ajoutez-les aux fruits; mettez-les dans un saladier. Ajoutez 100ml de jus d'orange et tenez au frais avant de servir.

medium-sized **moyen[ne]**
milk **le lait**
I mix **je mélange**
mixed **mélangé**
olive-oil **l'huile** (f) **d'olive**
pastry **la pâte**
    puff-pastry **la pâte feuilletée**
    short(crust) pastry **la pâte brisée**
peel **la pelure**
I peel **je pèle** (peler), **j'épluche**
peeled **pelé, épluché**
I pour **je verse**
rare **saignant**
recipe (for) **la recette (de)**
roast **le rôti**
I roast **je fais rôtir**
in sauce **en sauce**
I sift **je tamise, je passe au tamis**
I slice **je coupe (en tranches)**
sliced **(coupé) en tranches**
I spread **j'étends**
stewed **à l'étouffée**
sunflower oil **l'huile** (f) **de tournesol**
I toast **je fais griller**
toasted **grillé**
I wash up **je fais la vaisselle**
I weigh **je pèse** (peser)
well-done **bien cuit**
I whip **je fouette**
whipped **fouetté**
I whisk **je bats** (battre), **je remue, je fouette**
whisked **battu, fouetté**

Eating

additive **l'additif** (m)
I am hungry **j'ai faim**
I am thirsty **j'ai soif**
appetite **l'appétit** (m)
appetizing **appétissant**
bad **mauvais**
I bite **je mords**
bitter **amer [-ère]**

calorie **la calorie**
    low-calorie **à basses calories**
I chew **je mâche**
cold **froid**
delicious **délicieux [-se]**
diet **le régime**
    I'm on a diet **je suis/me mets** (se mettre) **au régime**
fatty/oily **gras[se]**
fresh **frais [fraîche]**
fresh(ly) **fraîche(ment)**
healthy (appetite) **bon[ne], robuste**
    healthy (food) **sain**
I help myself **je me sers** (servir)
hot **chaud**
hunger **la faim**
hungry **affamé, qui a faim**
I like **j'aime**
mild **doux [-ce], léger [-ère]**
I offer **j'offre** (offrir)
I pass (salt) **je passe (le sel)**
piece **le morceau**
I pour **je verse**
I provide **je fournis**
salty **salé**
I serve **je sers** (servir)
    dinner is served **le dîner est servi**
sharp **coupant**
slice **la tranche**
I smell **je sens** (sentir)
soft **doux [-ce]**
spicy **épicé**
stale (bread) **rassis**
    (cheese) **dur**
still **non gazeux [-se]**
strong **fort**
I swallow **j'avale**
tasty **qui a du goût**
thirst **la soif**
thirsty **assoiffé**
I try **j'essaie** (essayer)
vegan **végétalien[ne]**
vegetarian **végétarien[ne]**

Sickness & Health

11a Accidents & emergencies

accident **l'accident** *(m)*
ambulance **l'ambulance** *(f)*
I attack **j'attaque**
black eye **l'œil** *(m)* **poché**
I bleed **je saigne**
blood **le sang**
bomb **la bombe**
break **la fracture**
I break **je casse**
  I broke a leg **je me suis cassé la jambe**
breakage **la fracture, la rupture**
broken **cassé**
bruise **la contusion, l'hématome** *(m)*, **le bleu**
I bruise easily **je me fais facilement des bleus**
  I bruise (someone) **je fais un bleu à**
burn **la brûlure**
I burn **je (me) brûle**

casualty **l'urgence** *(f)*
casualty department **le service des urgences**
I collide **j'entre en collision**
collision **la collision**
I crash (into) **j'entre en collision (avec)**
crash **la collision, un accident**
I crush **j'écrase**
dead **mort**
death **la mort**
I die **je meurs** *(mourir)*
emergency **l'urgence** *(f)*
emergency exit **la sortie de secours**
emergency services **les services** *(m)* **de secours**
it explodes **il explose**
explosion **l'explosion** *(f)*
I extinguish **j'éteins** *(éteindre)*
I fall **je tombe**

There has been an accident! We need an ambulance quickly.

– My friend is injured. Are you a doctor? Do you know any revival techniques?
– I'm sorry, I have never done any First Aid training.
– Then where's the nearest hospital?

Il vient d'y avoir un accident. Il nous faut une ambulance, vite!

– **Mon ami est blessé. Vous êtes médecin?**

– **Je suis désolé. Je n'ai jamais fait de cours de secourisme.**
– **Où est l'hôpital le plus proche alors?**

---

fatal **fatal**
fine **bien**
fire **le feu**
fire brigade **les pompiers** *(m)*
fire engine **le camion des pompiers**
fire extinguisher **l'extincteur** *(m)*
fireman **le pompier**
first aid **les premiers secours** *(m)*
fracture **la fracture**
graze **l'écorchure** *(f)*
    I grazed my knee **je me suis écorché le genou**
I've had an accident **j'ai eu un accident**
hospital **l'hôpital** *(m)*
I've hurt myself **je me suis fait mal (à)**
impact **l'impact** *(m)*
incident **l'incident** *(m)*
I injure **je blesse**
injury **la blessure**
injured **blessé**
    I've injured myself **je me suis blessé[e]**
insurance **l'assurance** *(f)*
I insure **j'assure**
I kill **je tue**

killed **tué**
life-belt **la ceinture de sécurité**
life-jacket **le gilet de sauvetage**
oxygen **l'oxygène** *(f)*
paramedic **l'auxiliare** *(m/f)* **medical(e)**
I recover **je recupère, je me remets** *(-mettre)*
recovery **la récupération**
I rescue **je sauve**
rescue **le sauvetage**
rescue services **les services** *(m)* **de sauvetage**
I run over **j'écrase**
I rush **je me dépêche**
safe **sauf [-ve], sauvé**
safe and sound **sain et sauf [saine et sauve]**
safety-belt **la ceinture de sécurité**
salvage **la récupération**
I save **je sauve**
seatbelt **la ceinture de sécurité**
terrorist attack **l'attaque** *(f)* **de terroristes**
third-party **l'assurance** *(f)* **au tiers**
witness **le témoin**
I wound **je (me) blesse**
wounded **blessé**

Call the fire brigade! Someone is trapped in the wreckage of the car crash.

Appelez les pompiers! Quelqu'un est coincé dans les débris de la voiture.

She has cut her hand badly.

Elle s'est coupé profondément la main.

I think I have broken my arm. It hurts a lot.

Je crois que je me suis cassé le bras. Ça fait très mal.

It was your fault, not mine.

Vous êtes en tort, pas moi.

Statistics show that the most likely place for accidents is in the home.

Les statistiques montrent que la plupart des accidents se produisent à domicile.

➤ MEDICAL TREATMENT 11c; HEALTH & HYGIENE 11d

11b Illness & disability

alive **vivant**
all right **bien**
arthritis **l'arthrite** *(f)*
asthma **l'asthme**
I bleed **je saigne**
blind **aveugle**
blood **le sang**
breath **le souffle**
I breathe **je respire**
breathless **à bout de souffle**
broken **cassé**
cancer **le cancer**
catarrh **le catarrhe**
I catch cold **je prends** *(prendre)*
  froid
cold **le rhume**
constipated **constipé**
constipation **la constipation**
convalescence **la convalescence**
I am convalescing **je suis en**
  convalescence
cough **la toux**
I cough **je tousse**
I cry **je pleure**
I cut **je (me) coupe**

dead **mort**
deaf **sourd**
  deaf-mute **le sourd-muet, la**
  sourde-mouette
deafness **la surdité**
death **la mort**
depressed **déprimé**
depression **la dépression**
  (nerveuse)
diarrhoea **la diarrhée**
I die **je meurs** *(mourir)*
diet **le régime, la diète**
disabled **handicapé**
disease **la maladie**
dizziness **le vertige,**
  l'étourdissement *(m)*
dizzy **pris de vertige**
drug **le médicament, la drogue**
drugged **drogué**
drunk **ivre, saoul**
dumb **muet[te]**
earache **la douleur à l'oreille**
  I've earache **j'ai mal à l'oreille**
I feel dizzy **j'ai la tête qui tourne,**
  je suis pris *(prendre)* **de vertige**

– What's wrong?
– My foot hurts.

I can't breath very well.

I have been sick/thrown up several
times. I had the flu last week.

She said she felt very dizzy.

I feel dizzy if I stand up.

I don't usually faint!
But the dizziness is wearing off.

– Qu'est-ce qui ne va pas?
– J'ai mal au pied.

Je n'arrive pas à respirer
correctement.

J'ai vomi plusieurs fois. J'ai eu
la grippe la semaine dernière.

Elle a dit qu'elle était prise d'un
violent vertige.

J'ai la tête qui tourne si je me
lève.

Je m'évanouis très rarement.
Mais mon vertige a l'air de
s'atténuer.

I feel ill/unwell **je me sens** *(se sentir)* **mal, je ne me sens pas bien**
fever **la fièvre**
feverish **fièvreux [-se]**
flu **la grippe**
I get drunk **je me saoule**
I got better **je me suis remis** *(remettre)*
handicapped **le handicapé, la handicapée**
  handicapped *(adj)* **handicapé**
I had an operation **j'ai été opéré**
I have a headache **j'ai mal à la tête**
heart attack **la crise cardiaque**
high blood pressure **de la tension**
hurt **blessé**
I hurt … **j'ai mal à …**
it hurts **ça fait mal**
where does it hurt? **où avez-vous mal?**
illness **la maladie**
I am ill/sick **je suis malade**
I live **je vis** *(vivre)*, **je suis en vie**
I look (ill) **j'ai l'air (malade)**
mental illness **la maladie mentale**

mentally sick **malade mental**
migraine **la migraine**
mute **le muet, la muette**
  mute *(adj)* **muet[te]**
pain **la douleur**
painful **douloureux [-se]**
pale **pale**
paralyzed **paralysé**
paraplegic **paraplégique**
pregnant **enceinte**
pregnancy **la grossesse**
rheumatism **le rhumatisme**
sick **malade**
I am sick/vomit **je vomis**
I sneeze **j'éternue**
sore throat **le mal à la gorge**
sting **la piqûre**
it stings **ça pique**
stomach ache **le mal à l'estomac**
stomach upset **l'indigestion** *(f)*
symptom **le symptôme**
I take drugs **je me drogue**
temperature **la température**
I have a temperature **j'ai de la température/fièvre**
travel sickness **le mal des transports**

My children have diarrhoea; I seem to be constipated.	**Mes enfants ont la diarrhée; je pense que je suis constipé.**
I don't know what is wrong with you. It's only a stomach upset/stomachache.	**Je ne sais pas ce qui ne va pas chez toi. Ce n'est qu'une indigestion.**
I am pregnant!	**Je suis enceinte!**
He seems to have a temperature.	**Il a l'air d'avoir de la température**
He had an operation recently.	**Il a été opéré récemment.**
He seems to be recovering.	**Il a l'air de se remettre.**
I suffer from high blood-pressure.	**Je fais de l'hypertension.**
I have a sore throat.	**J'ai mal à la gorge.**
I have a migraine coming on.	**Je sens que je vais avoir une migraine.**

11c Medical treatment

antiseptic l'antiseptique *(m)*
appointment le rendez-vous
bandage la bande, le bandage
blood le sang
blood test l'analyse *(f)* de sang
blood pressure la tension arterielle
capsule la capsule
chemist le pharmacien, la pharmacienne
chemotherapy la chimiothérapie
critical critique
cure le traitement, la guérison
danger to life le danger mortel
dangerous dangereux [-se]
death la mort
doctor (Dr.) le médecin (Dr)

dressing le pansement, le bandage
drop la goutte
drug le médicament
E111-form le formulaire E111
I examine j'examine
examination l'examen *(m)*
I fill je remplis
four times a day quatre fois par jour
I have j'ai
heating le chauffage
hospital un hôpital
I improve je me rétablis, je me remets *(remettre)*
injection la piqûre
insurance certificate le certificat

Call a doctor!
Is he a good doctor?

Appelez un docteur!
C'est un bon médecin?

Will I need an operation? I have my medical insurance.

Est-ce que j'ai besoin d'une opération? J'ai mon assurance médicale.

He does not like injections.
He has never had an X-ray.

Il n'aime pas les piqûres.
On ne lui a jamais fait de radio.

Can I have a prescription? I have lost my tablets.

Est-ce que vous pouvez me faire une ordonnance? J'ai perdu mes comprimés.

An increasing number of people use alternative medicine and techniques, like homeopathy and reflexology.

Un nombre croissant de gens utilise les médecines parallèles ainsi que des techniques comme l'homéopathie et la réflexologie.

Stress-related illness is on the increase.

Les maladies provoquées par le stress augmentent.

médical
I look after **je m'occupe de**
medical **médical, l'examen** *(m)* **médical**
medicine **le médicament**
medicine *(science)* **la médecine**
midwife **la sage-femme**
nurse **un infirmier, une infirmière**
I nurse **je soigne**
I operate **j'opère**
operation **l'opération** *(f)*
pastille **la pastille**
patient **le malade, le patient**
physiotherapy **la kinésithérapie**
physiotherapist **le/la kinésithérapeute**
pill **la pillule**
plaster (of Paris) **le plâtre de Paris**
I prescribe **je prescris**
prescription **l'ordonnance** *(f)*
radio therapy **la radiothérapie**
receptionist **le/la réceptioniste**
service **le service**
I set **je fixe**
spa resort **la station thermale**
specialist **le spécialiste**
stitch **le point**
sticking plaster/Bandaid® **le sparadrap**
surgery **la chirurgie, le cabinet médical**
surgery hours **les heures** *(f)* **de consultation**
syringe **la seringue**
tablet **le comprimé**
therapeutic **thérapeutique**
therapy **les soins** *(m)*
therapist **le thérapeute**
thermometer **le thermomètre**
I treat **je soigne**
treatment **le traitement**
ward **la salle d'hôpital**
wound **la blessure**
I X-ray **la radiographie**

Dentist & optician

abscess **l'abcès** *(m)*
anaesthetic **l'anesthésique** *(m)*
bi-focals **à double foyer, bifocal**
contact lens **le verre de contact**
hard/soft lenses **les verres durs/souples**
contact lens fluid **le liquide pour verres de contact**
crown **la couronne**
dental treatment **le traitement dentaire**
dentist **le dentiste**
dentures **le dentier**
drill **la fraise**
drilling **le fraisage**
I extract **j'arrache**
eye **l'œil** *(m)* (pl **les yeux**)
eyesight **la vue**
eyestrain **la vue fatiguée**
eye test **l'examen** *(m)* **de la vue**
false **faux [fausse]**
filling **le plombage**
frame **la monture**
glasses/spectacles **les lunettes** *(f)*
gum **la gencive**
lens **le verre**
I'm long-sighted **je suis presbyte**
optician **un opticien, une opticienne**
pupil **la pupille**
I'm short-sighted **je suis myope**
spectacle case **l'étui** *(m)* **à lunettes**
stye **l'orgelet** *(m)*
sunglasses **une paire de lunettes de soleil**
tinted **teinté**
tooth **la dent**
I have toothache **j'ai mal aux dents**

11d Health & hygiene

Physical state

ache	**la douleur**
aching	**endolori, douloureux [-se]**
asleep	**endormi**
awake	**éveillé**
blister	**l'ampoule** *(f)*
boil	**le furoncle**
comfort	**le confort**
comfortable	**confortable, à l'aise**
discomfort	**le malaise**
dizziness	**le vertige**
dizzy	**pris de vertige**
drowsiness	**la somnolence**
drowsy	**somnolent**
faint	**pris de vertige**
I exercise	**je fais de l'exercice**
exercise bike	**le vélo de santé/d'apportement**
I faint	**je m'évanouis**
I feel (well)	**je me sens** *(se sentir)* **(bien)**
fit	**en forme**
fitness	**la forme**
I'm hot/cold	**j'ai chaud/froid**
health	**la santé**
healthy	**en bonne santé, sain**
hunger	**la faim**
hungry	**affamé**
ill/sick	**malade**
I lie down	**je m'allonge**
I look	**j'ai l'air**
queasy	**écœuré**
recovery	**la convalescence**

I recuperate/recover	**je me rétablis, je guéris**
I relax	**je me détends**
I rest/have a rest	**je me repose**
sick	**malade**
I sleep	**je dors** *(dormir)*
sleepy	**ensommeillé**
stamina	**la vigueur**
strange	**drôle, bizarre**
thirst	**la soif**
I am thirsty	**j'ai soif**
tired	**fatigué**
I am tired	**je suis fatigué**
tiredness	**la fatigue**
uncomfortable	**mal à l'aise**
under the weather	**mal en point**
unfit	**pas en forme**
unwell	**malade, indisposé**
virile	**viril**
I wake up	**je me réveille**
well	**bien**
well-being	**le bien-être**

Beauty & hygiene

acne	**l'acné** *(f)*
bath	**le bain**
beauty	**la beauté**
beauty contest	**le concours de beauté**
beauty salon/parlour	**l'institut** *(m)*/ **le salon de beauté**
beauty treatment	**les soins** *(m)* **de beauté**

– I don't feel at all well!	– **Je ne me sens pas bien du tout.**
– You should rest!	– **Vous devriez vous reposer!**
I need a shower.	**J'ai besoin de prendre une douche.**

I burp/belch **j'ai un renvoi**
I brush **je (me) brosse**
brush **la brosse**
I clean **je nettoie** *(nettoyer)* **, je (me) lave**
clean **propre**
I clean my teeth **je me lave les dents**
comb **je peigne**
I comb my hair **je me peigne les cheveux**
condom **le préservatif**
contraceptive **le moyen de contraception**
contraception **la contraception**
I cut **je coupe**
dandruff **les pellicules** *(f)*
I defecate **je défèque**
diet **le régime**
I am on a diet **je me mets** *(se mettre)* **au régime**
dirty **sale**
electric razor **le rasoir électrique**
flannel/face cloth **le gant de toilette**
fleas **les puces**
fresh air **l'air** *(m)*, **le frais**
hairbrush **la brosse à cheveux**
haircut **la coupe de cheveux**
I have my hair cut **je me fais couper les cheveux**
hairdo **la coiffure**
healthy *(person)* **en bonne santé**
healthy *(diet)* **hygiénique**
hungry **affamé**

I am hungry **j'ai faim**
hygienic **hygiénique**
hygiene **l'hygiène** *(f)*
laundry *(establishment)* **le pressing, la blanchisserie**
laundry *(linen)* **le linge**
lice/nits **les poux** *(m)*
I'm losing my hair **je perds mes cheveux**
I menstruate **j'ai mes règles**
menstruation **les règles** *(f)*, **la menstruation**
nailbrush **la brosse à ongles**
nutritious **nutritif [-ve]**
period **les règles** *(f)*
period pains **les douleurs** *(f)* **menstruelles**
razor **le rasoir**
sanitary **sanitaire**
sanitary towel **la serviette hygiénique/périodique**
scissors **les ciseaux** *(m)*
shampoo **le shampooing**
I shave **je (me) rase**
shower **la douche**
soap **le savon**
I take a bath/shower **je prends** *(prendre)* **un bain/une douche**
tampon **le tampon**
toothbrush **la brosse à dents**
toothpaste **le dentifrice**
towel **la serviette**
I wash **je (me) lave**

I'd like a hair-cut, please. Don't cut it too short.

Je voudrais me faire couper les cheveux, s'il vous plaît: pas trop court.

A little more off the back and sides, please.

Dégagez un peu plus derrière et les côtés.

Please trim my moustache.

Pourriez-vous me rafraîchir la moustache.

➤ TOILETRIES 9b; AT THE HAIRDRESSER App.11d

Social issues

12a Society

abnormal **anormal**
alternative **le choix**
amenity **l'équipement** *(m)*
anonymous **anonyme**
attitude **l'attitude** *(f)*
available **disponible**
basic **de base**
basis **la base**
burden **le fardeau**
campaign **la campagne**
care **le soin**
cause **la cause**
change **le changement**
circumstance **la circonstance**
community **la communauté**
compulsory **obligatoire**
contribution **la contribution**
cost **le coût**
I counsel **je conseille**
counselling **les conseils** *(m)*
criterion **le critère**
debt **la dette**
  I am in debt **je suis endetté**
dependence **la dépendance**
dependent **dépendant**
depressed *(region)*
  économiquement faible
depression **la dépression**
deprived **privé de**

difficulty **la difficulté**
effect **l'effet** *(m)*
effective **efficace**
fact **le fait**
finance **la finance**
financial **financier**
frustrated **frustré**
frustration **la frustration**
guidance **les conseils** *(m)*
increase **l'augmentation** *(f)*
inner city **les quartiers** *(m)*
  pauvres, les vieux quartiers
  déshérités
insecurity **l'insécurité** *(f)*
institution **l'institution** *(f)*
loneliness **la solitude**
lonely **seul**
long-term **à long terme**
measure **la mesure**
negative **négatif**
normal **normal**
policy/policies **la politique**
positive **positif [-ve]**
power **le pouvoir**
prestige **le prestige**
problem **le problème**
protest movement **le mouvement**
  de protestation
I provide (for/with) **je fournis**

– There are immense social
problems in the inner city.

– What are the causes?
– People are frustrated and lonely,
often as a result of unemployment.

– Il y a d'importants problèmes
sociaux dans les quartiers
défavorisés.

– Quelles en sont les causes?
– Les gens sont frustrés et
seuls, souvent à cause du
chômage.

➤ SOCIAL SERVICES, POVERTY 12b; HOUSING & HOMELESSNESS 12c

provision **la provision**
psychological **psychologique**
quality of life **la qualité de la vie**
question/issue **le problème,**
   la question
rate **le taux**
responsibility **la responsabilité**
responsible (ir-) **(ir)responsable**
result **le résultat**
right *(human)* **le droit**
role **le rôle**
rural **rural**
scarcity **la pénurie**
scheme **le projet**
I am on the scrap heap **je suis**
   mis *(mettre)* **au rebus**
secure (in-) **(pas) en sécurité**
security **la sécurité**
self-esteem **l'amour-propre** *(m)*
short-term **à court terme**
situation **la situation**
social **social**
society **la société**
stable (un-) **(in)stable**
stability (in-) **l'(in)stabilité** *(f)*
statistics **les statistiques** *(f)*
status **le statut**
stigma **le stigmate**
stress **le stress**
stressful **stressant**
structure **la structure**
superfluous **superflu**
support **le soutien**
urban **urbain**
value **la valeur**

Some useful verbs

it affects **il a des conséquences**
I can afford **je peux** *(pouvoir)*
   m'offrir
I am alienated **je suis exclu**
I break down **je craque**
I campaign **je fais campagne**
I care for **je m'occupe de**
I cause **j'occasionne**
it changes **il change**
I contribute **je contribue**
I cope **je me débrouille**
I depend on **je dépends de**
I deprive **je prive**
I discourage **je décourage**
I dominate **je domine**
I encourage **j'encourage**
I help **j'aide**
I increase **j'augmente**
I lack **je manque de**
I look after **je m'occupe de**
I need **j'ai besoin de**
I neglect **je néglige**
I owe **je dois** *(devoir)*
I protest **je proteste**
I put up with **je supporte**
I rely on **je compte sur**
I respect **je respecte**
I share **je partage**
I solve **je résous** *(résoudre)*
I suffer from **je souffre** *(souffrir)*
   de
I support **je soutiens** *(soutenir)*
I tackle **j'aborde**
I value **j'estime**

Financial difficulties lead to loss of status and family problems. The quality of life suffers because of it.

Les difficultés financières entraînent la perte de statut et les problèmes familiaux. La qualité de la vie en souffre.

We attempt to offer guidance and counselling.

Nous essayons de donner des conseils.

➤ ADDICTION & VIOLENCE 12d; PREJUDICE 12e

12b Social services and poverty

Social services

aid **l'aide** *(f)*
agency **l'agence** *(f)*
authority **l'autorité** *(f)*
benefit **l'allocation** *(f)*
I benefit **je bénéficie**
charity **l'organisation** *(f)* **caritative**
claim **la réclamation**
I claim **je réclame**
claimant **le demandeur**
disability **l'invalidité** *(f)*
disabled **invalide**
I am eligible for **j'ai droit à**
frail **fragile**
frailty **la fragilité**
grant **la bourse**
handicap **le handicap**
handicapped **handicapé**
ill-health **la mauvaise santé**
income support **l'allocation** *(f)* **chômage**
loan **le prêt**
maintenance **la pension alimentaire**
official **officiel[le]**
reception centre/center **le centre d'accueil**
Red Cross **la Croix Rouge**
refuge **le refuge**
refugee **le réfugié, la réfugiée**
I register **je m'inscris** *(s'inscrire)*
registration **l'inscription** *(f)*
Salvation Army **l'Armée** *(f)* **du Salut**
service **le service**
social security **la sécurité sociale**
social services **les services** *(m)* **sociaux**
social worker **un assistant social, une assistante sociale**
support **le soutien**
I support **je soutiens** *(soutenir)*
welfare **le bien-être**

Wealth & poverty

affluence **la richesse**
I beg **je mendie**
beggar **le mendiant, la mendiante**
I am broke **je suis fauché**
debt **la dette**
in debt **endetté**
deprivation **la privation**
deprived **privé de**
destitute **sans ressources**

There is a reception centre/center for the homeless which provides food and clothing.
Many charities are active in this way. The physically handicapped can apply for help too.

They are particularly vulnerable to unemployment.
Not everyone gets the dole, as many have not worked for a long time.

Il y a un centre d'accueil pour les sans-abris qui fournit de la nourriture et des vêtements.
De nombreuses œuvres de bienfaisance sont actives dans ce sens. Les handicapés physiques peuvent aussi demander de l'aide.

Ils sont particulièrement vulnérables au chômage.
Tout le monde n'a pas droit à l'allocation chômage, car beaucoup n'ont pas travaillé depuis longtemps.

living standards   **le niveau de vie**
millionaire   **le millionnaire**
need   **le besoin**
nutrition   **l'alimentation** *(f)*
poor   **pauvre**
poverty   **la pauvreté**
   I live in poverty   **je vis** *(vivre)*
   dans le besoin
rich   **riche**
subsistence   **la subsistance**
tramp/vagrant   **le clochard**
vulnerability   **la vulnérabilité**
vulnerable   **vulnérable**
wealth   **la richesse, les richesses**
I am well-off   **je vis** *(vivre)* **dans**
   l'aisance *(f)*

Unemployment

I cut back *(on jobs)*   **je réduis**
I dismiss   **je licencie, je congédie**
dismissal   **le licenciement**
dole   **l'indemnité** *(f)*, **le chômage**
I give notice   **je donne mon**
   préavis
job   **l'emploi** *(m)*
job centre/center   **l'agence** *(f)*
   nationale pour l'emploi, l'ANPE
job creation scheme   **le plan de**
   création d'emplois

long-term unemployed   **les**
   chômeurs *(m)* **de longue durée**
I have lost my job   **j'ai été privé de**
   mon emploi
part-time   **à temps partiel**
redundancy   **le licenciement**
redundant   **licencié**
   I am made redundant   **être**
   licencié
redundancy money   **l'indemnité** *(f)*
   de licenciement
retraining   **le recyclage**
   I am retrained   **je me recycle**
I refuse a job   **je rejette** *(rejeter)*
   une offre d'emploi
I resign   **je démissionne**
short-time working   **le chômage**
   partiel
skill   **la compétence**
training scheme/program   **le**
   programme de formation
unemployable   **incapable de travail**
unemployed   **au chômage**
unemployment   **le chômage**
unemployment benefit/insurance
   l'allocation *(f)* **de chômage**
unemployment rate   **le taux de**
   chômage
vacancy   **le poste vacant**

– How high is the level of
unemployment? – In some areas it
is about 15%.
– Can people retrain or work
part-time?

– Yes, sometimes, and many retire
early.

My brother was made redundant
some months ago. He has to
report every two weeks to the job
centre/employment office.

– **Quel est le niveau du**
chômage? – Dans certaines
régions, il est d'environ 15%.
– **Est-ce que les gens peuvent**
se recycler ou travailler à temps
partiel?
– **Oui, parfois, et beaucoup**
prennent une retraite anticipée.

Mon frère a été licencié il y a
quelques mois. Il doit venir
signer tous les quinze jours à
l'ANPE.

➤ JOB APPLICATION 14c; PERSONAL FINANCE 14e

12c Housing & homelessness

accommodation **le logement**
I build **je construis**
building **le bâtiment**
  building land **le terrain à bâtir**
  building site **le chantier de construction**
camp **le camp**
comfortable/homely **confortable, accueillant**
commune **la commune**
I commute **je fais la navette**
commuter **le navetteur [-se]**
council housing/public housing **les logements** *(m)* **sociaux**
delapidated **délabré**
I demolish **je démolis**
demolition **la démolition**
it deteriorates **il s'abîme**
digs/pad **les piaules** *(f)*
drab **morne, gris**

estate/real estate agent **l'agent** *(m)* **immobilier**
I evict **j'expulse**
it falls down **il tombe en ruine**
flat/apartment **l'appartement** *(m)*
  block of flats/apartment house **l'immeuble** *(m)*
furnished **meublé**
homeless **sans-abri**
homelessness **la vie sans domicile fixe**
hostel **l'auberge** *(f)*
house **la maison**
housing **le logement**
  housing association **l'association** *(f)* **de logement**
  housing policy **la politique de logement**
  housing shortage **la crise du logement**

– Are they hoping to renovate the city centre/downtown?
– Yes, many houses will be pulled down. Others will be modernized.

– Espèrent-ils rénover le centre-ville/en ville?
– Oui, de nombreuses maisons seront démolies. D'autres seront modernisées.

We live in a house near the shopping centre/center. The advantage is that we do not have to commute to work.

Nous habitons une maison près du centre commercial.
L'avantage est que nous ne faisons pas la navette pour aller au travail.

My sister lives on a new estate in the suburbs. She has a long journey every day to work.

Ma sœur habite dans un nouveau lotissement en banlieue. Elle a un long trajet pour aller au travail chaque jour.

It is impossible to find a furnished flat/apartment to rent.

C'est impossible de trouver un appartement meublé à louer.

inner city **les vieux quartiers** *(m)* **déshérités, les quartiers** *(m)* **défavorisés**
landlord **le/la propriétaire**
I let/rent **je loue**
living conditions **les conditions** *(f)* **de vie**
I maintain **j'entretiens** *(soutenir)*
I modernize **je modernise**
mortgage **l'emprunt-logement** *(m)*
I move (house) **je déménage**
I occupy **j'occupe**
overcrowded **surpeuplé**
overcrowding **le surpeuplement**
own *(adj)* **propre**
I own **je suis propriétaire de**
I pull down **je démolis**
I redevelop **je redéveloppe**
I renovate **je rénove**
I rent **je loue**
rent **le loyer**

I repair **je répare**
repairs **les réparations** *(f)*
shanty town **le bidonville**
shelter **l'abri** *(m)*
slum **le taudis**
I sleep rough **je couche dehors**
slum clearance **l'aménagement** *(m)* **des quartiers insalubres**
speculator **le spéculateur, la spéculatrice**
squalid **misérable, sordide**
I squat **je squatte**
squatter **le squatter**
suburb **la banlieue**
tenant **le/la locataire**
town planning **l'urbanisme** *(m)*
urban **urbain**
urban development **le développement urbain**
unfurnished **non-meublé**
waste land **le terrain vague**

– Why do so many houses in France stand empty?
The houses deteriorate fast and squatters move in.

Aren't the town planners intending to demolish the houses?

– Yes, but at the same time so many are homeless. They sleep rough or squat.
– Is the council/municipality still building council/public housing?

– Not enough. Living conditions in the blocks of flats/apartment houses are extremely poor. They are overcrowded and the landlords no longer repair them.

– **Pourquoi est-ce que tant de maisons en France sont vides?**
Les maisons se détériorent rapidement et les squatters emménagent.
Est-ce que les urbanistes n'envisagent pas de démolir les maisons?

– **Si, mais en même temps, il y a tant de sans-abri. Ils couchent dehors ou squattent.**
– **Est-ce que le conseil municipal construit toujours des immeubles?**

– **Pas assez. Les conditions de vie dans les immeubles sont extrêmement mauvaises. Ils sont surpeuplés et les propriétaires ne les réparent plus.**

12d Addiction & violence

abuse **le mauvais traitement**
I abuse *(person)* **je maltraite**
act of violence **l'acte** *(m)* **de violence**
addict **le/la toxicomane**
addiction **la dépendance**
addictive **qui crée une dépendance**
aggression **l'agression** *(f)*
aggressive **agressif [-ve]**
alcohol **l'alcool** *(m)*
alcoholic **un/une alcoolique**
alcoholism **l'alcoolisme** *(m)*
anger **la colère**
angry **en colère**
I attack **j'attaque**
attack **l'attaque** *(f)*
I beat up **je bats** *(battre)*
I bully **je brutalise**
bully **la brute**
consumption **la consommation**
dangerous **dangereux [-se]**
I drink **je bois** *(boire)*
I get drunk **je m'enivre**
drunk **ivre, soûl**
drunken driving **la conduite en**

état d'ivresse
I dry out **je suis** *(suivre)* **une cure de désintoxication**
effect **l'effet** *(m)*
fatal **fatal**
fear **la peur**
I fear **j'ai peur**
force **la force**
gang **le gang, la bande**
harassment **le harcèlement**
hooligan **le voyou**
hostile **hostile**
hostility **l'hostilité** *(f)*
insult **l'insulte** *(f)*
I insult **j'insulte**
intoxication **l'ivresse** *(f)*
legal (il-) **(il)légal**
I legalize **je légalise**
living off immoral earnings/procuring **le proxénétisme**
I mug **j'agresse**
mugger **l'agresseur** *(m)*
nervous **nerveux [-se]**
nervousness **la nervosité**
pimp **le souteneur, le proxénète**
porno **porno**

Violence and vandalism are common in the inner city. Sometimes gangs mug tourists on the streets or terrorize citizens.

La violence et le vandalisme sont choses communes en ville. Les bandes agressent parfois les touristes dans la rue ou terrorisent les citoyens.

They beat up rivals and threaten the safety of the community.

Ils se battent leurs rivaux et menacent la sécurité de la communauté.

Older people and women are sometimes afraid to go out alone.

Les personnes âgées et les femmes ont parfois peur de sortir seules.

pornography **la pornographie**
prostitution **la prostitution**
punk **le punk**
rehabilitation **la réhabilitation**
I revert **je retourne**
I seduce **je séduis** *(séduire)*
sexual harassment **le harcèlement sexuel**
skinhead **le skinhead**
I smoke **je fume**
stimulant **stimulant**
stimulation **la stimulation**
I terrorize **je terrorise**
I threaten **je menace**
thug **le voyou**
vandal **le/la vandale**
vandalism **le vandalisme**
victim **la victime**
violent **violent**

Drugs

addicted to drugs **intoxiqué**
AIDS **le SIDA**
angel dust **la poudre d'ange**
cannabis **le cannabis**
cocaine **la cocaïne**
crack **le crack**
I deal **je traite**

drug **la drogue**
drug scene **le monde de la drogue**
drug traffic **le trafic de la drogue**
ecstasy **l'ecstasy** *(m)*
I get infected **je suis contaminé**
glue **la colle**
hard drugs **les drogues** *(f)* **dures**
hashish **le hasch**
I have a fix **je me drogue**
heroin **l'héroïne** *(f)*
HIV-positive **séro-positif [-ve]**
I inject **je m'injecte, je me pique**
junkie **le drogué, la droguée**
I kick (the habit) **je renonce (à la drogue)**
LSD **le LSD**
narcotic **le narcotique**
pusher **le revendeur**
I sniff **j'inhale, je sniffe**
soft drugs **les drogues** *(f)* **douces**
solvent **le solvant**
stimulant **stimulant**
syringe **la seringue**
I take drugs/a fix **je me drogue**
tranquillizer **le tranquillisant**
withdrawal **l'état** *(m)* **de manque**

Many young people have a drug problem. They start by sniffing solvents, or by taking soft drugs. Cannabis is the most common.

Beaucoup de jeunes ont des problèmes de drogue. Ils commencent par inhaler des solvants, ou par prendre des drogues douces. Le cannabis est la drogue la plus commune.

They quickly become addicted. Then they go onto hard drugs.

Ils deviennent rapidement intoxiqués. Puis ils passent aux drogues dures.

The drug scene is worrying as so many people become dealers or turn to crime.

Le monde de la drogue est inquiétant car tant de gens deviennent fournisseurs ou criminels.

12e Prejudice

asylum seeker **la personne qui cherche asile**
I call names **j'injurie**
citizenship **la citoyenneté**
civil liberties **les libertés** (f) **civiques**
country of origin **le pays natal**
cultural **culturel[le]**
culture **la culture**
I discriminate **je fais une discrimination**
discrimination **la discrimination**
dual nationality **la double nationalité**
emigrant **un émigrant, une émigrante**
emigration **l'émigration** (f)
equal (un-) **(in)égal**
equal opportunities **l'égalité** (f) **des chances**
equal pay **le salaire égal**
equal rights **l'égalité** (f) **des droits**
equality (in-) **l'(in)égalité** (f)
ethnic **ethnique**
far right **l'extrême droite** (f)
fascism **le fascisme**
fascist **le/la fasciste**

foreign **étranger [-ère]**
foreign worker **un ouvrier étranger, une ouvrière étrangère**
freedom **la liberté**
freedom of movement **la liberté de mouvement**
freedom of speech **la liberté d'expression**
ghetto **le ghetto**
human rights **les droits** (m) **de l'homme**
I immigrate **j'immigre**
immigrant **un immigrant, une immigrante**
immigrant (settled) **un immigré, une immigrée**
immigration **l'immigration** (f)
I integrate **j'intègre** (intégrer)
integration **l'intégration** (f)
intolerance **l'intolérance** (f)
intolerant **intolérant**
majority **la majorité**
minority **la minorité**
mother tongue **la langue maternelle**
I persecute **je persécute**
persecution **la persécution**
politically correct **politiquement**

– Is racism a serious problem?

– Yes, black and dark-skinned people suffer particularly from discrimination.

Immigration is now restricted. Black or Asian immigrants are more often refused a residence permit or work permit.

– What about the ethnic minority population resident here?

– **Est-ce que le racisme est un problème grave?**
– **Oui, les noirs et les personnes à la peau brune souffrent particulièrement de discrimination.**
L'immigration est maintenant limitée. Les immigrants noirs et asiatiques se voient plus souvent refuser un permis de séjour ou de travail.
– **Et à propos de la population de minorité ethnique qui réside ici?**

correct
prejudice   le préjugé
prejudiced   **plein de préjugés**
rabid   **farouche**
race riot   **l'émeute** (f) **raciale**
racism   **le racisme**
racist   **le/la raciste**
   racist (adj)   **raciste**
refugee   **le réfugié, la réfugiée**
I repatriate   **je rapatrie**
residence permit   **le permis de séjour**
right   **le droit**
   right to asylum   **le droit d'asile**
   right to residence   **le droit de séjour**
stereotypical   **stéréotypique**
I stand up for   **je défends**
tolerance   **la tolérance**
tolerant (in-)   **(in)tolérant**
I tolerate   **je tolère** (tolérer)
work permit   **le permis de travail**

Race

anti-Semitic   **antisémite**
anti-Semitism   **l'antisémitisme** (m)
Asian   **un/une asiatique**
black   **le noir, la noire**
Caribbean   **les Antilles**

Caribbean   **un Antillais, une Antillaise**
coloured/colored   **de couleur**
dark-skinned   **à peau brune**
Jew   **le juif, la juive**
Jewish   **juif**
Neo-Nazism   **le Néo-Nazisme**
white   **le blanc, la blanche**

Sexuality

female   **la femme**
feminine   **féminin**
feminism   **le féminisme**
feminist   **la féministe**
heterosexual   **l'hétérosexuel** (m)
   heterosexual   **hétérosexuel[le]**
homosexual/gay   **l'homosexuel** (m)
   homosexual   **homosexuel[le]**
homosexuality   **l'homosexualité** (f)
lesbian   **la lesbienne**
   lesbian (adj)   **lesbienne**
male   **mâle**
sexual   **sexuel[le]**
sexuality   **la sexualité**
women's lib   **la libération de la femme**
women's rights   **les droits** (m) **de la femme**

– Unfortunately they tend to get the worst jobs and to be paid less.

The law still discriminates against male homosexuals, although society is getting more tolerant. Gay people have become more open about their sexuality.

The feminist movement is still demanding equal rights for women.

– **Malheureusement, ils ont tendance à récupérer les pires emplois et à être moins payés.**

La loi fait toujours une discrimination contre les homosexuels bien que la société devienne plus tolérante. Les homosexuels parlent plus ouvertement de leur sexualité.

Le mouvement féministe demande toujours l'égalité des droits pour les femmes.

➤ LOVE 7b

Religion

13a Ideas & doctrines

agnostic **agnostique**
anglican **anglican**
apostle **l'apôtre** *(m)*
atheism **l'athéisme** *(m)*
atheist **l'athée** *(m/f)*
atheistic **athée**
authority **l'autorité** *(f)*
belief **la croyance**
I believe (in) **je crois** *(croire)* **(en)**
believer **le croyant**
blessed **béni**
Buddha **le Bouddha**
Buddhism **le bouddhisme**
Buddhist **le/la Bouddhiste**
calvinist **le/la calviniste**
he canonizes **il canonise**
cantor **le chantre**
catholic **catholique**
charismatic **charismatique**
charity **la charité**
Christ **le Christ**
Christian **chrétien[ne]**
Christianity **le christianisme**
church **l'église** *(f)*
commentary **le commentaire**
conscience **la conscience**
conversion **la conversion**

covenant **l'alliance** *(f)*
disciple **le disciple**
divine **divin**
duty **le devoir**
ecumenism **l'œcuménisme** *(m)*
ethical **éthique, moral**
evil **le mal**
faith **la foi**
faithful **fidèle**
the faithful **les fidèles** *(m)*
I forgive **je pardonne à**
forgiveness **le pardon**
free will **le libre-arbitre**
fundamentalism **l'intégrisme** *(m)*
fundamentalist **intégriste**
god **le dieu**
goddess **la déesse**
Gospel **l'évangile** *(m)*
grace **la grâce**
heaven **le Ciel**
Hebrew **hébreu, hébraïque**
hell **l'enfer** *(m)*
heretical **hérétique**
Hindu **hindou**
Hinduism **l'Hindouisme** *(m)*
holiness **la sainteté**
holy **saint**

The five pillars of Islam are belief in the One True God and his Prophet, prayer, fasting, giving alms and pilgrimage to Mecca.

Les cinq piliers de l'Islam sont l'attestation de la foi (il n'est de divinité que Dieu et Mahomet est son prophète), la prière rituelle, le jeûne du ramadan, l'aumône légale, et le pèlerinage à La Mecque.

Holy Spirit **le Saint-Esprit**
hope **l'espoir** *(m)*
human **humain**
human being **l'être** *(m)* **humain**
humanism **l'humanisme** *(m)*
humanity **l'humanité** *(f)*
infallibility **l'infaillibilité** *(f)*
infallible **infaillible**
Islam **l'Islam** *(m)*
Islamic **islamique**
Jesus **Jésus**
Jew **le Juif, la Juive**
Jewish **juif [-ve]**
Judaic **judaïque**
Judaism **le judaïsme**
Lord **le Seigneur**
merciful **clément**
mercy **la miséricorde**
Messiah **le Messie**
Mohammed **Mohammed, Mahomet**
moral **moral**
morality **la moralité**
Muslim **le musulman, la musulmane**
 Muslim *(adj)* **musulman**
myth **le mythe**
New Testament **le Nouveau Testament**
nirvana **le nirvana**
Old Testament **l'Ancien Testament** *(m)*
orthodox **orthodoxe**
pagan **païen[ne]**

parish **la paroisse**
Pentateuch **le Pentateuque**
prophet **le prophète**
Q'uran/Koran **le Coran**
redemption **la rédemption**
religion **la religion**
sacred **sacré**
saint **le saint, la sainte**
Saint Peter **Saint Pierre**
he sanctifies **il sanctifie**
Satan **Satan** *(m)*
he saves **il sauve**
scripture **l'Écriture** *(f)*
service **le service**
Sikh **le Sikh**
Sikhism **le Sikhisme**
Shintoism **le Shintoïsme**
sin **le péché**
sinful **pécheur**
soul **l'âme** *(f)*
spirit **l'esprit** *(m)*
spiritual **spirituel**
spirituality **la spiritualité**
Talmud **le Talmud**
Taoism **le taoïsme**
theological **théologique**
theology **la théologie**
Torah **la Torah**
traditional **traditionnel**
Trinity **la Trinité**
true **vrai**
truth **la vérité**
vision **la vision**
vocation **la vocation**

Religious fundamentalism can lead to fanaticism and intolerance in any religion.

L'intégrisme religieux peut mener au fanatisme et à l'intolérance dans n'importe quelle religion.

There is considerable disagreement about the ordination of women to the priesthood.

Il existe énormément de désaccords sur la question des femmes prêtres et de leur ordination.

➤ CHRISTIAN GROUPS App.13b

archbishop **l'archevêque** *(m)*
baptism **le baptême**
bar-mitzvah **le bar-mitzva**
I bear witness to **je témoigne de**
Bible **la Bible**
biblical **biblique**
bishop **l'évêque** *(m)*
bishopric/see **l'évêché** *(m)*
cathedral **la cathédrale**
chapel **la chapelle**
christening **le baptême**
clergy **le clergé**
clergyman **l'ecclésiastique** *(m)*
communion **la communion**
  holy communion **la Sainte Communion**
community **la communauté**
I confess *(sins)* **je me confesse**
  I confess *(faith)* **je confesse**
confession **la confession**

confirmation **la confirmation**
congregation **l'assemblée** *(f)*
  congregation *(of cardinals)* **la congrégation**
convent **le couvent**
I convert *(others)* **je convertis**
  I convert *(self)* **je me convertis**
diocese **le diocèse**
Eucharist **l'Eucharistie** *(f)*
evangelical **évangélique**
evangelist **évangéliste**
I give alms **je fais l'aumône** *(f)*
I give thanks (to God) **je rends grâces (à Dieu)**
Imam **l'Imam, l'Iman** *(m)*
intercession **l'intercession** *(f)*
laity **les laïcs** *(m)*
lay **laïque**
layperson **le laïc**
the Lord's Supper **la Sainte Cène**

Bishops in the Church of England are not afraid to speak about social problems.	**Les évêques de l'Église Anglicane n'ont pas peur de se prononcer sur les problèmes sociaux.**
The sacrament of Holy Communion will be celebrated on Sunday at 9 o'clock.	**L'Eucharistie sera célébrée dimanche à 9 heures.**
The Parish Council meets regularly.	**Le conseil de la paroisse se réunit régulièrement.**
Those who are called to ministry must demonstrate their vocation before being accepted in theological colleges.	**Ceux qui ont la vocation du saint ministère doivent le démontrer avant qu'on les accepte pour faire des études en théologie.**
The Baptist tradition is very strong in the American South.	**La tradition baptiste est très forte dans le sud des États-Unis.**

Mass   **la Messe**
I meditate   **je médite**
meditation   **la méditation, le
    recueillement**
minister   **le pasteur (protestant)**
I minister to the parish   **je dessers
    (desservir) la paroisse**
ministry   **le saint ministère**
mission   **la mission**
missionary   **le missionnaire**
monastery   **le monastère**
monk   **le moine**
mosque   **la mosquée**
mullah   **le mollah**
nun   **la religieuse**
parish   **la paroisse**
parishioner   **le paroissien, la
    paroissienne**
pastor   **le pasteur**
pastoral   **pastoral**
Pope   **le Pape**
I praise   **je loue**
I pray (for)   **je prie (pour)**

prayer   **la prière**
prayerful   **recueilli, méditatif [-ve]**
priest   **le prêtre**
rabbi   **le rabbin**
I repent   **je me repens** *(se
    repentir)*
repentance   **le repentir**
repentant   **repenti**
I revere   **je vénère** *(vénérer)*
reverence   **la révérence**
reverent   **respectueux [-se]**
rite   **le rite**
ritual   **le rituel**
sacrament   **le sacrement**
synagogue   **la synagogue**
synod   **le synode**
temple   **le temple**
witness   **le témoin**
I witness   **je témoigne**
worship   **le culte, l'adoration** *(f)*
I worship   **j'adore**

A few Muslim schoolgirls in France have come into conflict with the authorities because they chose to wear the veil at school.	**Quelques collégiennes musulmanes en France sont entrées en conflit avec les autorités pour avoir choisi de porter le foulard islamique à l'école.**
Every Muslim is called to prayer five times a day.	**Tout musulman est appelé à la prière cinq fois par jour.**
During the Holy month of Ramadan, Muslims fast from dawn to dusk. The month ends with the celebrations of the festival of Eid.	**Pendant le mois sacré du ramadan, les musulmans jeûnent dès l'aube jusqu'au coucher du soleil. Le mois se termine par les fêtes de l'Id.**
Passover is the most important festival of Judaism.	**La Pâque est la fête la plus importante du judaïsme.**

Business & economics

14a The economics of work

I administer **j'administre**
I agree (to do) **je me mets** *(se mettre)* **d'accord (pour faire)**
agreement **l'accord** *(m)*
bureaucracy **la bureaucratie**
business **les affaires** *(f)*
 a business **une entreprise**
capacity *(industrial)* **les moyens** *(m)* **de production**
commerce **le commerce**
commercial **commercial**
company **la compagnie**
deal **l'affaire** *(f)*
I deliver **je livre**
demand **la demande**
 the product is in demand **le produit est très demandé**
development **le développement**
I earn (a living) **je gagne (ma vie)**
I employ **j'emploie** *(employer)*
employment **l'emploi** *(m)*
executive **le cadre**
I export **j'exporte**
exports **les exportations** *(f)*
fall **la chute, la baisse**
goods **les marchandises** *(f)*
it grows **il se développe**
I import **j'importe**
I increase **j'augmente**

increase **l'augmentation** *(f)*
industrial output **le rendement, la production**
industry **l'industrie** *(f)*
I invest **j'investis**
investment **l'investissement** *(m)*
lay-offs **des licenciements** *(m)*
living standards **le niveau de vie**
I manage **je gère** *(gérer)*
management **la gestion**
multinational **multinational**
I negotiate **je négocie**
one-to-one **face à face, seul à seul**
priority **la priorité**
I produce **je produis**
producer **le producteur**
production line **la chaîne de fabrication**
productivity **la productivité**
quality **la qualité**
I raise (prices) **je hausse (les prix)**
reliability **la fiabilité, la qualité**
rise **la hausse**
 wages rise **la hausse des salaires**
semi-skilled **spécialisé**
services **les services** *(m)*
I set (priorities) **je décide (des**

Unemployment is rising to 12%.

Le chômage monte à 12 pour cent.

The unions called for a reduction in the average weekly hours of work.

Les syndicats ont demandé une réduction des heures de travail hebdomadaires moyennes.

priorités)
sick-leave   **le congé de maladie**
I sign *(contracts)*   **je signe**
skilled labour/labor   **la main-d'œuvre qualifiée**
social unrest   **l'agitation** *(f)* **sociale, les troubles** *(m)* **sociaux**
social welfare   **la sécurité sociale**
I strengthen   **je renforce, je consolide**
supply   **la provision**
trade-unionism   **le syndicalisme**
unemployment   **le chômage**
unemployment benefit **l'allocation-chômage** *(f)*
unskilled labour/labor   **la main-d'œuvre non-spécialisée**
work ethic   **l'attitude** *(f)* **moraliste envers le travail**
workforce   **la main-d'œuvre**
working week   **la semaine de travail**

Industrial/Labor dispute

I am on strike   **je fais grève**
I blackleg   **je brise la grève**
I boycott   **je boycotte**
I cross the picket line   **je traverse le piquet de grève**
demonstration   **la manifestation**
dispute   **le conflit**
I go slow/slow down   **je fais la grève perlée**
industrial/labor dispute   **le conflit social**

I join the union   **je me syndique**
I lock-out   **je ferme l'usine aux ouvriers**
lock-out   **le lock-out**
minimum wage   **le SMIC**
I picket   **je fais partie d'un piquet de grève**
picket   **le piquet de grève**
productivity bonus   **la prime à la productivité**
I resume work   **je reprends le travail**
settlement   **l'accord** *(m)*
stoppage   **l'arrêt** *(m)* **de travail**
strike   **la grève**
   general strike   **la grève générale**
   unofficial strike   **la grève sauvage**
I strike/go on strike   **je fais grève**
strike ballot   **le scrutin**
strikebreaker   **le briseur de grève**
striker   **le gréviste**
trade union   **le syndicat**
unfair dismissal   **le licenciement injuste**
the profession is forming a union   **la profession se syndique**
unionized labour/labor   **la main-d'œuvre syndiquée**
unrest   **l'agitation** *(f)*
I am a union member   **je suis syndiqué**
wage demand   **la revendication salariale**
work to rule   **la grève du zèle**

The Department of Commerce hope these measures will enhance the country's competitiveness. The unions fear they will facilitate job losses.

Le Département du Commerce espère que ces mesures encourageront la compétitivité. Les syndicats craignent qu'elles rendent plus faciles les licenciements.

➤ AT WORK 14b; UNEMPLOYMENT 12b; JOBS & PROFESSIONS App.14b

14b At work

I am away on business **je suis en déplacement**

boring **ennuyeux [-se]**

business trip **le voyage d'affaires**

I buy **j'achète** *(acheter)*

canteen **la cantine**

career **la carrière**

disciplinary proceedings **des mesures** *(f)* **disciplinaires**

I follow a training course **je suis/fais un stage**

free **libre**

grant **la subvention**

I grant *(someone)* **j'accorde à**

holiday/vacation **les vacances** *(f)*, **le congé**

job **le poste, l'emploi** *(m)*

job satisfaction **la satisfaction au travail**

misconduct **l'inconduite** *(f)*

occupation **l'occupation** *(f)*

I'm off work **je ne travaille pas, je ne suis pas de service**

post **le poste**

profession **la profession**

professional **professionnel[le]**

I qualify **j'obtiens** *(obtenir)* **mon diplôme/brevet**

research **la recherche, les recherches**

I sell **je vends**

tax **la taxe, l'impôt** *(m)*

I tax **j'impose**

taxes **les impôts** *(m)*

I toil **je travaille dur**

training **la formation**

training course **le stage**

vocation **la vocation**

wage-earner **le salarié, la salariée**

warning *(verbal)* **l'avertissement** *(m)*

written warning **l'avis** *(m)*

I work **je travaille**

work **le travail, le boulot** *(fam)*

worker **l'ouvrier** *(m)*

Company personnel & structure

accounts department **le service de la comptabilité**

apprentice **l'apprentis** *(m)*

assistant **un/une assistant[e]**

associate **l'associé** *(m)*

board of directors **le conseil d'administration**

boss **le patron, la patronne**

colleague **le/la collègue**

I delegate **je délègue** *(déléguer)*

department **le département**

director **le directeur**

division **la division**

employee **un/une employé[e]**

employer **l'employeur** *(m)*

labour/labor **le travail**

line manager **le supérieur**

management **la direction, la gestion**

manager **le directeur**

manageress **la directrice**

managing director/CEO **le PDG**

marketing department **les responsables** *(m/f)* **du marketing**

personal assistant **le/la secrétaire particulier [-ère]**

president **le/la président[e]**

production department **les responsables** *(m/f)* **de la production**

I report to **je suis sous les ordres directs de**

I am responsible for **je suis responsable de**

sales department **les responsables** *(m/f)* **des ventes**

secretary **le/la secrétaire**

specialist **le/la spécialiste**

staff/personnel **le personnel**

team **l'équipe** *(f)*

trainee **le stagiaire**

I transfer **je suis muté**

vice president **le vice-président**

In the office

business lunch **le déjeuner d'affaires**
business meeting **la réunion**
computer **l'ordinateur** *(m)*
conference call **l'audioconférence** *(f)*
conference room **la salle de conférence**
desk **le bureau**
I dictate **je dicte**
dictating machine **le dictaphone®**
electronic mail **le courrier électronique**
extension **le poste**
fax **le fax, la télécopie**
fax machine **le télécopieur**
I fax **j'envoie** *(envoyer)* **par télécopie**
file **le dossier**
I file **je classe**
filing cabinet **le classeur (vertical)**
intercom **l'interphone** *(m)*
open-plan **non cloisonné**
photocopier **la photocopieuse**
photocopy **la photocopie**
I photocopy **je photocopie**
pigeonhole **le casier**
reception **la réception**
receptionist **le/la réceptionniste**
swivel chair **le fauteuil pivotant**
typing pool **la dactylo** *(fam)*
wastebasket **la poubelle**
word processor **la machine à traitement de texte**
work station **le poste de travail**

In the factory & on site

automation **l'automatisation** *(f)*
blue-collar worker **le col bleu**
bulldozer **le bulldozer**
car/automobile industry **l'industrie** *(f)* **automobile**
component **la pièce**
concrete **le béton**
construction industry **la construction**
crane **la grue**
foreman **le contremaître, le chef d'équipe**
fork-lift truck **le chariot de levage**
I forge **je forge**
industry **l'industrie** *(f)*
heavy/light **lourde/légère**
I manufacture **je fabrique**
manufacturing **la fabrication**
mass production **la production de masse**
mining **l'exploitation** *(f)* **minière**
power industry **l'énergie** *(f)*
precision tool **l'outil** *(m)* **de précision**
prefabricated **préfabriqué**
process **le processus**
I process **je traite**
product **le produit**
raw materials **les matières** *(f)* **premières, le matériau**
robot **le robot**
scaffolding **l'échafaudage** *(m)*
I smelt **je fonds**
steel smelting **la sidérurgie**
textile industry **le textile**

While my wife works for a bank, my son works in a factory on the production line and my daughter works in an office all day, I enjoy the peace and quiet to work from home as a writer.

Pendant que ma femme travaille dans une banque, mon fils travaille à la chaîne d'une usine, et ma fille travaille toute la journée dans un bureau, moi je profite de la tranquillité chez moi pour exercer le métier d'un écrivain.

➤ COMPUTERS 15d; STATIONERY App.22b

14c Working conditons

Conditions & remuneration

I am employed **je suis employé**
apprenticeship **l'apprentissage** *(m)*
benefit **l'allocation** *(f)*
I clock in **je pointe (à l'arrivée)**
I clock out **je pointe (à la sortie)**
company car **la voiture de fonction**
contract **le contrat**
expenses **les frais** *(m)*
expense account **les frais** *(m)* **de représentation**
flexi-time/flextime **l'horaire** *(m)* **mobile**
freelance **indépendant**
I work freelance **je travaille en free-lance**
full-time **à temps plein**
income **le revenu**
overtime **des heures** *(f)* **supplémentaires**

overworked **surchargé de travail**
part-time **à temps partiel**
payday **le jour de paie/paye**
payslip **la feuille de paie/paye**
payrise/pay raise **l'augmentation** *(f)* **de salaire**
payroll **le registre du personnel**
pension **la retraite, la pension**
permanent **permanent**
I retire **je prends** *(prendre)* **ma retraite**
retirement **la retraite**
salary **le salaire**
self-employed **qui travaille à son compte**
sexual harassment **le harcèlement sexuel**
shift **le poste/la période de travail d'équipe**
   day/night **le poste de jour/nuit**
temporary **temporaire**

– The conditions in this office are not good enough for your secretary, Mr Martin.

– What do you mean?
– The place is cold, badly lit, and poorly ventilated. And you have far too many electrical appliances plugged into one socket.
Unless you make considerable changes within three months, I shall be forced to close the office down. I shall come back next week to discuss your plans. Goodbye!

– **Les conditions de travail de ce bureau ne sont pas assez bonnes pour votre secrétaire, Monsieur Martin.**

– **Que voulez-vous dire?**
–**Les locaux sont froids, mal éclairés et mal ventilés. Et vous avez trop d'appareils électriques branchés à la même prise.**
Si vous n'effectuez pas de changements importants dans les trois mois à venir, je serai obligé de fermer ce bureau. Je reviens la semaine prochaine pour discuter de vos plans. Au revoir, monsieur!

Job application

I advertize for a secretary **je fais paraître une annonce pour trouver une sécretaire**
advertisement **l'annonce** *(f)*
I have been made redundant **j'ai été licencié**
I apply for a job **je fais une demande d'emploi**
classified ad **la petite annonce**
curriculum vitae/resumé **le curriculum vitae, le c.v.**
discrimination **la discrimination**
   racial **raciale**
   sexual **sexuelle**
employment agency **l'agence** *(f)* **de placement**
job centre *(government)* **l'Agence** *(f)* **Nationale pour l'Emploi (l'ANPE)**
I find a job **je trouve un emploi**
interesting **intéressant**
interview **l'entretien** *(m)*

I interview **je convoque pour un entretien**
job application **la demande d'emploi**
I look for **je cherche**
opening *(vacancy)* **le débouché**
I promote *(someone)* **je nomme ... à un poste**
I am promoted **je suis promu**
promotion **la promotion, l'avancement** *(m)*
qualification **le diplôme, le brevet**
qualified **qualifié, compétent**
situations vacant **Offres** *(f)* **d'emploi**
I start work (for) **je commence à travailler (pour)**
I take on *(employee)* **j'embauche**
trial period **la période d'éssai**
vacancy **le poste libre**
work experience **le stage (non rémunéré)**

– Hello. Could I speak to the Personnel Manager, please.

– Speaking. What can I do for you?
– I saw your advert in the local paper for a sales executive: to start work next month.

– That's right.
– Could you send me the job description and application forms?
– Certainly.

– How many referees are you asking for?
– Two, including your present or last employer.

– Allô. Je voudrais parler au directeur du personnel, s'il vous plaît.
– C'est moi-même. Que puis-je faire pour vous?
– J'ai vu l'annonce que vous avez fait paraître au journal régional pour chercher un cadre commercial: pouvant commencer le travail le mois prochain.
– C'est ça.
– Voulez-vous m'envoyer les détails du poste et le dossier à remplir pour faire ma demande, s'il vous plaît? – Bien sûr.
– Combien de noms faut-il donner en référence?
– Deux, dont votre employeur actuel, ou le plus récent.

➤ UNEMPLOYMENT 12b

14d Finance & industry

account **le compte bancaire**
advance **l'avance** *(f)*
advertising **la publicité**
advice note **l'avis** *(m)*
audit **la vérification des comptes,
l'audit** *(m)*
bill **la facture**
board **le conseil**
bonds **le bon, le titre**
branch *(of company)* **la
succursale, la branche**
budget **le budget**
capital **les capitaux** *(m)*
capital expenditure **la dépense
d'investissement**
Chamber of commerce **la
Chambre de commerce**
collateral **le nantissement**
company **la société, la compagnie**
I consume *(resources)* **je
consomme**
consumer goods **les biens** *(m)* **de
consommation**
consumer spending **les dépenses**
(f) **des ménages**
cost of living **le coût de la vie**
costing **l'estimation** *(f)* **du prix de
revient**
costs **les coûts** *(m)*
credit **le crédit**
debit **le débit**

deflation **la déflation**
economic **économique**
economy **l'économie** *(f)*
funds **les fonds** *(m)*
government spending **les
dépenses** *(f)* **publiques**
income **le revenu**
income tax **l'impôt** *(m)* **sur le
revenu**
instalment **l'acompte** *(m)*, **le
versement partiel**
interest rate **le taux d'intérêt**
I invest in **j'investis en/dans**
investment **le investissement**
invoice **la facture**
labour/labor costs **les coûts** *(m)*
de la main-d'œuvre
liability **la responsabilité**
manufacturing industry **la
fabrication industrielle**
market **le marché**
market economy **l'économie** *(f)* **de
marché**
marketing **la commercialisation,
le marketing**
merchandise **la marchandise**
national debt **l'endettement** *(m)*
national
I nationalize **je nationalise**
output **la production, le
rendement**

A spiralling budget deficit caused
panic on the stock exchange
today.

**Aujourd'hui, la spirale du déficit
budgétaire a causé la panique à
la Bourse.**

The company informed
shareholders that this year's
operating profits will not match the
level seen last year.

**L'entreprise a annoncé à ses
actionnaires que les profits
d'exploitation de cette année
seront moins avantageux que
ceux de l'année dernière.**

pay   **le salaire, la paie**
price   **le prix**
price war   **la guerre des prix**
private sector   **le secteur privé**
I privatise   **je privatise**
product   **le produit**
production   **la production, la fabrication**
public sector   **le secteur public**
quota   **le quota**
real estate/realty   **l'immobilier** *(m)*
retail sales   **les ventes** *(f)* **au détail**
retail trade   **la vente au détail**
salaries   **les salaires** *(m)*, **les traitements** *(m)*
sales tax   **la taxe à l'achat**
service sector   **le secteur tertiaire**
share   **l'action** *(f)*
shares going up/down   **des actions** *(f)* **en hausse/en baisse**
share index   **l'indice** *(m)* **de la Bourse**
statistics   **les statistiques** *(f)*
Stock Exchange   **la Bourse**
I subsidize   **je subventionne**
subsidy   **la subvention**
supply and demand   **l'offre** *(f)* **et la demande**
supply costs   **les coûts** *(m)* **de l'approvisionnement**
I tax   **je taxe, j'impose**
tax   **la taxe, l'impôt** *(m)*
tax increase   **la hausse des impôts**
taxation   **la taxation, l'imposition** *(f)*
taxation level   **le taux d'imposition**
turnover   **le chiffre d'affaires**
VAT/sales tax   **la T.V.A.**
viable   **viable, qui a des chances de réussir**
wages   **les salaires** *(m)*

Personnel

accountant   **le/la comptable**
actuary   **un/une actuaire**
auditor   **le vérificateur de comptes**
banker   **le banquier**
  investment banker   **le banquier d'acceptation**
  merchant banker   **le banquier de commerce**
bank manager   **le directeur d'agence bancaire**
broker   **le courtier**
  insurance broker   **le courtier d'assurances**
consumer   **le consommateur, la consommatrice**
investor   **l'investisseur** *(m)*
speculator   **le spéculateur, la spéculatrice**
stockbroker   **l'agent** *(m)* **de change**
trader *(Wall St.)*   **le contrepartiste**

There is no area of electrical retailing where there isn't strong competition.

The owners of high street stores are embarking on a program(me) of cuts in an effort to restore profitability.

La concurrence est très forte dans tous les domaines de l'électroménager.

Les propriétaires des commerces s'engagent dans un programme de réductions des coûts afin d'essayer de rétablir la rentabilité.

➤ BANKING, THE ECONOMY 14e

14e Banking & the economy

Banking & personal finance

account   **le compte**
automatic teller   **la caisse automatique**
bank   **la banque, l'agence** *(f)* **bancaire**
bank loan   **le crédit bancaire**
I bank (money)   **je dépose en banque**
bankrupt   **failli, en faillite**
building society   **la société de crédit immobilier**
cash   **les espèces** *(f)*
I cash a cheque/check   **je touche/j'encaisse un chèque**
cashcard   **la carte de retrait, la carte bleue**
cashdesk   **la caisse, le guichet**
cashpoint   **le distributeur automatique, la billetterie**
I change   **je change**
cheque/check   **le chèque**
credit card   **la carte de crédit**
currency   **la monnaie, la devise**
deposit *(in a bank)*   **le dépôt**
deposit *(returnable)*   **la caution**

down payment/deposit   **des arrhes** *(f)*
Eurocheque   **l'eurochèque** *(m)*
exchange rate   **le taux de change**
hire purchase/installment plan   **la vente à crédit**
I'm in credit by   **(j'ai) un crédit de**
in deficit   **en déficit**
in the red   **à découvert**
I lend   **je prête**
loan   **le prêt** *(m)*, **l'avance** *(f)*
mortgage   **l'emprunt-logement** *(m)*, **l'hypothèque** *(f)*
I mortgage   **j'obtiens** *(-tenir)* **un emprunt-logement, j'hypothèque**
I open (an account)   **j'ouvre** *(ouvrir)* **un compte**
overdraft   **le découvert**
repayment   **le remboursement**
I save   **je mets** *(mettre)* **de côté, je fais des économies**
savings   **l'épargne** *(f)*, **les économies** *(f)*
travellers' cheque/traveler's check   **le chèque de voyage**
I withdraw   **je retire (de)**

– Good morning. I'd like to open an account here, if possible.

– **Bonjour, madame. Je voudrais ouvrir un compte dans cette banque, si c'est possible.**

– Certainly, sir. What sort of account do you need?

– **Certainement, monsieur. Quel genre de compte vous faut-il?**

– Just a normal cheque account. Are overdraft facilities available for students?

– **Un compte courant, avec un carnet de chèques. Est-ce qu'il existe des possibilités de découvert pour les étudiants?**

– I need to check that for you, sir, but I don't think so.

– **Je dois vérifier cela pour vous, monsieur, mais je ne pense pas.**

Growth

amalgamation   **l'amalgamation** *(f)*, **la fusion**
appreciation   **la hausse, l'augmentation** *(f)*
assets   **les biens** *(m)*, **le capital**
assurance   **la garantie**
auction   **la vente aux enchères**
boom   **la montée en flèche, la forte hausse, le boom**
competition   **la concurrence**
economic miracle   **le miracle de l'économie**
efficiency   **la capacité, l'éfficacité** *(f)*
growth   **la croissance**
merger   **la fusion, le fusionnement**
profit   **le profit, le bénéfice**
profitable   **rentable, lucratif [-ve]**
progress   **le progrès**
prosperity   **la prospérité**
prosperous   **prospère, florissant**
quality control   **le contrôle/la gestion de la qualité**
recovery   **la reprise**
research and development   **la recherche-développement**

takeover   **le rachat**
takeover bid   **l'OPA** *(m)* **(offre publique d'achat)**

Decline

bankrupt   **failli, en faillite**
credit squeeze   **les restrictions** *(f)* **de crédit**
debt   **la dette**
it is declining   **il est en baisse**
deficit   **le déficit**
depreciation   **la dépréciation**
I dump   **je dépose**
inflation   **l'inflation** *(f)*
inflation rate   **le taux d'inflation**
loss   **la perte**
no-growth economy   **l'économie** *(f)* **sans croissance**
slow-down   **le ralentissement**
slump   **la récession, la crise**
spending cuts   **les compressions** *(f)* **budgétaires**
stagnant   **stagnant**
stagnation   **la stagnation**

– Did you hear about Woodland Toys plc? Unfortunately, they went bankrupt.
– Why was that?
– They borrowed too heavily in order to introduce a new line which just didn't sell!
– And what was it?
– A range of battery powered toys; just couldn't compete with the video and computer games !

– Tu as entendu la nouvelle des Jouets Woodland? Malheureusement, ils ont fait faillite.
– Pourquoi?
– Ils ont trop emprunté afin de lancer un nouveau produit qui n'a pas pris.
– Et qu'est-ce que c'était?
– Une gamme de jouets fonctionnant sur piles. Ça ne pouvait pas réussir contre la concurrence des jeux vidéo/jeux d'ordinateur!

➤ ECONOMICS OF WORK 14b; FINANCE & INDUSTRY 14d; TRADE 27c

Communicating with others

15a Social discourse

Meetings

I accept	**j'accepte**
appointment	**le rendez-vous**
I become	**je deviens** *(devenir)*
ball	**le bal**
banquet	**le banquet**
I'm busy	**je suis pris**
I celebrate	**je célébre, je fête**
celebration	**la fête, les festivités** *(f)*
club	**le club**
I come and see	**je viens** *(venir)* **voir**
I dance	**je danse**
date	**la date**
diary/datebook	**l'agenda** *(m)*
I drop in on	**je passe voir**
I expect	**je m'attends à**
I fetch	**je vais chercher**
I have fun	**je m'amuse**
I greet	**je salue**
guest	**un invité, une invitée**
handshake	**la poignée de main**
I invite	**j'invite**
invitation	**l'invitation** *(f)*
I join	**je rejoins** *(rejoindre)*
I keep	**je garde**
I meet	**je rencontre**
meeting	**la rencontre**
party	**la réunion**
reception	**la réception**
I see	**je vois** *(voir)*
I shake hands with	**je serre la main à/de**
I spend *(time)*	**je passe**
social life	**la vie mondaine**
I take part	**je participe**
I talk	**je parle**
I visit *(someone)*	**je rends visite à**
visit	**la visite**

Greetings & congratulations

bow/curtsey	**la révérence**
I bow/curtsey (to)	**je fais une révérence (à)**
Cheers!	**Santé!**
Come in!	**Entrez!**
I congratulate	**je félicite**
Congratulations!	**Félicitations!** *(f)*
Excuse me	**Excusez-moi**
Good evening	**Bonsoir**
Good morning/afternoon	**Bonjour**
Hallo/hello	**Salut!**
Happy Christmas	**Joyeux Noël**
Happy Easter	**Joyeuses Pâques**
Happy New Year	**Bonne Année**
Here's to …	**À la santé de …**
Hi!	**Salut!**
I toast	**je porte un toast**
toast	**le toast**
Well done!	**Félicitations!**

Introduction

Bill, meet Jane	**Bill, voici Jane**
How do you do?/How are you?	**Comment allez-vous?**
I introduce myself	**je me présente**
I introduce	**je présente**
introduction	**la présentation**
Ladies and Gentlemen	**Mesdames, Messieurs**
Madam	**Madame**
May I introduce ...?	**Puis-je vous présenter …?**
Miss	**Mademoiselle**
Mr.	**M. (Monsieur)**
Mrs.	**Mme (Madame)**
Ms.	**Madame**
I'd like you to meet	**j'aimerais vous faire rencontrer**

Pleased to meet you **Enchanté de faire votre connaissance**
I say! **dites donc!**
Sir **Monsieur**
This is ... **Voici ...**
I welcome **je souhaite la bienvenue (à)**
Welcome to **Bienvenue à**

Pleasantries

I address (someone) **je m'adresse à**
I address as tu **je tutoie (tutoyer)**
I address as vous **je vouvoie (vouvoyer)**
Best regards from ... **Meilleures salutations** (f) **de ...**
Bless you!/Gesundheit! **À vos souhaits!**
Much better, thank you **Beaucoup mieux, merci**
I'm fine, thank you **Je vais bien, merci**
I hope you get well soon **J'espère que vous irez bientôt mieux**
How are you keeping? **Comment vous portez-vous?**
My regards to ... **Mes amitiés à ...**
so-so **comme ci, comme ça**
Very well, thank you **Très bien, merci**
Your (very good) health! **À votre santé!**

Thanking

I thank **je remercie**
No, thank you! **Non, merci!**
thanks! **merci!**
thanking **le remerciement**
I'm grateful to you for **je vous suis reconnaissant de**
Nice/good of you to ... **C'est gentil à vous de ...**
It's a pleasure **C'est un plaisir**
Many thanks **Mille remerciements**
Not at all! **Pas de quoi!**

Thank you so much **Merci beaucoup**
With pleasure **Avec plaisir**

Apologizing

I apologize **je m'excuse**
I do apologize **je tiens (tenir) à m'excuser**
apology/excuse **l'excuse** (f)
Excuse me, please **Excusez-moi, s'il vous plaît**
I excuse **j'excuse**
Forget it! **N'en parlons plus!**
I forgive **je pardonne**
it doesn't matter (at all/a bit) **cela ne fait rien (du tout)**
it matters **c'est important**
not at all **pas du tout**
I beg your pardon **je vous demande pardon**
I'm (so very) sorry (that ...) **je suis (vraiment) désolé (que** +subj**)**
Unfortunately, I can't! **Malheureusement, je ne peux pas!**

Farewells

All the best! **Beaucoup de bonheur!**
Best wishes! **Mes/Nos meilleurs vœux!**
Bye! **Au revoir!**
Cheerio! **Salut!**
Good luck! **Bonne chance!**
Goodbye **Au revoir**
I say goodbye **je dis au revoir**
Good night! **Bonne nuit!**
Have a good time! **Amusez-vous bien!**
Have a safe journey home! **Rentrez bien!**
See you later! **À tout à l'heure!**
I will see you later/ tomorrow **Je vous verrai plus tard/demain**
Sweet dreams! **Faites de beaux rêves!**

▶ POST/MAIL & TELEPHONE 15c; COMPUTERS 15d

15b Comments & exclamations

Approval & disapproval

I approve **j'approuve**
Is this all right? **Est-ce que ça va?**
That's all right! **Ça va!**
Excellent! **Excellent!**
You should(n't) have ... **vous (n')auriez (pas) dû** +inf
Tut-tut *(clicks)* **Allons! Allons!**
What a shameful business! **Quelle honte!**

Permission & obligation

That's (quite) all right **C'est bon**
allowed **autorisé**
I allow **j'autorise**
I am allowed to ... **je suis autorisé à ...**
it is not allowed/permitted **ce n'est pas autorisé/permis**
Can I ...? **Puis-je ...?**
I can (not) **je (ne) peux (pas)**
you cannot/can't **vous ne pouvez pas**
I have to **je dois**
May I ...? **Pourrais-je ...?**
I may (not) **je (ne) pourrais (pas)**
I must (not) **je (ne) dois (pas)**
No **Non**
Not now/here/tonight **Pas maintenant/ici/ce soir**
obligation **l'obligation** *(f)*
I ought to ... **je devrais ...**
you ought to ... **vous devriez ...**
permitted **permis**
permission **la permission**
Please do! **Je vous en prie!**
I'm (not) supposed to **je (ne) suis (pas) censé**
Have you got time to ...? **Avez-vous le temps de ...?**

Surprise

oh dear! **oh mon Dieu!, oh là là!**
Fancy (that)! **Tiens!**

Good God! **Mon Dieu!**
Goodness! **Seigneur!**
Is that so? **Est-ce vrai?**
Really! **Vraiment!**
I surprise **je surprends**
surprising **surprenant**
Does that surprise you? **Est-ce que cela vous surprend?**
Ugh! **Pouah!**
Well? **Et bien?**
So what? **Et alors?**
Wow! **Super!**

Hesitating

Just a minute/moment! **Une minute/Un moment!**
I hesitate **j'hésite**
What's his/her name? **Quel est son nom?**
How shall I put it? **Comment dire?**
Now let me think **Laissez-moi réfléchir maintenant**
or rather ... **ou plutôt ...**
that is to say ... **c'est-à-dire ...**
That's not what I meant to say **Ce n'est pas ce que je voulais dire**
thingummyjig **le machin**
Well ... **Et bien ...**

Listening & agreeing

I believe so/not **je crois/je ne crois pas**
Certainly (not)! **Certainement (pas)!**
definite(ly) **certain, sûr, certainement, sûrement**
Don't you think (that) ...? **Ne crois-tu pas (que) ...?**
Exactly!/Just so! **Exactement!**
Indeed **En effet**
never **jamais**
no! **non!**
of course (not)! **bien sûr (que non)!**

Oh! **Oh!**
Quiet! **Silence!**
I quite agree **je suis entièrement d'accord**
Really? **Vraiment?, Ah bon?**
Rubbish! **Quelle blague!**
Shh! **Chut!**
That's correct **C'est exact**
That's not fair **Ce n'est pas juste**
That's not right **Ce n'est pas exact**
That's not so **Ce n'est pas ainsi**
That's wrong **C'est faux**
I think/don't think so **je pense que oui/non**
true **vrai**
Uh-huh! **Oui, oui!, Oh oui!**
wrong **faux**
Yes! **Oui!**
Yes, please **Oui, s'il vous plaît**
you're wrong **tu as tort**

Clarification & meaning

a kind/sort of ... **un genre/une sorte de ...**
Can you speak more slowly, please?
Pouvez-vous parler plus lentement, s'il vous plaît?
Could you repeat that, please?
Pourriez-vous répéter cela, s'il vous plaît?

Did you say ... ? **Avez-vous dit ...?**
Do you mean ... ? **Est-ce que vous voulez dire ...?**
er ... **euh ...**
Is that clear? **C'est clair?**
I mean **je veux dire**
I said that ... **j'ai dit que ...**
slowly **lentement**
The same to you *(polite)* **Vous de même**
That's just what I meant **C'est exactement ce que je voulais dire**
That's just what I had in mind
C'est exactement ce à quoi je pensais
That's not what I had in mind/meant
Ce n'est pas ce à quoi je pensais
That's just what I need **C'est précisément ce dont j'ai besoin**
What did you say? **Qu'est-ce que vous avez dit?**
What do you mean by ... ? **Que voulez-vous dire par ...?**
What I said was ... **J'ai dit que ...**
What is the matter? **Qu'est-ce qui se passe?**
you know **vous savez**

– What make of computer did you want, sir?

– Quel marque d'ordinateur désirez-vous, monsieur?

– Wait a moment. I'll have to think about it ...

– Attendez un instant. Il faut que je réfléchisse ...

– Was it this one?

– C'était celui-ci?

– No, I don't think so. I need one that is easy to use and has a lot of memory.

– Non, je ne pense pas. Il me faut un ordinateur qui soit facile à utiliser, et qui ait beaucoup de mémoire.

15c Post/mail & telephone

Post/Mail

abroad   **à l'étranger**
addressee   **le/la destinataire**
airmail letter   **la lettre par avion**
airmail   **par avion**
answer   **la réponse**
collection   **la levée**
I correspond   **je corresponds**
correspondence   **la correspondance**
correspondent   **le correspondant, la correspondante**
counter   **le guichet**
customs declaration   **la déclaration de douane**
envelope   **l'enveloppe** *(f)*
express delivery   **la distribution express**
I finish *(letter)*   **je termine**
first-class   **normal**
freepost   **port payé**
greetings   **les salutations** *(f)*
I hand in   **je remets** *(remettre)*
letter   **la lettre**
letter-box/mail box   **la boîte aux lettres**

letter-rate   **le tarif d'une lettre**
mail   **le courrier**
news   **les nouvelles** *(f)*
package   **l'emballage** *(m)*
parcel   **le colis**
parcel-rate   **le tarif d'un colis**
pen-friend/pal   **le correspondant, la correspondante**
I post/mail   **je poste**
post office   **la poste**
post restante   **la poste restante**
post/mail   **le courrier**
postage   **les tarifs** *(m)* **postaux**
postal order   **le mandat postal**
postcard   **la carte postale**
postcode   **le code postal**
postman   **le facteur, la factrice**
I receive   **je reçois** *(recevoir)*
recorded/registered mail   **le courrier recommandé**
reply   **la réponse**
sealed   **cacheté**
I send   **j'envoie** *(envoyer)*
sender   **un expéditeur, une expéditrice**
stamp   **le timbre**
I write   **j'écris** *(écrire)*

When does the post/mail arrive?	**Quand est-ce que le courrier arrive?**
I haven't heard from her for ages.	**Je n'ai pas eu de ses nouvelles depuis bien longtemps.**
Dear Sir,	**Monsieur,**
I am writing on behalf of my father, concerning...	**Je vous écris de la part de mon père, en ce qui concerne …**
I look forward to hearing from you.	**Dans l'attente de votre réponse …**
Yours sincerely	**Je vous prie d'agréer, monsieur/madame, l'expression de mes sentiments les meilleurs**

Telephone &
telecommunications

answering machine **le répondeur**
téléphonique
booth/kiosk **la cabine**
button **le bouton**
call-box **la cabine téléphonique**
chat-line **le téléphone rose**
conversation **la conversation**
dial **le cadran**
electronic mail (E-mail) **le courrier**
électronique
engaged *(phone)* **occupé**
ex-directory **sur la liste rouge**
extension **le poste**
fax **la télécopie, le fax**
fax modem **le modem de fax**
local call **la communication**
urbaine
long-distance call **la**
communication interurbaine
nought **le zéro**
operator **le/la standardiste**
out of order **en panne**
receiver **le combiné**
reverse charge call **l'appel** *(m)* **en**
P.C.V.
slot **la fente**
subscriber **un abonné, une**
abonnée
telecommunications links **les liai-**
sons *(f)* **de télécommunications**
telegram(me)/wire **le télégramme**
telegraph **le télégraphe**
telephone **le téléphone**
telephone directory **l'annuaire** *(m)*
téléphonique
telephone/phone **le téléphone**
wrong number **le mauvais numéro**

Telephoning

I call **j'appelle** *(appeler)*
I call again **je rappelle** *(rappeler)*
I connect **je mets** *(mettre)* **en**
communication
I dial **je compose**
I fax **j'envoie** *(envoyer)* **une**
télécopie/un fax
I hang up **je raccroche**
I hold **je patiente**
I pick up **je décroche**
I press **j'appuie** *(appuyer)*
I put ... through (to) **je passe ... (à)**
I speak to **je parle à**
I telephone/phone/call **je**
téléphone
I transmit **je transmets**
(transmettre)

Do you have change for the
telephone? Can I dial direct?

– This is Jean-Luc (speaking).
Could you put me through to
François?
– Please wait/hold! ... Are you still
there? I'm afraid he's not in.

– I will call back later.

This is Cambridge 503244.

**Avez-vous de la monnaie pour le
téléphone? Puis-je appeler par
l'automatique?**

**– C'est Jean-Luc à l'appareil.
Pourriez-vous me passer
François?**
**– Veuillez patienter!/Ne quittez pas!
... Vous êtes toujours en ligne? Je
regrette, il n'est pas ici.**

– Je rappellerai plus tard.

**Ici Cambridge 503244. (cinquante,
trente-deux, quarante quatre).**

15d Computers

Computer applications

adventure game   **le jeu d'aventure**
application   **l'application** (f)
artificial intelligence   **l'intelligence**
   (f) **artificielle**
bar code   **le code à barres**
bar code reader   **le lecteur de**
   code à barres
calculator   **la calculatrice**
computer   **l'ordinateur** (m)
computer control   **le contrôle par**
   ordinateur
computer science/studies
   l'informatique (f)
computerized   **informatisé**
desk-top publishing/DTP   **la**
   Publication Assistée par
   Ordinateur (PAO)
grammar checker   **le correcteur de**
   grammaire
information technology   **la**
   technologie de l'information
information   **une information**
office automation   **la bureautique**
optical reader   **le lecteur optique**

simulation   **la simulation**
simulator   **le simulateur**
spell-checker   **le correcteur**
   d'orthographe
synthesiser   **le synthétiseur**
thesaurus   **le thésaurus, le**
   dictionnaire de synonymes
word processor   **la machine de**
   traitement de texte
word-processing   **le traitement de**
   texte

Word processing & operating

I abort   **j'abandonne**
I access   **j'accède (accéder) à**
I append   **j'ajoute**
I back-up   **je sauvegarde**
I block (text)   **je sélectionne**
I browse   **je feuillette**
I cancel   **j'annule**
I click on   **je clique**
I communicate   **je communique**
I copy   **je copie**
I count   **je compte**
I create   **je crée**

Which disk drive are you using?	**Quel lecteur de disque utilisez-vous?**
What size disks does it use?	**De quelle taille de disque avez-vous besoin?**
Can you repair this keyboard?	**Pouvez-vous réparer le clavier?**
How do you turn down the brightness?	**Comment est-ce qu'on baisse l'intensité?**
What do the function keys do?	**À quoi servent les touches de fonction?**
The Macintosh and IBM systems are not yet compatible.	**Les systèmes Macintosh et IBM ne sont pas encore compatibles.**
These computers are on a local area network.	**Ces ordinateurs sont sur un réseau local.**

I cut and paste **je coupe et je colle**
I debug **je débogue**
I delete **j'efface**
I download **je transfère (transférer)**
I embolden **je mets (mettre) en caractères gras**
I emulate **j'imite**
I enter **j'entre**
I erase **j'efface**
I exit **je sors**
I export **j'exporte**
I file **je classe**
I format **je formate**
I handle (text) **je traite (texte)**
I import **j'importe**
I install **j'installe**
keyboard **le clavier**
keyboard operator **un opérateur/ une opératrice de saisie**
I list **je liste**
I log on/off **j'entre/je sors (sortir)**
I log **j'enregistre**
I merge **je fusionne**
I move **je déplace**
I open (a file) **j'ouvre (ouvrir) (un fichier)**
I print (out) **j'imprime**
I (word) process **je traite**
I program(me) **je programme**
I read **je lis (lire)**
I re-boot **je réinitialise, je réamorce**
I receive **je reçois (recevoir)**
I record **j'enregistre**
I remove **j'efface**
I replace **je remplace**
I retrieve **j'extrais**
I run **je parcours**
I save **je sauvegarde**
I search **je cherche**
I send **j'envoie**
I shift **je décale**
I simulate **je simule**
I sort **je classe**
I store **je mets (mettre) en mémoire**
I switch on/off **j'allume/j'éteins (éteindre)**
I tabulate **je mets (mettre) en colonnes**
I update **je mets (mettre) à jour**
I underline **je souligne**

– How easy is this spreadsheet to use?
– You can always consult the pull-down menu.

– Ce tableur est-il facile à utiliser?
– Vous pouvez toujours regarder le menu qui défile vers le bas.

This disk is corrupted. It has wiped my file!
Have you checked for a virus?

Ce disque est corrompu. Il a effacé mon fichier!
Avez-vous vérifié qu'il n'y a pas de virus?

Which operating system do you use?

Quel système d'exploitation utilises-tu?

Don't show me your password!

Ne me montrez pas votre mot de passe!

I don't like this software package.

Je n'aime pas ce progiciel.

Leisure & sport

16a Leisure

activity **l'activité** *(f)*
amateur **amateur**
archeology **l'archéologie** *(f)*
archery **le tir à l'arc**
I begin **je commence**
I belong to **je fais partie de**
book **le livre**
boring **ennuyeux [-se]**
camera **l'appareil** *(m)* **photo**
card **la carte**
card game **le jeu de cartes**
card table **la table de jeu**
casino **le casino**
cinema/movie house **le cinéma**
closed **fermé**
club **le club**
I collect **je collectionne**
coin **la pièce**
connoisseur (of) **le connaisseur/la connaisseuse (de)**
crossword puzzles **les mots** *(m)* **croisés**
collection **la collection**

collectors fair **la foire des collectionneurs**
I decide **je décide**
discotheque **la discothèque**
I dislike **je n'aime pas**
DIY/do-it-yourself **le bricolage**
energy **l'énergie** *(f)*
energetic **énergique**
enthusiasm **l'enthousiasme** *(m)*
entrance **l'entrée** *(f)*
entry fee **le prix d'entrée**
excitement **l'exaltation** *(f)*
exciting **passionnant**
excursion **l'excursion** *(f)*
exit **la sortie**
fair **la fête foraine**
fascinating **fascinant**
I fish **je pêche, je vais à la pêche**
finished **fini**
free time **le temps libre**
fun **amusant**
I gamble **je joue de l'argent**
I go out **je sors** *(sortir)*

– What is your favourite hobby?

– Well, I used to go for a drive in the country every Sunday, but I have no time for hobbies nowadays. Sometimes I go fishing, which is recommended for stressed executives.

I can meet you at the swimming pool or, if you prefer, at the gym.

– **Quel est ton passe-temps préféré?**
– **Eh bien, tous les dimanches, je partais en voiture à la campagne, mais maintenant, je n'ai plus de temps pour les passe-temps. Parfois, je vais à la pêche, ce qui est recommandé pour les cadres stressés.**

On peut se rencontrer à la piscine, ou si tu préfères, à la salle de gym/au gymnase.

guide **le/la guide**
guided tour **la visite guidée**
hobby/pastime **le passe-temps**
holiday/vacation **les vacances** *(f)*
interest **l'intérêt** *(m)*
interesting **intéressant**
I join **je m'inscris** *(s'inscrire)* **à**
leisure **le loisir**
I like **j'aime**
I listen to **j'écoute**
I look **je regarde**
market **le marché**
   antiques market **le marché d'antiquités**
   flea market **le marché aux puces**
I meet **je rencontre**
meeting place **le lieu de rencontre**
member **le membre**
membership **l'adhésion** *(f)*
nightclub **la boîte de nuit**
open **ouvert**
organization **une organisation**
I organize **j'organise**
picnic **le pique-nique**
place **le lieu**
I play **je joue**
pleasure **le plaisir**
politics **la politique**

I prefer **je préfère**
private **privé**
public **publique**
queue/line **la queue**
I queue/get in line **je fais la queue**
I read **je lis** *(lire)*
ready **prêt**
season **la saison**
season ticket **l'abonnement** *(m)*
secluded **isolé**
slide **la diapositive**
spectator **le spectateur, la spectatrice**
I start (doing) **je commence (à faire)**
I stop (doing) **j'arrête (de faire)**
I stroll **je me promène**
subscription **l'abonnement** *(m)*
television **la télévision**
ticket **le billet**
time **l'heure** *(f)*
theatre/theater **le théâtre**
tour/visit **la visite**
vacation **les vacances** *(f)*
I visit **je visite, je rends visite à**
visit **la visite**
I walk **je marche**
I watch **je regarde**
youth club **le centre de jeunes**
zoo **le zoo**

– What do you like doing on a rainy day?
– Perhaps playing cards but not with my brother: he cheats!

– Shall we take the children to the zoo?
– Good idea. If we take Eve's children and their school friends as well we can have a group reduction.

– **Qu'est-ce que tu aimes faire les jours de pluie?**
– **Peut-être jouer aux cartes mais pas avec mon frère: il triche!**

– **Et si nous emmenions les enfants au zoo?**
– **Bonne idée. Si nous emmenons les enfants d'Eve et leurs copains d'école, nous pourrons bénéficier d'un prix de groupe.**

➤ LEISURE WEAR & EQUIPMENT 16c; PHOTOGRAPHY App.16c

16b Sporting activity

against **contre**
I aim **je vise**
archer **l'archer** *(m)*
athlete **un/une athlète**
athletic **athlétique**
ball **la balle**
  ball *(large)* **le ballon**
bathtowel **la serviette de bain**
bet **le pari**
boat **le bateau**
boxer **le boxeur**
I bowl **je joue aux boules**
captain **le capitaine**
I catch **j'attrape**
champion **le champion, la champione**
championship **le championnat**
changing/locker room **le vestiaire**
I climb **je grimpe**
climber **le grimpeur, la grimpeuse**
coach **un entraîneur, une entraîneuse**
cup *(sport)* **la coupe**
cycle **le vélo**
I cycle **je fais du vélo**
defeat **la défaite**
I dive **je plonge**
I do (sport) **je fais (du sport)**
I draw *(tie)* **je fais match nul**
draw *(tie)* **le match nul**
effort **l'effort** *(m)*
endurance **l'endurance** *(f)*
equipment **le matériel**
I exercize **je fais des exercices**
I fall **je tombe**
fall **la chute**

finals **la finale**
fit **en pleine forme**
fitness **la forme**
game **le jeu**
I get fit **je me mets** *(se mettre)* **en forme**
goal **le but**
ground/stadium **le terrain**
gym(nasium) **la salle de gym, le gymnase**
I hit **je frappe, je touche**
hit **la frappe**
ice-rink **la patinoire**
I ice skate **je fais du patin à glace**
injury **la blessure**
instructor **le moniteur, la monitrice**
I jog **je fais du jogging**
jogger **le jogger**
I jump **je saute**
jump **le saut**
I kick (ball) **je shoote (dans le ballon)**
lawn **la pelouse**
  lawn *(tennis)* **le gazon**
league **la ligue**
locker room **le vestiaire**
I lose **je perds** *(perdre)*
I lift weights **je fais des haltères**
marathon **le marathon**
match **le match**
medal **la médaille**
  gold/silver/bronze **d'or/ d'argent/de bronze**
muscle **le muscle**
Olympic Games (Winter) **les Jeux**

It is a remarkable achievement for the national team, which has performed extremely well.

C'est un exploit remarquable pour l'équipe nationale qui a extrêmement bien joué.

(m) **Olympiques (d'hiver)**
opponent **un/une adversaire**
pedal **la pédale**
pentathlon **le pentathlon**
physical **physique**
I pitch **je lance**
pitcher **le lanceur**
I play **je joue**
player **le joueur, la joueuse**
point **le point**
professional **le professionnel, la professionnelle**
I race **je fais une course**
race **la course**
referee **l'arbitre** *(m)*
rest **le repos**
result **le résultat**
I ride **je fais du cheval**
riding-school **l'école** *(f)* **d'équitation**
roller-skating **le patinage à roulettes**
I row **je fais de l'aviron**
I run **je cours** *(courir)*
run **la course**
runner **le coureur**
sailing school **l'école** *(f)* **de voile**
I sail **je fais de la voile**
sail **la voile**
I score (a goal) **je marque (un but)**
score **le score**
I shoot *(ball, puck)* **je shoote**
I shoot (at a target) **je tire (sur la cible)**
I shoot pool **je joue au billard américain**
I ski **je fais du ski**
ski-slope **la piste**

show **le spectacle**
skier **le skieur, la skieuse**
ski-lift **le remonte-pente**
sponsor **le sponsor**
sponsorship **le sponsoring**
sport **le sport**
sports field **le terrain de sport**
sprint **le sprint**
stadium **le stade**
stamina **l'endurance** *(f)*
strength **la force**
supporter **le/la supporter**
I swim **je nage**
table tennis **le tennis de table**
team **l'équipe** *(f)*
team sport **le sport d'équipe**
I throw **je lance**
timing/timekeeping **le chronométrage**
touch-down **le but**
tournament **le tournoi**
track **la piste**
I train **je m'entraîne**
trainer **un entraîneur, une entraîneuse**
training **l'entraînement** *(m)*
triumph **le triomphe**
trophy **le trophée**
I am unfit **je ne suis pas en forme**
victory **la victoire**
I win **je gagne**
work-out **la séance d'entraînement**
world championship **le championnat du monde**
world cup **la coupe du monde**

The team has been training in very trying weather conditions and each athlete was ready to give his best.

L'équipe s'est entraînée dans des conditions climatiques très pénibles et chaque athlète était prêt à donner le meilleur de lui-même.

➤ PHYSICAL STATE 11d

16c Sports & equipment

Sports

aerobics **l'aérobic** *(m)*
archery **le tir à l'arc**
athletics **l'athlétisme** *(m)*
badminton **le badminton**
baseball **le baseball**
basketball **le basketball**
bowling **le jeu de boules**
  ten-pin bowling/tenpins **le bowling (à dix quilles)**
boxing **la boxe**
climbing (rock) **l'escalade** *(f)*
  free climbing **la libre escalade** *(f)*
crew **l'équipage** *(m)*
cricket **le cricket**
cycling **le cyclisme**
decathlon **le décathlon**
diving **la plongée**
  deep sea diving **la plongée sous-marine**
football **le football**
handball **le handball**
hockey **le hockey**
horse-racing **les courses** *(f)* **de chevaux**
horse-riding **l'équitation** *(f)*
ice-hockey **le hockey sur glace**
ice-skating **le patinage (sur glace)**
jogging **le jogging**
motor-racing **les courses** *(f)* **automobiles**
paragliding **le delta-plane**
parapenting **le parapente**
polo **le polo**
pool **le billard américain**
racing **les courses** *(f)*
riding **l'équitation** *(f)*
rugby **le rugby**
sailing **la navigation à voile**
skiing **le ski**
  alpine skiing **le ski alpin**
  cross-country skiing **le ski de fond**

down-hill skiing **le ski de descente**
snooker **le billard**
soccer **le football**
swimming **la natation**
table tennis **le tennis de table**
tennis **le tennis**
volleyball **le volleyball**
water-polo **le water-polo**
weightlifting **l'haltérophilie** *(f)*
weight training **la musculation (en salle)**
windsurfing **la planche à voile**

Leisure wear and sports clothes

anorak **l'anorak** *(m)*
bathing suit **le maillot de bain**
boots **les bottes** *(f)*
cycling shorts **le short de cycliste**
dancing shoes **les chaussures** *(f)* **de danse**
gardening gloves **les gants** *(m)* **de jardinage**
leotard **le collant**
parka **le parka**
rugby shirt **la chemise de rugby**
salopette **la salopette**
swimsuit/bathing suit **le maillot de bain**
swimming trunks **le maillot de bain**
track suit **le survêtement**
trainers **les chaussures** *(f)* **de sport, les baskets** *(f)*
walking boots **les chaussures** *(f)* **de marche**
waterproof jacket **la veste imperméable**
Wellington boots **les bottes** *(f)* **en caoutchouc**
wet suit **la combinaison de plongée**

Leisure and sport equipment

arrow **la flèche**
ball **la balle**
bat *(cricket, baseball)* **la batte**
bat (table tennis) **la raquette de tennis de table**
binoculars **les jumelles** *(f)*
boxing gloves **les gants** *(m)* **de boxe**
bow **le flèche**
camera **l'appareil** *(m)* **photo**
crash helmet **le casque**
equipment **le matériel**
exercise bike **le vélo de santé/d'appartement**
fishing rod **la canne à pêche**
headphone **le casque (à écouteurs)**
hi-fi **la chaîne hi-fi**
knapsack **le sac à dos**
knitting needles **les aiguilles** *(f)* **à tricoter**
javelin **le javelot**
mountain bike **le Vélo Tout Terrain (V.T.T.)**
net **le filet**
outrigger **l'outrigger** *(m)*

puck **le palet**
racket **la raquette**
rifle **le fusil**
roller skates **les patins** *(m)* **à roulettes**
rowing machine **la machine à ramer**
rowing boat **le canot (à rames)**
rucksack **le sac à dos**
sailing-boat **le voilier**
sewing kit **la boîte à couture**
secateurs **les sécateurs** *(m)*
skate **le patin**
skis **les skis** *(m)*
ski boots **les chaussures** *(f)* **de ski**
ski sticks/poles **les bâtons** *(m)* **de ski**
spinning wheel **le rouet**
sports bag **le sac de sport**
stick *(hockey)* **le crosse (de hockey)**
surf board **la planche de surf**
stopwatch **le chronomètre**
weights **les poids** *(m)*
yacht **le yacht**
zoom lens **le zoom**

– Did you watch the game?

– No, I had to leave before the end. Who won?

– We lost 3 - 1. I still cannot understand how such a capable team could lose so disastrously after a brilliant season.

All sports commentators agree that they were particularly unlucky when the referee insisted on the penalty.

– **As-tu regardé le match?**

– **Non, j'ai dû partir avant la fin. Qui a gagné?**

– **Nous avons perdu 3 à 1. Je ne peux toujours pas comprendre comment une équipe aussi compétente a pu perdre de façon aussi désastreuse après une saison remarquable.**

Tous les commentateurs sportifs sont d'accord pour dire qu'ils n'ont surtout pas eu de chance quand l'arbitre a insisté sur le pénalty.

➤ GARDENING 24c; TOOLS App.8b; PHOTOGRAPHY App.16a

The Arts

17a Appreciation and criticism

abstract **abstrait**
abstruse **obscur, abstrus**
action **l'action** *(f)*
aesthete **l'esthète** *(m)*
aesthetics **l'esthétisme**
I appreciate **j'apprécie**
appreciation **l'appréciation** *(f)*
art **l'art** *(m)*
artist **l'artiste** *(m)*
artistic **artistique**
atmosphere **l'atmosphère** *(f)*
atmospheric **atmosphérique**
author **l'auteur** *(m)*
award **le prix**
I analyze **j'analyse**
avant-guarde **d'avant-garde**
believable **croyable**
character **le personnage**
characterization **la description des personnages**
characteristic **caractéristique**
climax **le point culminant**
it closes **il termine**
comic **comique, drôle**
commentary **le commentaire**
conflict **le conflit**
contemporary **contemporain**
contrast **le contraste**
it creates **il crée**
creativity **la créativité**
credible **crédible**
critic **le critique**
criticism **la critique**
cultivated **cultivé**
culture **la culture**
it deals with **il traite de**
it describes **il décrit**
it develops **il développe**
development **le développement**
device **la technique**

dialogue **le dialogue**
disturbing **inquiétant**
empathy **l'empathie** *(f)*
ending **la fin**
endless **interminable**
it ends **il se termine**
entertaining **distrayant**
entertainment **la distraction**
epic **l'aventure** *(f)* **épique**
event **l'événement** *(m)*
eventful **plein d'aventures**
example **l'exemple** *(m)*
exciting **palpitant, passionnant**
I explain **j'explique**
explanation **l'explication** *(f)*
it explores **il explore**
it expresses **il exprime**
extravagant **extravagant, excessif**
fake *(adj)* **faux [-se]**
fantastic **fantastique**
fantasy **la fantaisie**
figure **le personnage, la figure**
funny **amusant, drôle**
image **l'image** *(f)*
imaginary **imaginaire**
imagination **l'imagination** *(f)*
inspiration **l'inspiration** *(f)*
inspired (by) **inspiré (de)**
intense **intense**
intensity **l'intensité** *(f)*
interpretation **l'interprétation** *(f)*
invention **l'invention** *(f)*
inventive **inventif [-ve]**
ironic **ironique**
irony **l'ironie** *(f)*
issue **le problème**
life **la vie**
long-winded **long[ue] et laborieux [-se]**

lyrical **lyrique**
modern **moderne**
mood **l'humeur** *(f)*
moral **la morale**
  moral *(adj)* **moral**
morality **la moralité**
moving **émouvant**
mystery **le mystère**
mysterious **mystérieux [-se]**
mystical **mystique**
mysticism **le mysticisme**
nature **la nature**
obscure **obscur**
obscene **obscène**
obscenity **l'obscénité** *(f)*
opinion **l'opinion** *(f)*
optimism **l'optimisme** *(m)*
optimistic **optimiste**
parody **la parodie**
passion **la passion**
passionate **passionné**
pessimistic **pessimiste**
pessimism **le pessimisme**
poetic **poétique**
it portrays **il dresse le portrait (de)**
portrayal **le portrait**
precious **précieux [-se]**
protagonist **le protagoniste**

I read **j'étudie**
reader **le lecteur, la lectrice**
realistic **réaliste**
reference **la référence**
I reflect **je réfléchis**
reflection **la réflexion**
relationship **les rapports** *(m)*
review **la revue**
sad **triste**
satire **la satire**
it satirizes **il satirise**
satirical **satirique**
style **le style**
  in the style of … **à la manière de …**
stylish **stylé, élégant**
subject **le sujet**
technique **la technique**
tension **la tension**
theme **le thème**
tone **le ton**
tragedy **la tragédie**
tragic **tragique**
true **vrai**
vivid **éclatant, vif [vive]**
viewpoint **le point de vue**
witty **spirituel[le], amusant**
work of art **l'œuvre** *(f)* **d'art**

Artistic styles & periods

Art Nouveau **l'art** *(m)* **nouveau**
Baroque **baroque**
Bronze Age **l'âge** *(m)* **de bronze**
Classical period **la période classique**
Dadaist **dada**
Enlightenment **le siècle des lumières**
expressionism **l'expressionisme** *(m)*
Futurist(ic) **futuriste**
Georgian **georgien[ne]**
Gothic **gothique**
Greek **grec[que]**
Middle Ages **le Moyen Âge**

moorish **mauresque, maure**
naturalistic **naturaliste**
Neolithic Age **l'âge néolithique**
Norman **normand**
Post- **post-**
realism **le réalisme**
Renaissance **la renaissance**
Rococo **rococo**
Roman Empire **l'empire** *(m)* **romain**
Romanesque **romanesque**
Romantic period **la période romantique**
structuralist **structuraliste**
surrealism **le surréalisme**
symbolism **le symbolisme**

17b Art & architecture

antique l'antiquité *(f)*
antiquity l'antiquité *(f)*
architect l'architecte *(m)*
art l'art *(m)*
artefact l'objet *(m)* d'art
artist l'artiste *(m)*
art student l'étudiant *(f)* des beaux-arts
auction sale la vente aux enchères
auctioneer le commissaire-priseur
balance l'équilibre *(m)*
baroque baroque
beam la poutre
bronze le bronze
brush le pinceau
I build je construis
building le bâtiment
bust le buste
caricature la caricature
I carve je sculpte, je taille
I cast je moule, je coule
ceramics la céramique
charcoal le fusain
chisel le ciseau
chiselled ciselé
classical classique
clay l'argile *(f)*
collage le collage
creative créatif [-ve]
creativity la créativité
decorated orné, décoré
decoration la décoration
decorative arts les arts *(m)* décoratifs
I design je crée
design la création, le design, le motif
dimension la dimension
I draw je dessine
drawing le dessin
easel le chevalet
elevation l'élévation *(f)*
enamel l'émail *(m)*
I engrave je grave
engraving l'estampe *(f)*
I etch je grave
etching la gravure
exhibition l'exposition *(f)*
figure la figure
figurine la figurine
fine arts les beaux-arts *(m)*
flamboyant flamboyant
form la forme
free-hand à main levée
fresco la fresque
frieze la frise
genre le genre
graphic arts les arts *(m)* graphiques
gravity la gravité
holograph l'hologramme *(f)*
interior intérieur
intricate compliqué
ironwork la ferronnerie
landscape le paysage
landscape architect l'architecte

Here, we are probably in the best place. Look, in the foreground you can see the monastery, which dates back from 1679 and which is such a good example of religious architecture and in the background the medieval towers are still visible.

Ici, nous sommes sans doute au meilleur endroit. Regardez, au premier plan on peut voir le monastère, qui date de 1679 et qui est un si bel exemple d'architecture religieuse, et à l'arrière plan on peut encore voir les tours médiévales.

(m) **paysagiste**
landscape painter **le peintre paysagiste**
large-scale work **l'œuvre** *(f)* **de grande échelle**
later works **les œuvres** *(f)* **postérieures/plus récentes**
light **la lumière**
light *(adj)* **clair**
lithography **la lithographie**
luminosity **la luminosité**
luminous **lumineux [-se]**
masterpiece **le chef-d'œuvre**
metal **le métal**
miniature **la miniature**
model **le modèle**
monochrome **monochrome**
mosaic **la mosaïque**
museum **le musée**
oil painting **la peinture à l'huile**
ornate **orné**
I paint **je peins** *(peindre)*, **je fais de la peinture**
paint **la peinture**
painting **le tableau**
pastel **le pastel**
portrait **le portrait**
potter **le potier**
pottery **la poterie**
it represents **il représente**
representation **la représentation**
reproduction **la reproduction**
restoration **la restauration**
I restore **je restaure**
restored **restauré**

restorer **le restaurateur**
roughcast **l'ébauche** *(f)*
school **l'école** *(f)*
I sculpt **je sculpte**
sculptor **le sculpteur**
sculpture **la sculpture**
seascape **le paysage marin**
shadow **l'ombre** *(f)*
shape **la forme**
I shape **je forme**
sketch(ing) **l'esquisse** *(f)*
I sketch **j'esquisse**
stained glass **le verre teint**
 stained glass window **le vitrail**
statuary **la statuaire**
statue **la statue**
still-life **la nature morte**
I stipple **je pointille**
studio **le studio**
style **le style**
tapestry **la tapisserie**
tempera **la détrempe**
town-planning **l'urbanisme** *(m)*
traditional **traditionnel**
translucent **translucide**
transparent **transparent**
visual arts **les arts** *(m)* **plastiques**
water-colour/color **l'aquarelle** *(f)*
weathering **le vieillissement**
wood **le bois**
wood-carving **la sculpture sur bois**
woodcut **la sculpture sur bois**
wood-engraving **la gravure sur bois**

I have just been to the exhibition at the Academy, which has already attracted thousands of visitors. There is the most wonderful collection of drawings and sculptures.

Je viens de voir l'exposition à l'Academy, qui a déjà attiré des milliers de visiteurs. Il y a une collection vraiment merveilleuse de dessins et de sculptures.

➤ ARCHITECTURAL FEATURES App.17b

17c Literature

autograph **l'autographe** *(m)*
book **le livre**
bookshop/store **la librairie**
bookseller **le libraire**
character **le personnage**
  main character **le/la protagoniste**
comic **comique**
dialogue/dialog **le dialogue**
fictional **fictif [-ve], fictionnel[le]**
hardback *(adj)* **relié**
I imagine **j'imagine**
imagination **l'imagination** *(f)*
inspiration **l'inspiration** *(f)*
inspired by **inspiré par/de**
it introduces **il introduit**
introduction **l'introduction** *(f)*
I leaf through **je feuillette**
librarian **le/la bibliothécaire**
library **la bibliothèque**
  public library **la bibliothèque municipale**
  reference library **la bibliothèque de consultation**
literal(ly) **littéral(ement)**
map **la carte**
myth **le mythe**
mythology **la mythologie**
it narrates **il raconte, il narre**
narrative **le narratif**
narrator **le narrateur**
page **la page**
paperback **le livre de poche**
poem **le poème**

poetic **poétique**
poetry **la poésie**
punctuation **la ponctuation**
quote **la citation**
I quote **je cite**
I read **je lis** *(lire)*
I recount **je rapporte**
rhyme **la rime**
it is set in **il se situe en**
text **le texte**
title **le titre**
verse **le vers**

Types of books

adventure story **le roman d'aventure**
atlas **l'atlas** *(m)*
autobiography **l'autobiographie** *(f)*
biography **la biographie**
children's literature **la littérature enfantine**
comic novel **le roman comique**
cookbook/cookery book **le livre de recettes/cuisine**
crime novel **le roman policier**
dictionary **le dictionnaire**
  bilingual **bilingue**
  monolingual **monolingue**
diary **le journal**
encyclopedia **l'encyclopédie** *(f)*
epic poem **le poème épique**
essay **l'essai** *(m)*
fable **la fable**
fairy tale **le conte de fée**

– What are you all reading at the moment?

–A spine-chilling story with a tragic conclusion. It is set in contemporary Los Angeles.

– Qu'est ce que vous lisez en ce moment?

– Un récit à vous glacer le sang avec une conclusion tragique. Il se situe dans le Los Angeles d'aujourd'hui.

feminist novel   **le roman féministe**
fiction   **la fiction**
Greek tragedy   **la tragédie grecque**
horror story   **le récit d'épouvante**
letters   **les lettres, la correspondance**
manual   **le manuel**
memoirs   **les mémoires** *(m)*
modern play   **la pièce moderne**
non-fiction   **le documentaire**
novel   **le roman**
picaresque   **picaresque**
poetry   **la poésie**
reference book   **l'ouvrage** *(m)* **de référence**
satirical poem   **le poème satirique**
science fiction   **la science-fiction**
short story   **la nouvelle**
spy story   **le roman d'espionnage**
teenage fiction   **la littérature pour les jeunes**
travel book   **le guide/le récit de voyage**
war novel   **le roman de guerre**

Publishing

abridged version   **la version abrégée**
acknowledgements   **les remerciements** *(m)*
appendix   **l'appendice** *(m)*
artwork   **les illustrations**
author   **l'auteur** *(m)*
best-seller   **le best-seller, le livre à succès**

bibliography   **la bibliographie**
book fair   **la foire du livre**
catalogue   **le catalogue**
chapter   **le chapitre**
contents   **la table des matières**
contract   **le contrat**
copy   **l'exemplaire** *(m)*
copyright   **les droits** *(m)* **d'auteur**
cover (of book)   **la couverture**
deadline   **la date limite**
dedicated to   **dédié à**
edition   **l'édition** *(f)*
   latest edition   **l'édition la plus récente**
editor   **le rédacteur**
   desk editor   **le rédacteur technique**
footnotes   **les annotations** *(f)*
illustrations   **les illustrations** *(f)*
manuscript   **le manuscript**
paperback   **le livre de poche**
preface   **la préface**
proof-reading   **la correction**
publication date   **la date de publication**
publisher   **l'éditeur** *(m)*
publishing house   **la maison d'édition**
quote   **la citation**
review   **la critique**
reviewer   **le critique**
subtitle   **le sous-titre**
translation   **la traduction**
version   **la version**
with a forward by   **préfacé par**

– A vivid account of life in the Thirties. The writer explores the theme of lost innocence.

– I'm reading a collection of modern foreign fiction.

– Un tableau évocateur de la vie dans les années trente. L'auteur explore le thème de l'innocence perdue.

– Je lis un recueil d'ouvrages de fiction en langue étrangère.

17d Music & dance

acoustics l'acoustique *(f)*
adjudicator l'adjudicateur *(m)*
agent l'agent *(m)*, l'impresario *(m)*
album l'album *(m)*
amplifier l'amplificateur *(m)*
audience le public, les spectateurs *(m)*
audition l'audition *(f)*
auditorium l'auditorium *(m)*
ballet la danse classique, le ballet
band leader le leader du groupe
baton la baguette
brass band la fanfare
canned music la musique d'ambiance
cassette tape la cassette audio
cassette-deck le lecteur de cassettes
chamber music la musique de chambre
chart/hit parade le hit-parade
choir le choeur
choral choral
choreography la chorégraphie
chorister le choriste
chorus le choeur
classical music la musique classique
compact disc/disk (CD) le disque compact, le CD
competition la compétition

compilation le recueil
I compose je compose
composer le compositeur
composition la composition
concert le concert
concert hall la salle de concerts
conductor le chef d'orchestre
I conduct je dirige l'orchestre
dance la danse
I dance je danse
dancer le danseur, la danseuse
dance music la musique de ballet
discotheque la discothèque
disc jockey l'animateur *(m)*, le disc-jockey
drummer le batteur
ensemble l'ensemble *(m)*
folk music la musique folklorique
group le groupe
harmony l'harmonie *(f)*
harmonic harmonique
hit (song) le tube
I hum je chantonne
instrument l'instrument *(m)*
instrument maker le luthier
instrument repairer le réparateur d'instruments de musique
instrumental music la musique instrumentale
instrumentalist le musicien instrumentaliste
I interpret j'interprète *(interpréter)*

– Do you play an instrument?
– I play the viola.
– I never learned to play an instrument but I have just bought an electric guitar.

– I like traditional jazz.
– I prefer easy listening music.

– Jouez-vous d'un instrument?
– Je joue de l'alto.
– Je n'ai jamais appris à jouer d'un instrument mais je viens d'acheter une guitare électrique.

– J'aime le jazz traditionnel.
– Je préfère la musique d'ambiance.

interpretation l'**interprétation** (f)
jazz **le jazz**
juke-box **le juke-box**
key **la clé**
lesson **la leçon**
I listen to **j'écoute**
listening l'**écoute** (f)
microphone **le micro**
music **la musique**
musical(ly) **musical(ement)**
musician **le musicien, la**
  musicienne
note **la note**
orchestra l'**orchestre** (f)
orchestration l'**orchestration** (f)
it is performed **on joue**
performance **la représentation**
performed by **interprété par**
performer **un/une interprète**
pianist **le/la pianiste**
piano **le piano**
piece **le morceau**
I play **je joue**
player **le joueur, la joueuse**
popular music **la musique**
  populaire
portable **portatif [-ve]**
I practice **je m'entraîne**
promotional video **la vidéo**
  promotionnelle
I put on a record **je mets** (mettre)
  un disque
recital **le récital**
record **le disque**
I record **j'enregistre**

recording l'**enregistrement** (m)
recording studio **le studio**
  d'enregistrement
reed l'**anche** (f)
refrain **le refrain**
I rehearse **je répète** (répéter)
rehearsal **la répétition**
repertoire **le répertoire**
rhythm **le rythme**
rhythmic(ally) **rythmique(ment)**
rock **le rock**
show **le spectacle**
I sing **je chante**
singer **le chanteur, la chanteuse**
solo **le solo**
soloist **le/la soliste**
song **la chanson**
song-writer **le compositeur**
string **les cordes** (f)
string orchestra l'**ensemble** (m) à
  cordes
symphony **la symphonie**
tape **la bande (sonore)**
tour **la tournée**
  on tour **en tournée**
tune l'**air** (m)
  in tune **juste**
  out of tune **faux [-se]**
I tune **j'accorde**
vocal music **la musique vocale**
voice **la voix**
I whistle **je siffle**
whistling **le sifflement**
wind band l'**ensemble** (m)
  d'instruments à vent

– There is a rave concert at the
Students' Union/college hall.
– What is the name of the band?
– I don't know. Their lyrics aren't
bad but their music is dire.

Some people have perfect pitch.

– Il y a un concert branché dans
la salle des étudiants.
– **Comment s'appelle ce groupe?**
– **Je ne sais pas. Les paroles ne**
sont pas mal mais la musique
est nulle.

Il y a des gens qui ont la voix
très juste.

17e Theatre & cinema/Theater & the movies

act **l'acte** (f)
I act **je joue**
acting school **le conservatoire de théâtre**
actor **l'acteur** (m)
actress **l'actrice** (f)
I applaud **j'applaudis**
applause/clapping **les applaudissements** (m)
assistant director **le régisseur**
audience **le public, les spectateurs** (m)
auditorium **la salle**
I book **je réserve**
box **la loge**
box-office **le bureau des réservations**
cabaret **le cabaret**
camera **la caméra**
camera crew **l'équipe** (f) **de tournage**
cameraman **le caméraman**
cartoons **les dessins** (m) **animés**
choreographer **le /la chorégraphe**
cinema/movies **le cinéma**
cinema/movie buff **le/la cinéphile**
circle **la galerie**
circus **le cirque**
I clap **j'applaudis**
cloakroom **les vestiaires** (m)

comedian **le comédien**
comedienne **la comédienne**
curtain **le rideau**
I design **je crée**
designer **le créateur**
I direct **je dirige**
director **le réalisateur**
drama **le drame**
dress rehearsal **la répétition générale**
dubbed **doublé**
dubbing **le doublage**
expectation **l'attente** (f)
farce **la farce**
farcical **ridicule**
film/movie **le film**
film/movie maker **le cinéaste**
filmstar/movie star **la vedette de cinéma**
film/movie producer **le producteur de cinéma**
first night **la première**
floor-show **le spectacle de variétés**
flop **le navet, le fiasco**
gaffer **l'éclairagiste** (m)
intermission **l'entracte** (m)
interval **l'entracte** (m)
lights **l'éclairage** (m)
limelights **les projecteurs** (m)
in the limelight **en vedette**

Foreign films are usually dubbed, but some cinema/movie clubs show them in the original language.	**Les films en langue étrangère sont en général doublés, mais certains ciné-clubs les passent en version originale.**
Sci-fi films were popular in the Sixties.	**Les films de science-fiction étaient en vogue dans les années soixante.**
The director has been nominated for an Oscar.	**Le réalisateur a été désigné pour un oscar.**

lobby **l'entrée** (f)
I make a film/movie **je fais un film**
masterpiece **le chef-d'œuvre**
matinée **la séance en matinée**
melodrama **le mélodrame**
mime **le mime**
movie **le film**
music-hall **le music-hall**
off-stage **dans les coulisses**
opening night **la première**
ovation **l'ovation** (f)
pantomime **la pantomime**
performance **la représentation, le spectacle**
photography **la photographie**
play **la pièce**
I play **je joue**
playwright **l'auteur** (m) **de pièces de théâtre**
premiere **la première**
I produce **je suis le producteur/la productrice**
producer **le producteur, la productrice**
production **la production**
public **le public**
retrospective **la rétrospective**
role **le rôle**
row **la rangée**
scene **la scène**
scenery **le décor**
screen **l'écran** (m)

screen test **l'audition** (f)
screening **la projection**
I shoot (a film/movie) **je tourne**
script **le script**
scriptwriter **l'auteur** (m) **du script**
seat **le siège**
    seat (cinema/movies) **le fauteuil**
sequel **la suite**
sequence **la séquence**
set (cinema/movie) **le plateau**
I show (film/movie) **je montre, je passe**
it is shown at **on le passe à**
it is sold-out **c'est complet**
sound-track **la bande sonore**
special effects **les effets** (m) **spéciaux**
stage (theatre/theater) **la scène**
stage directions **les indications** (f) **scéniques**
stage effects **les effets** (m) **de scène**
stage-fright **le trac**
stalls **les places** (f) **à l'orchestre**
stunt person **le cascadeur, la cascadeuse**
trailer **la présentation d'un nouveau film**
understudy **la doublure**
usherette **l'ouvreuse** (f)
I zoom **je zoome**

He is playing one of the most demanding roles of his career.	**Il joue l'un des rôles les plus difficiles de sa carrière.**
I want to see the latest production of her three-act play. All the critics will attend the opening night.	**Je veux voir la production la plus récente de sa pièce en trois actes. Tous les critiques assisteront à la première.**
The matinée is sold-out.	**La séance en matinée est complète.**

The Media

18a General terms

admission **l'entrée** *(f)*
I admit **je laisse entrer**
I analyze **j'analyse**
analysis **l'analyse** *(f)*
I appeal to **je fais appel à**
I argue **j'argumente**
argument **la dispute**
attitude **l'attitude** *(f)*
biased **partial**
campaign **la campagne**
censorship **la censure**
cogent **convaincant**
comment **le commentaire**
conspiracy **la conspiration**
criticism **la critique**
critique **la critique**
cultural **culturel[le]**
culture **la culture**
cultured **cultivé**
current events **l'actualité** *(f)*
declaration **la déclaration**
it declares **il déclare**

detailed **détaillé**
it discriminates **il fait une discrimination**
disaster **le désastre**
disinformation **la désinformation**
educational **pédagogique**
I entertain **je divertis**
ethical **moral**
event **l'événement** *(m)*
example **l'exemple** *(m)*
expectations **les attentes** *(f)*
I exploit **j'exploite**
fallacious **trompeur**
fallacy **l'illusion** *(f)*
freedom **la liberté**
full/detailed **rempli**
gullible **crédule**
hidden **caché**
ignorance **l'ignorance** *(f)*
I ignore **j'ignore**
influential **influent**
information **l'information** *(f)*

During the recent elections it was difficult to find an example of unbiased reporting.

In recent years many war correspondent have lost their lives while reporting from the front or have been taken as hostages.

Pendant les récentes élections, il était difficile de trouver un exemple de reportage impartial.

Ces dernières années, de nombreux correspondants de guerre ont péri alors qu'ils faisaient un reportage depuis le front ou ont été pris en otage.

informative **informatif [-ve]**
it interferes **il s'ingère** *(s'ingérer)*
interview **l'entretien** *(m)*
intrusion **l'intrusion** *(f)*
intrusive **importun**
issue *(problem)* **la question**
I keep up with (news) **je me tiens**
(se tenir) **au courant (des**
actualités)
libel **la diffamation**
libellous **diffamatoire**
it is likely **il est probable**
local interest news **l'actualité** *(f)*
d'intérêt local
material **le matériel**
meddling **indiscrèt**
news **les informations** *(f)*
news item **l'information** *(f)*
partisan **partisan**
persuasive **persuasif [-ve]**
prejudice **le préjugé**
political **politique**
politics **la politique**
press **la presse**
privacy **l'intimité** *(f)*
privacy law **la loi sur la protection**
de la vie privée
problem **le problème**
review **la revue**

I review **je passe en revue**
scoop **le scoop**
sensational **sensationnel[le]**
sensationalism **la recherche du**
sensationnel
sexism **le sexisme**
sexist **sexiste**
silence **le silence**
silent **silencieux [-se]**
social **social**
society **la société**
specious **spécieux [-se]**
summary **le résumé**
summary *(adj)* **sommaire**
it takes place **il a lieu**
trust **la confiance**
I trust **je fais confiance**
trustworthy **digne de confiance**
truth **la vérité**
truthful **véridique**
unbiased **impartial**
untrustworthy **indigne de**
confiance
up to date **à jour**
violent **violent**
violence **la violence**
weekly *(adj)* **hebdomadaire**

European current affairs are not
always reported in the British
press, though all quality papers
have foreign correspondents in all
the European capitals.

La presse britannique ne fait
pas toujours un reportage sur
l'actualité européenne, bien que
tous les journaux de qualité
aient des correspondants
étrangers dans toutes les
capitales européennes.

Media barons have dominated the
press in many western countries.

Les magnats des média ont
dominé la presse dans de
nombreux pays occidentaux.

agony aunt **le/la journaliste responsable du courrier du cœur**

article **l'article** *(m)*

back page **la dernière page**

barons **les magnats** *(m)*

broadsheet **le journal plein format**

cartoon **le dessin (humoristique)**

chief editor **le rédacteur/la rédactrice en chef**

circulation **le tirage**

colour/color supplement **le supplément illustré**

column **la colonne**

comic-strip **la bande dessiné**

correspondent **le correspondant, la correspondante**

foreign **à l'étranger**

crossword puzzle **les mots** *(m)* **croisés**

daily newspaper **le quotidien**

I edit **je suis le rédacteur/la rédactrice en chef**

edition **l'édition** *(f)*

editor **le rédacteur, la rédactrice**

editorial **l'éditorial** *(m)*

forgotten **oublié**

front page **la une**

glossy magazine **le magazine de luxe**

gutter press **la presse à scandales**

headline **le (gros) titre, la manchette**

heading **la rubrique**

horoscope **l'horoscope** *(m)*

illustration **l'illustration** *(f)*

it is published **il est publié**

journalist **le/la journaliste**

layout **la mise en page**

leader **l'article** *(m)* **de tête**

local paper **la presse locale**

magazine **le magazine**

monthly **la revue mensuelle, le mensuel**

national newspaper **la grande presse**

newsagent **le marchand/la marchande de journaux**

newspaper **le journal**

news stand **le kiosque (à journaux)**

page **la page**

pamphlet **la brochure**

periodical **le périodique**

The gutter press has a surprisingly high readership.

La presse à scandales a un nombre étonnamment élevé de lecteurs.

The Sunday edition has so many supplements that I can't find the personal ads.

Il y a tellement de suppléments dans l'édition de dimanche que je ne peux pas trouver les annonces personnelles.

The leader in the Examiner breaks the sensational news. What a scoop!

L'éditorial de l'édition de l'Examiner révèle la nouvelle sensationnelle. Quel scoop!

power **le pouvoir**
powerful **puissant**
press agency **l'agence** *(f)* de
presse
press conference **la conférence
de presse**
I print **j'imprime**
print **les caractères** *(m)*
print room **l'imprimerie** *(f)*
problem page **le courier du cœur**
I publish **je publie**
publisher **un éditeur, une éditrice**
publishing company **la maison
d'édition**
quality press **la presse sérieuse/
de qualité**
reader **le lecteur**
I report **je fais un reportage**
report **le reportage**
reporter **le/la journaliste**
short news item **l'information** *(f)*
brève
small ad **la petite annonce**
special correspondent **un envoyé
spécial, une envoyée spéciale**
special issue **le numéro spécial**
sports page **la page sportive**
I subscribe to **je m'abonne à**
subscription **l'abonnement** *(m)*
tabloid **le tabloïd**

type(face) **le caractère**
weekly **l'hebdomadaire** *(m)*

Newspaper sections

Announcements **Annonces** *(f)*
Arts **Arts** *(m)*
Economy **Économie** *(f)*
Editorial **Éditorial** *(m)*
Entertainment **Divertissements**
(m)
Food and drink **Nourriture** *(f)* et
Boissons *(f)*
Games **Jeux** *(m)*
Gossip column **Échos** *(m)*
Home news **Nouvelles** *(f)*
nationales
Horoscope **Horoscope** *(m)*
International news **Nouvelles** *(f)*
internationales
Obituary **Notices** *(f)*, **Nécrologie**
(f)
Finance **Finances** *(f)*
Problems page **Courrier** *(m)* du
cœur
Property **Immobilier** *(m)*
Sports section **Sport** *(m)*
Travel **Voyage** *(m)*
Weather **Météo** *(f)*
Women page **Page** *(f)* des
lectrices

When is the colour/color
supplement published?

– What is the frequency, circulation
and readership of the magazine?

– It's published monthly, is aimed
at motorbike enthusiasts and has
over 30,000 subscribers
worldwide.

**Quand est-ce qu'on publie le
supplément illustré?**

**– Quels sont la fréquence et le
tirage de ce magazine, et qui
sont les lecteurs?**

**– C'est un mensuel qui vise les
fanas de la moto et qui compte
plus de 30.000 abonnés dans le
monde entier.**

18c Television & radio

aerial   **l'antenne** *(f)*
anchorman   **le présentateur**
anchorwoman   **la présentatrice**
announcer   **le speaker, la speakerine**
audience   **le public**
I broadcast   **je diffuse**
broadcasting station   **la station de radio**
cable TV   **la télévision par câble, le câble**
cameraman   **le cadreur, le cameraman**
channel   **la chaîne**
commercial   **la publicité**
couch potato   **le lézard**
dubbed   **doublé**
earphones   **les écouteurs** *(m)*
episode   **l'épisode** *(m)*
high-frequency   **à haute fréquence**
interactive   **conversationnel[le], interactif [-ve]**
listener   **un auditeur, une auditrice**

live broadcast   **la diffusion en direct**
live coverage/commentary   **le reportage en direct**
loudspeaker   **le haut-parleur**
low-frequency   **à basse fréquence**
microphone   **le microphone**
body mike   **le micro portatif**
newsreader   **le présentateur, la présentatrice**
personal stereo   **le baladeur, le walkman®**
production studio   **le studio de production**
program(me)   **le programme**
radio   **la radio**
on radio   **à la radio**
I record   **j'enregistre**
recording   **l'enregistrement** *(m)*
remote control   **la télécommande**
repeat   **la rediffusion**
satellite dish   **l'antenne** *(f)* **parabolique**

– What! Still glued to the set? You have been watching the box all evening! You have become a real couch potato!

– Quoi! Encore cloué devant le poste? Tu as regardé la télé toute la soirée! Tu es devenu un vrai lézard!

– I'm just going to record this film/movie, then I'll join you. Have we got a blank videocassette?

–Je vais juste enregistrer ce film et je te rejoins. Est-ce que tu as des cassettes-vidéos vierges?

Was the Pink Floyd concert broadcast live from Venice?

Est-ce que le concert des Pink Floyd a été diffusé en direct de Venise?

Until recently most TV spots portrayed women in exclusively traditional roles.

Jusqu'à ces derniers temps, la plupart des publicités à la télévision représentaient les femmes dans des rôles exclusivement traditionnels.

satellite TV **la télévision satellite**
screen **l'écran** *(m)*
I show **je montre**
signal **le signal**
station **la station**
subtitles **les sous-titres** *(m)*
I switch off **j'éteins** *(éteindre)*
I switch on **j'allume**
teletext **le télétexte**
television **la télévision**
    on television **à la télévision**
telly/TV **la télé**
I transmit **je transmets**
    (transmettre)
TV film/movie **le téléfilm**
TV set **le téléviseur**
TV studio **le studio de télévision**
video clip **le clip vidéo**
videogame **le jeu vidéo**
video library **la vidéothèque**
video recorder **le magnétoscope**
viewer **le téléspectateur, la**
    téléspectatrice
I watch **je regarde**

TV and radio program(me)s

cartoons **les dessins** *(m)* **animés**
chat show **le talk-show**
children's program(me) **l'émission**
    (f) **pour enfants**
comedy **la comédie**
current affairs **les actualités** *(f)*
drama **le drame**
documentary **le documentaire**
feature film **le long métrage**
game show **le jeu télévisé**
light entertainment **les**
    divertissements *(m)* **légers**
news **les informations** *(f)*
quiz program(me)s **le quiz**
regional news **les informations** *(f)*
    régionales
soap **le feuilleton (à l'eau de**
    rose)
series **la série**
show **le spectacle**
sitcom **le sitcom**
sports program(me) **l'émission** *(f)*
    sportive
weather report **le bulletin météo**

There should be a program(me) on students grants on this channel but perhaps the children would prefer watching the cartoons. Where is the TV listings?

Il devrait y avoir un programme sur les bourses des étudiants, sur cette chaîne, mais les enfants préfèrent peut-être regarder les dessins animés. Où est le programme de télé?

During the summer the traffic bulletin is broadcast every hour in four languages for the benefit of foreign visitors.

Pendant l'été, le bulletin de la circulation est diffusé toutes les heures en quatres langues au bénéfice des touristes étrangers.

– What are you watching now?
– Nothing, but I can't find the remote control to switch the TV off.

– Qu'est-ce que tu es en train de regarder? – Rien, mais je ne trouve pas la télécommande pour éteindre la télé.

– There's a good program(me) on this channel at 9 o'clock.

– Il y a un bon programme sur cette chaîne à 9 heures.

➤ FILM/MOVIE GENRES App.17e

18d Advertising

I advertise   **je fais de la publicité**
advertisment   **la publicité**
advertising   **la publicité**
advertising industry   **l'industrie** *(f)* **de la publicité**
appeal   **l'attrait** *(m)*
it appeals to   **il plaît** *(plaire)* **à, il attire**
billboard   **le panneau d'affichage**
brochure   **le prospectus, la brochure**
campaign   **la campagne**
catalog(ue)   **la brochure**
it catches the eye   **il attire l'attention**
commercial   **la publicité**
commercial *(adj)*   **commercial**
competition *(rival)*   **la concurrence**
competition *(game)*   **le concours**
consumer   **le consommateur, la consommatrice**
consumer society   **la société de consommation**
copywriter   **le rédacteur/la rédactrice publicitaire**

I covet   **je convoite**
it creates a need   **il crée un besoin**
demand   **la demand**
direct mail   **le mailing, le publipostage**
disposable income   **le revenu net**
distributor   **le concessionnaire**
ethical   **éthique**
goods   **la marchandise**
hidden persuasion   **la persuasion cachée**
image   **l'image** *(f)*
junk mail   **les prospectus** *(m)* **adressés par la poste**
I launch   **je lance**
life-style   **le mode de vie**
market   **le marché**
    down-market   **bas de gamme**
    up-market   **haut de gamme**
market research   **l'étude** *(f)* **de marché**
materialism   **le matérialisme**
model   **le modèle**
I motivate   **je motive**
need   **le besoin**

This has been his least successful campaign: next time we will use another agency or perhaps a freelance copywriter.

Cette campagne a été la plus désastreuse pour lui: la prochaine fois, nous utiliserons une autre agence ou peut-être un rédacteur indépendant.

– Do you think that TV advertisements are more effective than advertisements in newspapers?

– Pensez-vous que les publicités à la télévision ont plus d'effet que les publicités dans les journaux?

– National TV reaches many more potential consumers but is extemely expensive.

– Les grandes chaînes de télévision touchent un plus grand nombre de consommateurs potentiels mais elles coûtent extrêmement cher.

persuasion **la persuasion**
poster **l'affiche** *(f)*
product **le produit**
I promote/publicize **je fais de la publicité (pour)**
promotion **la promotion**
publicity **la publicité**
public relations **les relations** *(f)* **publiques**
purchasing power **le pouvoir d'achat**
radio advertisements **les spots** *(m)* **publicitaires à la radio**
it sells **il (se) vend**
slogan **le slogan**
status symbol **le signe de prestige/richesse**
stunt **l'exploit** *(m)*
I target **je vise**
target group **le groupe cible**
I tempt **je tente**
trend **la mode**
trendy **dernier cri, à la dernière mode**
truthful **véridique**
TV advertisements **les spots** *(m)* **publicitaires à la télévision, la**

«pub»
unethical **immoral**

Small ads

accommodation **les logements** *(m)*
appointments **les offres** *(f)* **d'emplois**
births **les naissances** *(f)*
courses and conferences **les cours** *(m)* **et les conférences** *(f)*
deaths **les décès** *(m)*
engagements **les fiançailles** *(f)*
exchange **l'échange**
exhibitions **les expositions** *(f)*
for sale **à vendre**
health **la santé**
holidays **les vacances** *(f)*
lonely hearts **les cœurs** *(m)* **à prendre**
marriages **les mariages** *(m)*
personal services **les services** *(m)* **personnels**
property/real estate **l'immobilier** *(m)*
travel **le voyage**
wanted **les demandes** *(f)*

Our market survey shows that customers tend to buy items at supermarket check-outs on impulse.

SPECIAL OFFER! For one week only! Buy 2 and get 1 free! Plus 20% discount on your next purchase!

This publicity can be offensive to some ethnic groups.

Notre enquête montre que les clients ont tendance à faire des achats d'impulsion aux caisses de supermarché.

OFFRE SPÉCIALE! **Pendant une semaine seulement! Achetez deux produits et le troisième vous est offert! Plus 20% de réduction sur votre prochain achat!**

Cette publicité peut être blessante pour certains groupes ethniques.

Travel

19a General terms

I accelerate/speed up **j'accélère** *(accélérer)*
accident **l'accident** *(m)*
adult **un/une adulte**
announcement **l'annonce** *(f)*
arrival **l'arrivée** *(f)*
I arrive (at) **j'arrive (à)**
assistance **l'aide** *(f)*
I ask for assistance **je demande de l'aide**
bag **le sac**
baggage **les bagages** *(m)*
I book **je réserve**
booking office **le guichet des réservations**
business trip **le voyage d'affaires**
I buy a ticket **j'achète** *(acheter)* **un billet**
I call at **je me présente à**
I cancel **j'annule**
I carry **je porte**
I catch **j'attrape**
I check *(tickets)* **je contrôle**
child **l'enfant** *(m)*
class **la classe**
I confirm **je confirme**
connection **la correspondance**
I cross **je traverse**
delay **le retard**
I am delayed **je suis retardé**
I depart **je pars** *(partir)*
departure **le départ**
destination **la destination**
direct **direct**
direction **la direction**
disabled **handicapé**
distance **la distance**
documents **les papiers** *(m)* **d'identité**
driver *(car)* **le chauffeur**

early **tôt**
emergency **l'urgence** *(f)*
emergency call **l'appel** *(m)* **d'urgence**
I enquire **je me renseigne**
enquiry **le renseignement**
en route **en route**
entrance **l'entrée** *(f)*
exit **la sortie**
extra charge **le supplément**
fare **le tarif**
fare reduction **la réduction sur le prix du billet**
reduced fare **le tarif réduit**
fast **rapide**
I fill a form **je remplis un formulaire**
free **gratuit**
information **les renseignements** *(m)*
information office **le bureau d'information**
insurance **l'assurance** *(f)*
help **l'aide** *(f)*
helpful (un-) **(in)utile**
late **tard**
I leave *(place)* **je quitte**
I leave *(person/object)* **je laisse**
I leave at **je pars** *(partir)* **à**
left-luggage office **la consigne**
lost **perdu**
lost property/lost and found office **les objets** *(m)* **trouvés**
loudspeaker **le haut-parleur**
luggage **les bagages** *(m)*
message **le message**
I miss the train **je rate le train**
non-smoker **le non-fumeur**
notice **l'avis** *(m)*
nuisance **l'ennui** *(m)*

occupied **occupé**
on board **à bord**
on time **à l'heure**
I pack **je fais mes valises**
passenger **le passager, la passagère**
porter *(hotel)* **le portier**
perfect timing **juste au bon moment**
reduction **la réduction**
rescue **les secours** *(m)*
reservation **la réservation**
I reserve **je réserve**
I return **je reviens** *(revenir)*
return **le retour**
return/round-trip ticket **le billet aller-retour**
safe **sûr**
safety **la sécurité**
season ticket (weekly/monthly) **la carte de transport (hebdomadaire/mensuelle)**
seat **le siège, la place**
seatbelt **la ceinture de sécurité**
I set off **je pars** *(partir)*
signal **le signal**
single/one-way ticket **un aller simple**
slow **lent**
I slow down **je ralentis**
smoking **fumeur**
speed **la vitesse**
staff **le personnel**
I start from **je pars** *(partir)* **de**
stop **l'arrêt** *(m)*
I stop **je m'arrête**

on strike **en grève**
I take *(the bus, train)* **je prends**
ticket **le billet**
ticket desk **la billetterie**
ticket office **le guichet**
timetable **l'horaire** *(m)*
toilet **les toilettes** *(f)*
I travel **je voyage**
travel **le voyage**
travel agent/agency **un agent/une agence de voyage**
travel documents **les documents** *(m)* **de voyage**
travel information **les informations** *(f)* **routières**
travel pass **la carte d'abonnement**
travel sickness **le mal des transports**
traveller **le voyageur, la voyageuse**
tunnel **le tunnel**
turn **le virage**
I turn **je tourne**
I unpack **je défais** *(défaire)* **mes bagages**
valid **valable**
via/through **par, via**
visitor **le visiteur, la visiteuse**
warning **la mise en garde**
weekdays **les jours** *(m)* **de la semaine**
week-end **la fin de la semaine**
window **la fenêtre**
window seat **le fauteuil côté fenêtre**

Does public transport operate after midnight?

Y a-t-il des transports en commun après minuit?

Have a pleasant journey.

Faites un bon voyage.

Where is the lost-property/lost and found office? I have lost my suitcase.

Où est le bureau des objets trouvés? J'ai perdu ma valise.

➤ DIRECTIONS 2b; MOVEMENT 2c; MEANS OF TRANSPORT App.19a

19b Going abroad & travel by boat

Going abroad

I cross (the English Channel) je **traverse (la Manche)**
currency **la devise**
currency exchange office **le bureau de change**
customs **la douane**
customs control **le contrôle douanier**
customs officer **l'officier** (m) **des douanes**
customs regulations **les règlements** (m) **douaniers**
declaration **la déclaration**
I declare **je déclare**
duty **la taxe douanière**
duty-free goods **les produits** (m) **détaxés**
duty-free shop **le magasin de produits détaxés**
English Channel **la Manche**
Channel Tunnel **le Tunnel sous la Manche**
exchange rate **le taux de change**
expired (document) **périmé**
foreign currency **la devise étrangère**
frontier **la frontière**
I go through customs **je passe la douane**
I go through passport control **je passe le contrôle des passeports**
immigration office **le bureau d'immigration**
immigration rules **les lois** (f) **sur l'immigration**
passport **le passeport**
I pay duty on **je paie** (payer) **la taxe sur**
smuggler **le contrebandier, la contrebandière**
smuggling **la contrebande**
visa **le visa**

– Here are my documents. My final destination is Palermo.
– Thank you. Have a good trip!

– **Voici mes papiers. Je descends à Palerme.**
– **Merci, et bon voyage!**

I have nothing to declare.
This is for my personal use.

Je n'ai rien à déclarer.
C'est pour mon usage personnel.

For your comfort and safety, please fasten your seatbelts.

Pour votre confort et votre sécurité, veuillez attacher vos ceintures.

Travel by boat

boat/ship **le bateau**
bridge **le pont**
cabin **la cabine**
calm sea **la mer calme**
captain **le capitaine**
car-ferry **le bac, le ferry**
coast **la côte**
crew **l'équipage** *(m)*
crossing **la traversée**
cruise **la croisière**
deck **le pont**
    lower deck **le pont inférieur**
    upper deck **le pont supérieur**
deck chair **la chaise longue**
I disembark **je débarque**
disembarkation **le débarquement**
dock **les docks** *(m)*
I embark **j'embarque**
embarkation card **la carte
    d'embarquement**
I go on board **je monte à bord**
harbour **le port**
lifejacket **le gilet de sauvetage**
lifeboat **le canot de sauvetage**
lounge **le salon**
officer **l'officier** *(m)*

off-shore **au large**
on board **à bord**
overboard **par-dessus bord**
port **le port**
    port of call **le port d'escale**
on the port (side) **à bâbord**
purser **le commissaire de bord**
quay **le quai**
reclining seat **le siège inclinable**
sea **la mer**
    calm sea **la mer calme**
    choppy sea **la mer houleuse**
    heavy sea **la mer agitée**
    stormy sea **la mer houleuse**
sea-sickness **le mal de mer**
seaman **le marin**
shipping forecast **les prévisions
    (f) marines**
shipyard **la marina**
smooth **calme**
starboard **à tribord**
storm **l'orage** *(m)*
tide **la marée**
waves **les vagues** *(f)*
wind **le vent**
windy **venteux**
yachting **faire du yachting**

– Have you got any remedy
against sea-sickness?
– Yes, I have some pills in my
cabin. Meet me on C deck in 10
minutes.
– I don't think I'll survive that long.

**– Avez-vous un remède contre
le mal de mer?**
**– Oui, j'ai des comprimés dans
ma cabine. Retrouvez-moi sur le
pont C dans dix minutes.**
**– Je ne crois pas que je vais
tenir jusque-là.**

From which quay does the ship
leave?

De quel quai part le bateau?

Is passport control carried out on
board?

**Les passeports sont-ils
contrôlés à bord?**

▶ SHIPS & BOATS App.19b; WEATHER 24d

19c Travel by road

access l'accès (m)
I allow j'autorise
articulated lorry le semi-remorque
automatic automatique
I back up/reverse je fais marche arrière
bike/bicycle le vélo
black ice le verglas
bottleneck le rétrécissement
breathalyzer le ballon (de l'alcootest)
breathalyzing test l'alcootest (m)
breakdown la panne
I breakdown je tombe en panne
breakdown service l'assistance (f) autoroute
broken cassé
bus l'autobus (m)
bus fare le tarif de bus
bus stop l'arrêt (m) de bus
car/automobile la voiture
car hire/rental la location de voiture
car park/parking lot le parking
  multistorey/multistoried le parking à niveaux multiples
car parts les pièces (f) détachées
car wash le lavage de voiture
caravan/trailer la caravane
careful driver le chauffeur prudent
careless driving la conduite négligente
caution la prudence
caution (legal) la réprimande
I change gear je change de vitesse
chauffeur le chauffeur
check le contrôle
I collide (with) j'entre en collision (avec)
collision la collision
company car la voiture de service
competent qualifié
conductor/conductress (bus) le receveur, la receveuse
I cross je traverse
dangerous dangereux [-se]
detour la déviation
diesel le gas-oil, le gazole
I do 30 mph je roule à 30 mph
I drive je conduis
drive la conduite
driver le conducteur, la conductrice
driving conduire
  driving instructor le moniteur, la monitrice
  driving lesson la leçon de conduite
  driving licence/driver's license le permis de conduire
  driving school l'auto-école (f)
  driving test l'examen (m) de

I have a puncture/flat tire. Could you also have a look at the clutch?

J'ai un pneu crévé. Pouvez-vous aussi vérifier l'embrayage?

Fill it up with unleaded, please.

Le plein d'essence sans plomb, s'il vous plaît!

I had to stop on the hard shoulder. Fortunately, emergency phones are found on all motorways/expressways.

J'ai dû m'arrêter sur la bande d'arrêt d'urgence. Heureusement, on trouve des bornes téléphoniques sur toutes les autoroutes.

conduite

drunken driving **la conduite en état d'ébriété**

emergency stop **l'arrêt** *(m)* **d'urgence**

engine trouble **le problème de moteur**

I fasten the seatbelt **j'attache la ceinture**

I fill up **je fais le plein**

filling station **la station-service**

fine **la contravention**

I fix/repair **je répare**

forbidden **interdit**

garage **le garage**

gear **les vitesses** *(f)*

    I put the car in first gear **je passe la première**

    neutral **le point mort**

    reverse gear **la marche arrière**

I get in the car **je monte dans la voiture**

I get in lane **je me mets** *(se mettre)* **dans la file**

I get out **je sors** *(sortir)*

I give way **je cède** *(céder)* **le passage**

Highway Code **le code de la route**

highway police **la police de la route**

I hire/rent **je loue**

hired/rental car **la voiture de location**

I hitchhike **je fais de l'auto-stop**

hitchhiking **l'auto-stop** *(m)*

hitchhiker **un auto-stoppeur, une auto-stoppeuse**

insurance **l'assurance** *(f)*

I am insured **je suis assuré**

insurance policy **la police d'assurance**

I keep my distance **je garde mes distances**

key **la clef**

key-ring **le porte-clefs**

learner driver **un élève conducteur, une élève conductrice**

line of cars **la file de voitures**

logbook **le journal de bord**

lorry **le camion**

lorry driver **le routier**

make of car **la marque de voiture**

MOT/vehicle certification **le certificat de contrôle**

maximum speed **la vitesse maximum**

mechanic **le mécanicien, la mécanicienne**

mechanical **mécanique**

motel **le motel**

motor caravan/trailer **le camping-car**

motor show **le salon automobile**

one-way only **le sens unique**

I overtake/pass **je double**

overtaking/passing **le dépassement**

– Here is my driving licence/ driver's license: as you can see it is still perfectly valid.

Voici mon permis de conduire: comme vous pouvez le voir il est parfaitement valable.

I wonder how much the toll is for this motorway/expressway section?

Je me demande combien coûte le péage sur ce tronçon d'autoroute.

This new model has very low petrol/gas consumption.

Cette nouvelle voiture consomme très peu.

I park   **je me gare**
parking   **le stationnement**
parking ban   **l'interdiction** (f) **de stationner**
parking fine   **la contravention**
parking meter   **le parcmètre**
parking ticket (permit)   **le ticket de stationnement**
I pass   **je passe**
passage   **le passage**
passenger   **le passager, la passagère**
pedestrian   **le piéton, la piétonne**
petrol/gasoline   **l'essence** (f)
   super/four star   **le super**
   two star   **l'essence normale**
   unleaded   **l'essence sans plomb**
picnic area   **l'aire** (f) **de pique-nique**
police   **la police**
police station   **le commissariat**
private car   **la voiture privée**
public transport   **le transport public**
puncture/flat tire   **la crevaison, le pneu crevé**
I put on my seat belt   **j'attache ma ceinture**
registration papers   **les papiers** (m) **d'immatriculation**
rental charge   **les frais de location**
repair   **la réparation**
I repair   **je répare**
I reverse   **je fais marche arrière**
right of way   **la priorité**
road   **la route, le chemin**
   by road   **par la route**
road accident   **l'accident** (m) **de la route**
road block   **le barrage routier**
road hog   **le chauffard**
road map   **la carte routière**
road sign   **le panneau indicateur**
road signals   **la signalisation**
road works   **les travaux** (m)
route   **l'itinéraire** (m)

I run over   **j'écrase**
rush hour   **les heures** (f) **de pointe**
second-hand car   **la voiture d'occasion**
self-service   **le libre-service**
service   **le service**
service area   **l'aire** (f) **de service**
I set off   **je me mets** (se mettre) **en route**
signal   **le signal**
signpost   **le poteau indicateur**
slippery   **glissant**
slow   **lent**
I slow down   **je ralentis**
I sound the horn/honk   **je klaxonne**
speed   **la vitesse**
I speed up   **j'accélère** (accélérer)
speed limit   **la limitation de vitesse**
spot fine   **la contravention pour stationnement illégal**
I start (engine)   **je démarre**
statement   **la déclaration**
I switch off   **j'éteins** (éteindre)
I switch on   **j'allume**
taxi/cab   **le taxi**
taxi/cab driver   **le chauffeur de taxi**
taxi rank   **la station de taxis**
I test   **je teste**
toll   **le péage**
I tow away   **je remorque**
town plan   **le plan de la ville**
town traffic   **le trafic urbain**
traffic   **la circulation**
traffic jam   **l'embouteillage** (m)
traffic light   **les feux** (m) **de signalisation**
traffic offence/violation   **l'infraction** (f) **au code de la route**
traffic news   **l'information** (f) **routière**
traffic police   **la police de la route**
traffic warden   **l'agent** (m) **de la circulation**
traffic-free zone   **la zone piétonne**
trip   **le voyage**
I turn left   **je tourne à gauche**

I turn right **je tourne à droite**
I turn off (engine) **j'arrête le moteur**
underground garage **le parking souterrain**
U-turn **le demi-tour**
vehicle **le véhicule**
I wait **j'attends**
warning **l'avertisseur** (m)
witness **le témoin**

Roads & streets

alley **l'allée** (f)
avenue **l'avenue** (f)
bend/curve **le virage**
bridge **le pont**
built-up area **l'agglomération** (f)
bump **la bosse**
bypass **la rocade**
central reservation **le terre-plein central**
closed (road) **barrée**
corner **le coin**
crossing **le croisement**
crossroad **le carrefour**
cul-de-sac **la voie sans issue, l'impasse** (f)
hard shoulder **la bande d'arrêt d'urgence**
inside lane **la voie de droite**
intersection **l'intersection** (f)
junction **la sortie**

lane **la voie**
lay-by **l'aire** (f) **de stationnement**
level crossing **le passage à niveau**
main street **la rue principale**
motorway/expressway **l'autoroute** (f)
    entry **l'entrée** (f) **d'autoroute**
    exit **la sortie d'autoroute**
    junction **la sortie d'autoroute**
one-way street **la rue à sens unique**
outside lane **la voie de gauche**
pedestrian crossing **le passage pour piétons**
pedestrian island **le refuge pour piétons**
ramp **la dénivellation**
ring road **la rocade**
road **la route, le chemin**
roundabout **le rond-point**
side street **la petite rue**
sleeping policeman/speed bump **le ralentisseur**
slip road **la bretelle d'accès**
square **la place**
street **la rue**
underground passage **le passage souterrain**
white/yellow line **la ligne blanche/jaune**

There has been a serious accident on the motorway A1 between junction 7 and 8. A lorry travelling towards Paris has crashed against the central barrier.
Three vehicles are involved and one of the drivers is seriously injured. I have put on the hazard lights.

Delays are expected at the next junction.

Il y a eu un sérieux accident sur l'autoroute A1 entre la sortie 7 et 8. Un camion qui voyageait vers Paris s'est écrasé contre la barrière de sécurité.
Trois véhicules sont impliqués et un des conducteurs est sérieusement blessé. J'ai mis mes feux de détresse.

On s'attend à des encombrements à la prochaine sortie.

➤ ROAD SIGNS, PARTS OF THE CAR App.19c; DIRECTIONS 2b

19d Travel by air

aeroplane/airplane **l'aéroplane** *(m)*
aircraft **l'avion** *(m)*
air hostess/stewardess **l'hôtesse** *(f)* **de l'air**
airline **la ligne aérienne**
airline desk **le guichet de la ligne aérienne**
air travel **le voyage en avion**
airport **l'aéroport** *(m)*
I am airsick **j'ai le mal de l'air**
baggage **les bagages** *(m)*
body search **la fouille corporelle**
I board a plane **j'embarque à bord d'un avion**
boarding card **la carte d'embarquement**
business class **la classe affaires**
by air **par avion**
cabin **la cabine**
cancelled flight **le vol annulé**
carousel **le tapis roulant à bagages**
charter flight **le vol charter**

I check in **j'enregistre**
check-in operations **l'enregistrement** *(m)*
control tower **la tour de contrôle**
co-pilot **le copilote**
crew **l'équipage** *(m)*
desk **le guichet**
direct flight **le vol direct**
domestic flights **le vol intérieur**
during the flight **pendant le vol**
duty-free goods **les produits** *(m)* **détaxés**
economy class **la classe économique**
emergency exit **la sortie de secours**
emergency landing **l'atterrissage** *(m)* **d'urgence**
excess baggage **le surplus de bagages**
I fasten **j'attache**
flight **le vol**
flight attendant **un accompagnateur/une**

Can I make a connection to Lyons? Do I have to change flight?

Puis-je avoir une correspondance pour Lyon? Est-ce que je dois changer d'avion?

– I have some excess luggage.

– J'ai un surplus de bagages.

– Have you packed your luggage yourself?

– Avez-vous fait vos bagages vous-même?

Will Mr and Mrs Lebrun travelling on flight AZ 131 to Paris-Orly please contact Information desk immediately.

Monsieur et madame Lebrun voyageant sur le vol AZ 131 à destination de Paris-Orly sont priés de contacter le bureau d'informations immédiatement.

Where do I check-in for flight AZ 537?

Où dois-je enregistrer mes bagages pour le vol AZ 537?

accompagnatrice de vol

I fly   **je vole**

I fly at a height of   **je vole à une altitude de**

flying   **l'aviation** (f)

fuselage   **le fuselage**

gate   **la porte**

instruction   **les instructions** (f)

hand luggage   **les bagages** (m) **à main**

headphones   **les écouteurs** (m)

highjacker   **le pirate de l'air**

immigrant   **un immigré, une immigrée**

immigration   **l'immigration** (f)

immigration rules   **les lois** (f) **d'immigration**

I land   **j'atterris**

landing   **l'atterrissage** (m)

landing lights   **les lumières d'atterrissage**

no-smoking sign   **le panneau non-fumeur**

non-stop   **sans escale**

on board   **à bord**

parachute   **le parachute**

passenger   **le passager, la passagère**

passengers lounge   **la salle d'embarquement**

passport control   **le contrôle des passeports**

pilot   **le pilote**

plane   **l'avion** (m)

refreshments   **le repas (léger), les rafraîchissements** (m)

runway   **la piste**

safety jacket   **le gilet de sauvetage**

security measures   **les mesures** (f) **de sécurité**

security staff   **le personnel de sécurité**

steward   **le steward**

stewardess   **l'hôtesse** (f) **de l'air**

I take off   **je décolle**

take off   **le décollage**

terminal   **le terminal**

tray   **le plateau**

turbulence   **la perturbation**

view   **la vue**

window seat   **le fauteuil côté fenêtre**

There is some turbulence on the Alps. The expected landing time is at 11:40, local time.	**Il y a des perturbations au-dessus des Alpes. L'atterrissage est prévu pour 11h40, heure locale.**
This is the last call for passengers travelling on flght BZ 881 to Marseilles.	**Dernier appel pour les passagers du vol BZ 881 à destination de Marseille.**
My luggage has not yet been unloaded.	**Mes bagages n'ont pas encore été déchargés.**
How long is the delay?	**Combien de temps va durer le retard?**
What is the flight number?	**Quel est le numéro du vol?**

19e Travel by rail

announcement **l'annonce** *(f)*
barrier **la barrière**
buffet **le buffet**
buffet-car **la voiture-buffet**
coach **le wagon**
compartment **le compartiment**
connection **la correspondance**
dining-car **le wagon-restaurant**
exemption **l'exemption** *(f)*
fare **le prix du billet**
inspector **le contrôleur**
I lean out **je me penche à la fenêtre**
level crossing **le passage à niveau**
luggage rack **le porte-bagages**
I miss **je rate**
non-refundable **non-remboursable**

non smoker **le non-fumeur**
occupied **occupé**
on time **à l'heure**
platform **le quai**
porter **le porteur**
I punch (ticket) **je poinçonne**
rail station **la gare**
rail tracks **les rails**
railway/railroad **le chemin de fer**
elevated railway **le métro aérien**
ramp **la rampe**
reduction **la réduction**
reservation **la réservation**
reserved **réservé**
sleeper **la couchette**
smoker **le fumeur, la fumeuse**
speed **la vitesse**

A special announcement:
On Sundays and (Bank) Holidays the service to Toulon does not operate and on weekdays after 9 a.m. fares are subject to supplementary charges.
In addition, reservations are required for seats in the non-smoking compartments on the Bordeaux service.

We apologise for any inconvenience.

The 11.45 to Orleans is now leaving from platform 10.

The express train to Lille will depart from platform 4 in 5 minutes.

Une annonce spéciale:
Le service de Toulon ne circule pas les dimanche et jours fériers, et est sujet à supplément les jours de la semaine après 9 heures.
D'autre part, une réservation est obligatoire pour les places assises dans les compartiments non-fumeurs sur le service de Bordeaux.
Nous vous prions de nous excuser pour tout désagrément.

Le train de 11h45 à destination d'Orléans au départ quai numéro 10.

Le train express à destination de Lille partira dans 5 minutes, quai numéro 4.

stairs   **les escaliers** *(m)*
station master   **le chef de gare**
stop   **un arrêt**
subway/underground   **le métro**
supplement   **le supplément**
ticket   **le billet**
  first/second class ticket   **un billet de première/deuxième classe**
  group ticket   **un billet de groupe**
  single/one way ticket   **un aller simple**
  return ticket   **un aller-retour**
ticket collector   **le contrôleur de billets**
ticket office   **le guichet**
timetable   **l'horaire** *(m)*
  summer/winter timetable   **l'horaire d'été/hiver**

timetable changes   **les changements** *(m)* **d'horaire**
track   **la voie**
traveller   **le voyageur, la voyageuse**
train   **le train**
  direct train   **le train direct**
  express train   **l'express** *(m)*
  Intercity train   **l'inter-urbain** *(m)*
  local train   **le train de banlieue**
  night train   **le train de nuit**
trolley/cart   **le chariot**
underground/subway   **le métro**
user   **l'usager** *(m)*
I wait   **j'attends** *(attendre)*
waiting-room   **la salle d'attente**
wagon-lits   **le wagon-lit**
warning   **la mise en garde, un avertissement**
window   **la fenêtre**

– Where do I have to change?
– To go to the Eiffel Tower, you need to change at the next stop. Take the line to Nation and get off at Champ de Mars.

– Où dois-je changer?
Pour aller à la tour Eiffel, il faut changer au prochain arrêt. Prenez la direction Nation et descendez à Champ de Mars.

Excuse me, this a non-smoking compartment.

Excusez-moi, ceci est un compartiment non-fumeur.

This is a public announcement for all passengers travelling to Geneva. We are sorry to announce that this service is subject to delays. There will also be a platform change.

Ceci est un message pour tous les passagers à destination de Genève. Nous sommes désolés de vous annoncer que cette ligne sera sujette à des retards. Il y aura également un changement de quai.

There are no facilities for disabled travellers on this train.

Ce train n'est pas aménagé pour les handicapés.

Holidays/Vacation

20a General terms

abroad   à l'étranger
accommodation   le logement
alone   seul
area   la région
arrival   l'arrivée (f)
available   libre
beach   la plage
camera   l'appareil (m) photo
clean   propre
climate   le climat
closed   fermé
clothes   les vêtements (m)
cold   froid
comfort   le confort
comfortable   confortable
congested   encombré
cost   le coût
country   le pays
countryside   la campagne
dirty   sale
disadvantage   l'inconvénient (m)
disorganized   désorganisé
exchange   l'échange (m)
fire   le feu
folding chair   la chaise pliante
folding table   la table pliante
food   la nourriture
free   gratuit
full   plein
full-up   complet
I go   je vais (aller)
group   le groupe
group travel   le voyage en groupe
guide   le/la guide
guide book   le guide (de voyage)
guided tour   la visite guidée
guided walk   la promenade guidée
holidays/vacation   les vacances (f)
land   le terrain
landscape   le paysage

journey   le trajet
mild (climate)   doux [-se]
money   l'argent (m)
open   ouvert
organization   l'organisation (f)
I organize   j'organise
   organized   organisé
plan (town)   le plan (de la ville)
I plan   j'envisage
portable   portable
I return (to a place)   je retourne (à
   un lieu)
rucksack/knapsack   le sac à dos
sea   la mer
seascape   le panorama marin
seaside resort   la station balnéaire
show   un spectacle
I show   je montre
sight   la vue
I spend time   je passe du temps à
stay   le séjour
I stay   je reste
sun   le soleil
sunny   ensoleillé
I sunbathe   je prends (prendre) un
   bain de soleil
I tan/go brown   je bronze
tour   la visite
tourism   le tourisme
tourist   le/la touriste
tourist menu   le menu touristique
tourist office   l'office (m) du
   tourisme
town   la ville
town plan   le plan de la ville
travel   le voyage
I travel   je voyage
travel adaptor   l'adaptateur (m)
trip   l'excursion (f)
I understand   je comprends

I unpack **je défais** *(défaire)* **mes bagages**
visit **la visite**
I visit **je visite**
visiting hours **les heures** *(f)* **de visite**
visitors **les visiteurs** *(m)*
welcome **la bienvenue**
worth seeing **qui vaut la peine d'être vu**

Holiday/Vacation activities

beach holiday/vacation **à la plage**
boating holiday/vacation **les vacances** *(m)* **en bateau**
camping **faire du camping**
canoing **faire du canoë**
coach holiday/vacation **les vacances** *(m)* **en car**
cruise **faire une croisière**
cycling **faire du vélo**

fishing **la pêche**
fruit picking **cueillir des fruits**
home exchange **l'échange** *(m)* **de maison**
hunting **la chasse**
motoring holiday/vacation **les vacances** *(f)* **en voiture/auto**
mountain climbing **l'alpinisme** *(m)*
rock climbing **l'escalade** *(f)*
safari **faire un safari**
sailing **la voile**
shopping **les courses** *(f)*
sightseeing **le tourisme**
skiing **faire du ski**
study holiday/vacation **le voyage/ les vacances** *(f)* **d'études**
sunbathing **le bain de soleil**
trekking **le voyage-randonnée**
volunteer work **le travail bénévole**
walking **la marche**
wine tasting **la dégustation de vins**

Dear all at work

Having a wonderful holiday/ vacation. The weather is hot (I've a great tan), the campsite is clean and the local food is excellent.

The kids are having a great time too, enjoying playing in the water, building sandcastles and making lots of friends.

I'm not looking forward to coming home!

Best wishes, Sarah.

Chers collègues

Vacances merveilleuses. Il fait chaud (je suis bien bronzée), le camping est propre et la cuisine locale excellente.

Les enfants aussi s'amusent beaucoup, ils aiment jouer dans l'eau, faire des châteaux de sable et se sont fait beaucoup d'amis.

La perspective du retour ne me réjouit pas!

Meilleurs vœux, Sarah.

➤ HOBBIES 16a; ON THE BEACH App. 20a; WEATHER 24d

20b Accommodation & hotel

Accommodation

apartment **l'appartement** *(m)*
bed & breakfast **la chambre d'hôte**
campsite **le camping**
caravan/trailer **la caravane**
chalet **le chalet**
country cottage **le gîte rural**
farm **la ferme**
full board **la pension complète**
half board **la demi-pension**
home exchange **l'échange** *(m)* **de maison**
hotel **l'hôtel** *(m)*
mobile home **le mobile home**
inn **l'auberge** *(f)*, **l'hôtel** *(m)*
self-catering/service **le meublé, les vacances** *(f)* **en location**
villa **la villa** *(f)*
youth hostel **l'auberge** *(f)* **de jeunesse**

Booking & payment

affordable **qu'on peut se permettre**
all included **tout compris**
bill **la note**
I book **je réserve**
brochure **la brochure**
I cash **j'encaisse**
cheap **bon marché**
cheque/check **le chèque**
cost **le coût**
credit card **la carte de crédit**

credit **le crédit**
economical **économique, pas cher [chère]**
Eurocheque **l'eurochèque** *(m)*
expensive **cher [chère]**
excluding **non compris**
exclusive **en sus**
extra charge **le supplément**
extravagant **exorbitant**
fee **les droits** *(m)*
I fill in **je remplis**
form **le formulaire**
free **libre, gratuit**
inclusive **(y) compris**
I pay **je paie** *(payer)*
payment **le paiement**
price-list **le tarif**
receipt **le reçu**
reduction **la réduction**
refund **le remboursement**
I reserve **je réserve**
reservation **la réservation**
I sign **je signe**
signature **la signature**
traveller's cheque/traveler's check **le chèque de voyage**

Hotel

air-conditioning **la climatisation**
amenities **les aménagements** *(m)*
balcony **le balcon**
bath **le bain**
bed **le lit**
bed linen/bedding **la literie**

I'd like to complain.
The hot water tap does not work
and the lift is out of order.
There is only one coathanger in
the wardrobe; and I asked for a
room with a view.

**Je veux faire une réclamation.
Le robinet d'eau chaude ne
marche pas et l'ascenseur est
en panne. Il n'y a qu'un porte-
manteau dans l'armoire, et
j'avais demandé une chambre
avec vue.**

bedspread **le couvre-lit**
billiard room **la salle de billard**
board **la pension**
 full board **la pension complète**
 half board **la demi-pension**
breakfast **le petit déjeuner**
broken **cassé**
call **l'appel** *(m)*
I check in **je remplis une fiche**
I check out **je règle ma note**
comfortable **confortable**
I complain **je me plains**
complaint **la plainte**
conference **la conférence**
conference facilities **la possibilité de conférence**
damage **les dégâts** *(m)*
dining-room **la salle à manger**
early morning call **le réveil matinal**
en-suite bathroom **la salle de bains attenante**
evening meal **le dîner**
facilities **les locaux** *(m)*
fire exit **la sortie de secours**
fire extinguisher **l'extincteur** *(m)*
guest **le client, la cliente**
hairdresser **le coiffeur, la coiffeuse**
hairdryer **le sèche-cheveux**
hall **le hall**
heating **le chauffage**
hotel **l'hôtel** *(m)*
laundry **le linge**
laundry service **le service de blanchisserie**
laundry-bag **le bac à linge**

lift **l'ascenseur** *(m)*
meal **le repas**
night porter **le portier de service de nuit**
noisy **bruyant**
overnight bag **le nécessaire de voyage**
parking space **la place de parking**
plug *(bath)* **la bonde**
 plug *(electric)* **la prise**
porter **le porteur**
privacy **l'intimité** *(f)*
private toilet **les toilettes** *(f)* **privées**
reception **la réception**
receptionist **le/la réceptionniste**
room **la chambre**
 double room **la chambre double/pour deux personnes**
 family room **la chambre familiale**
 twin-beds room **la chambre à lits jumeaux**
room service **le service des chambres**
service **le service**
shower **la douche**
shower-cap **le bonnet de douche**
stay **le séjour**
I stay **je reste**
trouser/pants-press **le presse-pantalon**
view **la vue**
water **l'eau** *(f)*
 hot water **l'eau chaude** *(f)*
welcome **la bienvenue**

I'd like to reserve a room with a double bed and en-suite bathroom for three days from March 4th.

Je voudrais réserver une chambre avec un lit pour deux personnes et salle de bains pour trois jours à partir du 4 mars.

DO NOT DISTURB
PRESS THE BUTTON

NE PAS DÉRANGER
APPUYEZ SUR LE BOUTON

➤ ROOMS 8a; FURNISHINGS 8b, 8c; EATING OUT 10a

20c Camping & self-catering/service

Camping

air bed   **le matelas pneumatique**
antihistamine cream   **la crème antihistaminique**
ants   **les fourmis** *(f)*
barbeque   **le barbecue**
battery   **la pile**
camp bed   **le lit de camp**
camper   **le campeur, la campeuse**
camping equipment/gear
  l'équipement *(m)* **de camping**
camping   **faire du camping**
camping gas   **le butane**
campsite   **le terrain de camping**
caravan/trailer   **la caravane**
connected   **branché**
cooking facilities   **les cuisines** *(f)*
disconnected   **débranché**
drinking water   **l'eau** *(f)* **potable**
dustbin/ashcan   **la poubelle**
extension lead   **la rallonge**
forbidden   **interdit**

gas cooker   **la cuisinière à gaz**
gas cylinder   **la bouteille de gaz**
ground-sheet   **le tapis de sol**
I camp   **je campe**
I pitch/put up my tent   **je plante/dresse la tente**
I take down my tent   **je démonte la tente**
in the dark   **dans le noir**
launderette   **la laverie automatique**
mosquito bite   **la piqûre de moustique**
mosquito net   **la moustiquaire**
mosquitos   **les moustiques** *(m)*
pans   **les casseroles** *(f)*
potty   **le pot (de bébé)**
registration   **l'inscription** *(f)*
services   **les services** *(m)*
sheet   **le drap**
showers   **les douches** *(f)*
site/space   **l'emplacement** *(m)*

– Where shall we put up the tent?
– Away from the main block.
– I'll pitch it in the shade.
– No, it is a bit damp there. This is better here and there are no mosquitos.

– Où va-t-on dresser la tente?
– Loin du pavillon principal.
– Je la planterai à l'ombre.
– Non, c'est un peu humide là. Ici c'est mieux; il n'y a pas de moustique.

– Where's the torch/flashlight? It's not in the tent.
– It was in your rucksack/knapsack just now.
– Keep your voice down, please, we are trying to sleep!

– Où est la lampe de poche? Elle n'est pas dans la tente.
– Elle était dans ton sac à dos à l'instant.
– Taisez-vous un peu, s'il vous plaît, nous essayons de dormir!

Do you have a few spare pegs?

Avez-vous des pinces à linge en trop?

Did you bring a bottle-opener?

As-tu apporté un ouvre-boîtes?

sleeping bag **le sac de couchage**
sheet sleeping bag **le sac à viande**
space **la place**
tent **la tente**
tent-peg **le piquet**
tin opener **l'ouvre-boîtes** *(m)*
toilet/restroom **les toilettes** *(f)*
torch/flashlight **la lampe de poche**
vehicles **les véhicules** *(m)*
washing facilities **les sanitaires** *(m)*, **le bloc sanitaire**
water filter **le filtre d'eau**

Self-catering/service

agency **l'agence** *(f)*
agreement **l'accord** *(m)*
amenities **les aménagements** *(m)*
apartment **l'appartement** *(m)*
clean **propre**
I clean **je nettoie** *(nettoyer)*
I cook **je fais la cuisine**
damaged **endommagé**
damages **les dégâts** *(m)*

dangerous **dangereux**
electricity **l'électricité** *(f)*
equipment **le matériel**
farm **la ferme**
maid **la bonne**
meter *(electricity, etc.)* **le compteur**
owner **le/la propriétaire**
rent **le loyer**
I rent **je loue**
I rent out **je donne en location**
repair **la réparation**
I repair **je répare**
I return *(give back)* **je rends**
ruined **en ruine**
self-service **le libre-service**
set of keys **le jeu de clés**
I share **je partage**
shutters **les volets** *(m)*
smelly **malodorant**
spare keys **le double des clés**
water supply **la provision d'eau**
well **le puit**
well kept **bien entretenu**

The apartment is close to all amenities, just a few kilometres/kilometers from the nearest shops and convenient for the swimming pool.

L'appartement est proche de tous les aménagements, se situe à quelques kilomètres des magasins les plus proches et est commode pour la piscine.

There are no blankets, the cooker/stove doesn't work and there is a frog in the bathroom.

Il n'y a pas de couvertures, le four ne marche pas, et il y a une grenouille dans la salle de bains.

How do you lock the door?

Comment fermez-vous la porte à clé?

Are there any spare bulbs?

Y a-t-il des ampoules de rechange?

You will find the electricity meter under the stairs.

Vous trouverez le compteur d'électricité sous les escaliers.

➤ GENERAL HOLIDAY/VACTION TERMS 20a

Language

21a General terms

accuracy **la fidélité**
accurate **fidèle**
I adapt **j'adapte**
I adopt **je choisis**
advanced **supérieur**
aptitude **l'aptitude** *(f)*
artificial language **le langage artificiel**
based on **basé sur**
bilingual **bilingue**
bilingualism **le bilinguisme**
borrowing **l'emprunt** *(m)*
branch **le rameau**
classical languages **les langues** *(f)* **classiques**
it is derived from **il dérive de**
development **le développement**
difficult **difficile**
easy **facile**
error **l'erreur** *(f)*
foreign language **la langue étrangère**
foreign language *(to learn)* **une langue d'apprentissage**
I forget **j'oublie**
French speaker **le francophone**
French-speaking countries **les**

pays *(m)* **francophones**
grammar **la grammaire**
grammatical **grammatical**
I improve **je fais des progrès**
influence **l'influence** *(f)*
known **connu**
language **la langue**
language course **le cours de langues**
language family **la famille linguistique**
language school **l'école** *(m)* **de langues**
language skills **les compétences** *(f)* **linguistiques**
Latin **le latin**
I learn **j'apprends** *(apprendre)*
learning **l'apprentissage** *(m)*
level **le niveau**
linguistics **la linguistique**
link **la liaison, le lien**
living **vivant**
major languages **les langues** *(f)* **principales**
it means **il signifie**
I mime **je mime**
minor languages **les langues** *(f)*

I am not very good at languages but my sister is a gifted linguist.	Je ne suis pas très doué pour les langues, mais ma sœur est une excellente linguiste.
She learned French and Italian in school, then she travelled extensively and picked up Bulgarian and Urdu while working as a volunteer.	Elle a appris le français et l'italien à l'école, puis le bulgare et l'ourdou à l'occasion des nombreux voyages qu'elle a faits quand elle travaillait en tant que volontaire/bénévole.

secondaires
mistake   **la faute**
modern languages   **les langues** *(f)*
   vivantes
monolingual   **monolingue**
mother tongue   **la langue**
   maternelle
mutation   **la mutation**
name   **le nom**
nation   **la nation**
national   **national**
native speaker   **le locuteur nativ,**
   la locutrice native
natural   **naturel[le]**
official   **officiel[le]**
offshoot   **la conséquence**
origin   **l'origine** *(f)*
phenomenon   **le phénomène**
I practice   **je m'exerce**
preserved   **entretenu**
question   **la question**
register   **le registre**
self-assessment   **l'auto-évaluation**
   (f)
separate   **distinct**
sign language   **le langage par**
   signes
survival   **la survivance**
it survives   **il survit** *(survivre)*
target language   **la langue cible**
I teach   **j'enseigne**
teacher   **un enseignant, une**
   enseignante

teaching   **l'enseignement** *(m)*
test   **l'interrogation** *(f)*
I test   **j'interroge**
I translate   **je traduis** *(traduire)*
translation   **la traduction**
I understand   **je comprends**
unknown   **inconnu**
widely   **généralement**

Words & vocabulary

antonym   **l'antonyme** *(m)*
colloquial   **familier [-ère]**
consonant   **la consonne**
dictionary   **le dictionnaire**
expression   **l'expression** *(f)*
idiom   **l'idiome** *(m)*
idiomatic   **idiomatique**
jargon   **le jargon**
lexicographer   **le lexicographe**
lexicon   **le lexique**
phrase   **la locution**
phrase book   **le guide de**
   conversation
sentence   **la phrase**
slang   **l'argot** *(m)*
syllable   **la syllabe**
synonym   **le synonyme**
vocabulary   **le vocabulaire**
vowel   **la voyelle**
witticism   **le mot d'esprit**
word   **le mot**
word game   **le jeu de mots**

Lesser languages may disappear. However, thanks to the oral tradition in some communities, a few have been preserved.

Les langues moins importantes ont peut-être tendance à disparaître. Toutefois grâce à la tradition orale de certaines communautés, quelques-unes ont pu être préservées.

21b Using language

Speaking & listening

accent **l'accent** *(m)*
　regional accent **l'accent régional**
articulate **bien articulé**
I articulate **j'articule**
clear **clair**
I communicate **je communique**
conversation **la conversation**
I converse **je converse**
dialect **le dialecte**
diction **la diction**
I express myself **je m'exprime**
fluent **qui parle couramment**
fluently **couramment**
I interpret **je fais l'interprète**
interpreter **un/une interprète**
intonation **l'intonation** *(f)*
lisp **le zézaiement**
I lisp **je zézaie**
I listen **j'écoute**
listener **un auditeur, une auditrice**
listening **l'écoute** *(f)*
listening skills **la compréhension orale**

I mispronounce **je prononce mal**
mispronunciation **la faute de prononciation**
oral(ly) **oral, à l'oral**
phonetics **la phonétique**
I pronounce **je prononce**
pronunciation **la prononciation**
rhythm **le rythme**
sound **le son**
he sounds French **il a un accent français**
I speak **je parle**
speaker **un interlocuteur, une interlocutrice**
speaking **parlant**
speaking skills **l'art** *(m)* **oratoire**
speech **l'élocution** *(f)*
speed **la vitesse**
spoken **parlé**
spoken language **le langage parlé**
stress **l'accentuation** *(f)*
stressed (un-) **(in)accentué**
I stutter/stammer **je bégaie (bégayer)**
unpronounceable **imprononçable**
verbally **verbalement**

– I have no difficulty in reading French, but I don't understand it when people speak very fast or with a strong regional accent.

– Do you practise/practice French with a native speaker?
– No, I prefer to attend a class.

Do you have any previous knowledge of Russian?

– Je lis le français sans problème, mais je ne le comprends pas quand on parle très vite ou avec un fort accent régional.
– Pratiquez-vous le français avec un francophone?
– Non, je préfère suivre des cours.

Connaissez-vous déjà le russe?

Writing & reading

accent l'accent *(m)*
  grave/acute/circumflex
  grave/aigu/circonflexe
alphabet l'alphabet *(m)*
alphabetically **par ordre**
  alphabétique
in bold **en gras**
Braille **braille**
character **le caractère**
code **le code**
I correspond (with) **je**
  corresponds (avec)
correspondence **la**
  correspondance
I decypher **je déchiffre**
graphic **graphique**
handwriting **l'écriture** *(f)*
icon **l'icône** *(f)*
ideogram(me)/ideograph
  l'idéogramme *(m)*
illiterate **analphabète**
in italics **en italique**
I italicize **je mets** *(mettre)* **en**
  italique
letter *(of alphabet)* **la lettre**
literate **instruit, qui sait lire et**
  écrire

literature **la littérature**
note **la note**
paragraph **le paragraphe**
philology **la philologie**
philologist **le/la philologue**
pictograph **l'idéogramme** *(m)*
plain text **le texte simple**
I print **j'imprime**
I read **je lis** *(lire)*
reading **la lecture**
reading skills **l'aptitude** *(f)* **à lire**
I re-write **je récris** *(récrire)*
scribble **la gribouillage**
I scribble **je gribouille**
sign **le signe**
I sign **je signe**
signature **la signature**
I spell **j'épelle** *(épeler)*
spelling **l'orthographe** *(f)*
text **le texte**
I transcribe **je transcris**
transcription **la transcription**
I underline **je souligne**
I write **j'écris** *(écrire)*
writing **l'écriture** *(f)*
writing skills **l'art** *(m)* **d'écrire**
written language **la langue écrite**

Which languages have a Slavonic alphabet?

Quelles langues ont un alphabet slave?

– Which is the easiest language to learn for an English speaker? – French, of course!

– Quelle est la langue la plus facile à apprendre pour un anglophone? – Le français, naturellement!

Portuguese spoken here.

Ici on parle portugais.

Don't worry about spelling mistakes for the moment.

Ne vous souciez pas des fautes d'orthographe pour l'instant.

22 Education

22a General terms

achievement   **la réussite**
admission   **l'admission** (f)
   I am admitted to school   **je suis
   admis** (admettre) **à l'école**
absent   **absent**
age group   **le groupe d'âge**
I am away   **je suis absent**
aptitude   **l'aptitude** (f)
I analyze   **j'analyse**
answer   **la réponse**
I answer   **je réponds (à)**
I ask (a question)   **je pose (une
   question)**
   I ask (someone)   **je demande
   (à)**
I attend (a school)   **je suis élève (à
   l'école)**
boring   **ennuyeux [-se], barbant**
career   **la carrière**
careers advice   **le conseil
   d'orientation**
careers teacher   **le conseiller/la
   conseillère d'orientation**
caretaker   **le/la concierge**
I catch up   **je rattrape**
chapter   **le chapitre**
cheat   **le tricheur, la tricheuse**
class   **la classe**
class council   **le conseil de classe**
class representative   **le délégué de
   classe**
class teacher   **le professeur**
class trip   **le voyage scolaire**
club   **le club**
I complete   **je termine**
comprehension   **la compréhension**
compulsory schooling   **la scolarité**

   obligatoire
concept   **le concept**
I copy (out)   **je recopie**
copy   **l'exemplaire** (m)
course   **des cours** (m)
deputy head   **le directeur-adjoint**
detention   **la retenue, la colle**
   I am in detention   **je suis en
   retenue, je suis collé**
difficult   **difficile**
I discuss   **je discute**
easy   **facile**
education   **l'éducation** (f),
   l'enseignement (m)
educational system   **le système
   pédagogique**
I encourage   **j'encourage**
essay   **la dissertation, la
   rédaction**
example   **l'exemple** (m)
excellent   **excellent**
favourite/favorite   **préféré**
favourite/favorite subject   **la
   matière préférée**
I forget   **j'oublie**
governing body   **l'administration**
holidays/vacation   **les vacances** (f)
headteacher/principal   **le directeur,
   la directrice, le principal**
homework   **les devoirs** (m)
instruction   **des cours** (m)
interesting   **intéressant**
I learn   **j'apprends** (apprendre)
I leave   **je quitte**
lesson (class)   **le cours**
   lesson (chapter)   **la leçon**
I listen   **j'écoute**

local education authority **le rectorat, l'académie** (f)

I look at **je regarde**

I misunderstand **je ne comprends pas**

mixed ability group **le groupe de plusieurs niveaux**

modular **par module**

module **le module**

oral **oral**

outdoor **à l'extérieur, en plein air**

out of school/extra-curricular activity **les activités** (m) **parascolaires**

parents' evening **la réunion parents-enseignants**

pastoral care **l'éducation** (f) **religieuse**

I play truant **je sèche** (sécher) **les cours** (fam), **je fais l'école buissonnière** (fam)

I praise **j'admire**

principal (adj) **principal**

project **la recherche**

punctual **ponctuel[le]**

I punctuate **je ponctue**

punctuation mark **la ponctuation**

I punish **je punis**

punishment **la punition**

pupil **un/une élève**

qualification **les qualifications** (f)

I qualify **je suis qualifié**

question **la question**

I question **je mets** (mettre) **en doute**

I read **je lis** (lire)

reading **la lecture**

I repeat a year **je redouble**

repeating a year **le redoublement**

report **le bulletin**

research **la recherche**

I research **je fais de la recherche**

resources centre/center **le centre de documentation**

scheme of work **le plan de travail**

school book **le livre de classe**

school council **le conseil d'administration**

school-friend/pal **le camarade**

set **le groupe de niveau**

setted (by ability) **classés par groupes de niveau**

skill **l'aptitude** (f)

specialist teacher **le professeur** (m) **spécialisé**

spelling **l'orthographe** (f)

staff **le personnel (enseignant)**

I stay in **je reste**

I stay down (a year) **je ne passe pas**

stream **le groupe de niveau**

strict **sévère**

I study **j'étudie**

sum **la somme**

I summarize **je résume**

I swot **je bûche** (fam)

task **l'exercice** (m)

I teach **j'enseigne**

teacher **l'enseignant** (m), **l'enseignante** (f)

teaching **l'enseignement** (m)

term/semester **le trimestre**

I train **je suis** (suivre) **une formation (de)**

training **la formation**

I translate **je traduis**

translation **la traduction**

tutor **le tuteur**

I understand **je comprends**

understanding **la compréhension**

unit (of work) **le chapitre**

I work **je travaille**

I work hard (at) **je travaille dur, je bosse (sur)**

work experience **l'expérience** (f) **professionnelle**

I write **j'écris** (écrire)

written (work) **(le travail) écrit**

22b School

blackboard **le tableau**
book **le livre**
break **la récréation**
briefcase **le cartable**
canteen **la cantine**
cassette (audio/video) **la cassette (audio/vidéo)**
cassette recorder **le magnétophone**
classroom **la salle de classe**
computer **l'ordinateur** *(m)*
desk **le bureau**
dormitory **le dortoir**
gym(nasium) **le gymnase**
headphone **les écouteurs** *(m)*
interactive TV **la télévision interactive**
(language) laboratory **le laboratoire (de langues)**
library **la bibliothèque**
lunch-hour **l'heure** *(f)* **du repas**
note **le message**
office **le bureau**
playground **la cour de récréation**
radio **la radio**
ruler **la règle**
slide **la diapositive**
satellite TV **la télévision par satellite**
school hall **le hall de réunion**
schoolbag/satchel/bookbag **le cartable**

sports field **le terrain de sport**
sports hall **le gymnase**
staffroom **la salle des professeurs**
studio **le studio**
timetable **l'emploi** *(m)* **du temps**
video camera **le caméscope**
video cassette **la cassette-vidéo**
video recorder **le magnétoscope**
workshop **l'atelier** *(m)*

Type of school

boarding school **le pensionnat**
boarder **la pensionnaire**
comprehensive school **le collège**
day school **le collège (pour externes)**
further education **la formation continue**
grammar school **le lycée**
infant/nursery school **l'école** *(f)* **maternelle**
playgroup **la garderie**
primary school **l'école** *(f)* **primaire**
school **l'école** *(f)*
school type **le type d'école**
of school age **d'âge scolaire**
secondary **secondaire**
secondary school/junior high school **le collège**
sixth form/senior year **la terminale**
sixth-form college **le lycée**

– At what age do children start school?
– They have to go to school when they are six.
Our son already goes to the kindergarten and is looking forward to school.
Our daughter goes to the primary school/elementary school.

– **À quel âge les enfants commencent-ils l'école?**
– **Ils doivent aller à l'école dès l'âge de six ans.**
Notre fils va déjà à l'école maternelle et il lui tarde d'aller à l'école.
Notre fille va à l'école primaire/élémentaire.

special school **l'école** (f) **spécialisée**

technical school **le collège technique**

Classroom commands

Answer the question! **Répondez à la question!**

Ask your friend a question! **Posez une question à votre camarade!**

Be careful! **Attention!**

Be quiet! **Silence!**

Be quick! **Dépêchez-vous!**

Bring me your work! **Apportez-moi votre travail!**

Clean the blackboard! **Effacez le tableau!**

Close the door! **Fermez la porte!**

Come here! **Venez ici!**

Come in! **Entrez!**

Copy these sentences! **Écrivez ces phrases!**

Do your homework! **Faites vos devoirs!**

Don't talk/chatter! **Taisez-vous!**

Fast forward! *(tape)* **Faites avancez rapidement la bande!**

Go out! **Sortez!**

Learn by heart! **Apprenez par cœur!**

Learn the vocabulary! **Apprenez le vocabulaire!**

Listen carefully! **Écoutez bien!**

Make less noise! **Faites moins de bruit!**

Make notes! **Prenez des notes!**

Open the window! **Ouvrez la fenêtre!**

Pay attention! **Écoutez bien!**

Put on the headphones! **Mettez vos écouteurs!**

Read the text! **Lisez le texte!**

Rewind the tape! **Rembobinez la cassette!**

Take this to the office! **Apportez ceci au secrétariat!**

Show me your books! **Montrez-moi vos cahiers!**

Sit down! **Asseyez-vous!**

Stand up! **Levez-vous!**

Switch off the cassette recorder! **Éteignez le magnétophone!**

Switch on the OHP! **Allumez le rétroprojecteur!**

Tick the boxes! **Cochez les cases!**

Work in pairs! **Travaillez par deux!**

Work in groups! **Travaillez en groupes!**

Write an essay! **Écrivez une dissertation/rédaction!**

Write it down! **Écrivez ceci!**

Write out in neat/neatly! **Écrivez-le au propre!**

Write out in rough! **Écrivez-le au brouillon!**

She reads to her teacher every day and can read well now.	**Elle fait de la lecture en classe tous les jours et elle sait bien lire maintenant.**
– Do you move up a class every year?	**– Est-ce que vous passez d'une classe à l'autre tous les ans?**
– No, last year I had to stay down a year.	**– Non, l'année dernière j'ai dû redoubler.**

➤ EXAMINATIONS 22c; STATIONERY App.22b

171

22c School subjects & examinations

School subjects

arithmetic **l'arithmétique** *(f)*
art **le dessin**
biology **la biologie**
business studies **les études** *(f)* **commerciales**
careers education **l'orientation** *(f)*
chemistry **la chimie**
commerce **le commerce**
compulsory subject **la matière obligatoire**
computer studies **l'informatique** *(f)*
cookery **la cuisine**
CDT/craft, design and technology **les travaux manuels/pratiques**
design technology **la technologie (du design)**
economics **l'économie** *(f)*
foreign language **la langue étrangère**
French **le français**
geography **la géographie**
gymnastics **la gymnastique**

history **l'histoire** *(f)*
home economics **les arts** *(m)* **ménagers**
information technology **l'informatique** *(f)*
main subject **la matière principale**
mathematics **les mathématiques** *(f)*
music **la musique**
needlework **la couture**
option(al subject) **la matière facultative**
philosophy **la philosophie**
physical education **l'éducation** *(f)* **physique**
physics **la physique**
religious education **l'éducation** *(f)* **religieuse**
science **les sciences** *(f)*
sex education **l'éducation** *(f)* **sexuelle**
social studies **les études** *(f)* **sociales**

– Which school do you go to?
– I go to the comprehensive/public school. I enjoy it a lot. There are lots of clubs and activities.
– Which is your favourite subject?

– I like maths/math, but prefer physics. My favourite/favorite subject is PE. I don't like history, it is so boring.

I'm good at English, since I did an exchange. I work very hard at it.

– **À quelle école vas-tu?**
– **Je vais au collège. Je m'y plais beaucoup. Il y a beaucoup de clubs et d'activités.**
– **Quelle est ta matière préférée?**
– **J'aime bien les maths, mais je préfère la physique. Ma matière préférée c'est l'éducation physique. Je n'aime pas l'histoire, c'est tellement barbant.**
Je suis fort en anglais depuis que j'ai fait un échange. Je travaille beaucoup dans cette matière.

sociology **la sociologie**
sport **le sport**
subject **la matière**
subsidiary subject **la matière secondaire**
technical drawing **le dessin technique**
woodwork **la menuiserie**

Examinations

I assess **j'évalue**
assessment **l'évaluation** *(f)*
certificate **le certificat**
degree **la licence**
   higher degree **la maîtrise, le doctorat**
diploma **le diplome**
dissertation **la dissertation**
distinction **la mention**
doctorate **le doctorat**
examination **l'examen** *(m)*
   external **public/national**
   final **de fin d'études**
grade **la mention**
I grade **je classe**

graduate (engineer) **(l'ingénieur) diplômé**
listening comprehension **l'examen** *(m)* **oral, la compréhension orale**
mark **la note**
mark system **le barême/le système de notation**
masters **la maitrise**
merit **la mention (bien/très bien)**
oral **oral**
post-graduate course **la maîtrise, le doctorat**
reading comprehension **l'explication** *(f)* **de texte**
I pass (an exam) **je suis reçu** *(recevoir)* **(à un examen)**
I sit/take an exam **je passe un examen**
syllabus **le programme**
I test **je teste**
test **le contrôle**
thesis **la thèse**
trainee **le stagiaire**
written test **le contrôle écrit**

– Here are your marks!
Marie-Claire, you have done excellent work. Well done!
Jerome, you will need to work harder. Your spelling is very poor.

Anna, this is very satisfactory, but please improve your handwriting. Your work is so sloppily presented.

In June we are going on a class trip to the Vosges. You will do a project on the geography and wildlife of the area.

– **Voici vos notes!**
Marie-Claire, ton travail était excellent. Très bien!
Jérôme, il faut t'appliquer davantage, tu fais beaucoup de fautes d'orthographe.
Anna, c'est très satisfaisant, mais fais un effort pour améliorer ton écriture. Ton travail est si mal présenté

En juin nous ferons un voyage scolaire dans les Vosges. Vous ferez un projet d'études sur la géographie et la faune de la région.

➤ SCHOOL 22b; FURTHER EDUCATION SUBJECTS 22d

22d Further and higher education

adult **adulte**

adult education **la formation continue**

alumnus **un ancien élève, une ancienne élève**

apprentice **un apprenti, une apprenti**

apprenticeship **l'apprentissage** *(m)*

chair **la chaire**

college **la faculté**

college of further education **le centre de formation continue**

course of study **des études** *(f)*

diploma **le diplôme**

faculty **la faculté**

further education **des études** *(f)* **supérieures**

hall of residence/residence hall **la résidence/cité universitaire, le foyer**

higher education **les études** *(f)* **supérieures**

in-service training **le stage de formation**

lecture **la conférence**

lecture hall **l'amphi(théâtre)** *(m)*

lecturer **un (maître) assistant**

masters degree **la maîtrise**

part-time education **des études** *(f)* **à temps partiel**

postgraduate/graduate **le licencié/ la licenciée (de lettres/de sciences)**

professor/college professor **le professeur**

quota *(for university entry)* **le nombre de places à l'université**

research **la recherche**

retraining **le recyclage**

I retrain **je me recycle**

scholarship **la bourse**

seminar **le séminaire**

student **un étudiant, une étudiante**

student grant **la bourse d'étude**

student union **le syndicat des étudiants**

I would like to go to college to study environmental science.

J'aimerais aller en faculté pour étudier les sciences de l'environnement.

We have increased the number of universities and are aiming for a broader provision.

Nous avons augmenté le nombre des universités et nous visons de plus amples effectifs.

The technical colleges now belong to the university sector and we now speak of a comprehensive university.

Les instituts techniques font maintenant partie de l'université et nous parlons maintenant d'études universitaires globales.

The length of course is four years (eight semesters).

Les études prennent quatre ans (huit semestres).

Many students want vocational/job qualifications. They can easily transfer between courses.

De nombreux étudiants désirent une formation spécialisée. Ils peuvent facilement changer de filière.

teacher training college **le centre de formation pédagogique**

technical college **l'institut** *(m)* **technique**

university/college **l'université** *(f)*

university entrance qualification **les qualifications requises pour entrer à l'université**

vocational route **la formation spécialisée**

Faculties & subjects

accountancy/accounting **la comptabilité**

anthropology **l'anthropologie** *(f)*

architecture **l'architecture** *(f)*

business management **la gestion**

catering **la restauration**

classics **les lettres classiques**

civil engineering **le génie civil**

commerce **le commerce**

computer studies **l'informatique** *(f)*

construction **la construction**

education **l'enseignement** *(m)*

electronics **l'électronique** *(f)*

electrical engineering **(des études) d'ingénieur en électronique**

economics **l'économie, les sciences économiques**

engineering **(des études) d'ingénieur**

environmental sciences **les sciences de l'environnement**

geology **la géologie**

history of art **l'histoire** *(f)* **de l'art**

hotel management **l'hôtellerie** *(f)*

languages **les langues** *(f)*

law **le droit**

leisure and tourism **le tourisme et les loisirs** *(m)*

literature **la littérature**

mechanical engineering **le génie mécanique**

medicine **la médecine**

pharmacy **la pharmacie**

nuclear science **les sciences** *(f)* **nucléaires**

philosophy **la philosophie**

psychology **la psychologie**

sociology **la sociologie**

theology **la théologie**

Financial support is of the greatest importance. Many students get a state grant.

Many students apply for places but they can not all be admitted to university.

There is now an entrance restriction. The right to a place depends on marks in the *Baccalauréat*. They require particularly high marks for medicine. Our results are always outstanding.

Le financement des études est primordial. Beaucoup d'étudiants reçoivent une bourse d'état.
De nombreux étudiants posent leur candidature mais ils ne peuvent pas tous être admis à l'université.

Il y a maintenant des restrictions pour l'entrée en université. Le droit d'entrée dépend des résultats au baccalauréat. Il faut de très bonnes notes surtout en médecine. Nos résultats sont toujours excellents.

Science: the changing world

23a Scientific method & life sciences

Scientific method

academic paper **l'exposé** *(m)*, **la communication**
I analyze **j'analyse**
authentic **authentique**
I challenge **je mets** *(mettre)* **en question**
I check **je vérifie**
classification **la classification**
I classify **je classe**
I conduct (an experiment) **je fais une expérience**
control **le cas témoin**
I discover **je découvre** *(découvrir)*
discovery **la découverte**
experiment **l'expérience** *(f)*
I experiment **je fais une expérience**
flask **le ballon**
hypothesis **l'hypothèse** *(f)*
I identify **j'identifie**
I investigate **j'examine, j'étudie**
laboratory **le laboratoire**
material **le matériau**
measurement **le mesurage**
I observe **j'observe**

origin **l'origine** *(f)*
pipette **la pipette**
process **le processus**
research **la recherche, les recherches**
I research **je fais des recherches**
result **le résultat**
I solve *(a problem)* **je résouds** *(résoudre)*
test **l'analyse** *(f)*
I test **je fais une analyse**
test-tube **l'éprouvette** *(f)*
theory **la théorie**
I transfer **je transfère** *(transférer)*

Biology

bacteria **la bactérie**
botanical **botanique**
I breathe **je respire**
cell **la cellule**
chlorophyll **la chlorophylle**
it circulates **il circule**
decay **le pourrissement**
decline **le déclin**
it declines **il décline**
it excretes **il excrète** *(excréter)*, **il sécrète** *(sécréter)*

The researcher took a sample, mounted it on a slide and put it under the microscope for examination. All the results from the experiments support her hypothesis.

La chercheuse a pris un échantillon qu'elle a attaché à un porte-objet. Elle l'a examiné sous le microscope. Tous les résultats des expériences confirment son hypothèse.

excretion **l'excrétion** *(f)*, **la sécrétion**
it feeds **il mange**
food chain **la chaîne alimentaire**
gene **le gène**
genetic **génétique**
genetic disorder **la maladie/ malformation d'origine génétique**
it grows **il croît** *(croître)*
growth **la croissance**
habitat **l'habitat** *(m)*
it inherits **il hérite**
membrane **la membrane**
it mutates **il subit une mutation**
nucleus **le nucléus**
organic **organique**
organism **l'organisme** *(m)*
photosynthesis **la photosynthèse**
population **la population**
it reproduces **il se reproduit** *(se reproduire)*
respiration **la respiration**
sensitivity **la sensibilité**
survival **la survie**
it survives **il survit** *(survivre)*
virus **le virus**

Medical science & research

ante-natal tests *(on foetus)* **le diagnostic prénatal (le DPN)**
cosmetic/plastic surgery **la chirurgie esthétique**
DNA **l'ADN** *(m)*

donor **le donneur, la donneuse**
embryo **l'embryon** *(m)*
embryo research **les recherches** *(f)* **sur l'embryon**
ethical consideration **la considération éthique**
ethics of human reproduction **la bioéthique**
experiments on animals **les expériences** *(f)* **sur des animaux**
hereditary illness **la maladie héréditaire**
IVF (in vitro fertilisation) **FIV (la fécondation in vitro)**
I justify **je justifie**
microorganism **le micro-organisme**
organ transplant **la greffe d'organe**
pacemaker **le stimulateur (cardiaque)**
I permit **je permets** *(permettre)*
psychology **la psychologie**
recipient **la personne qui reçoit**
I reject (an organ) **je rejette**
risk **le risque**
I risk **je risque**
survival rate (Fr. = death rate) **le taux de mortalité**
test-tube baby **le bébé-éprouvette**
transplant **la greffe**
X-ray **le rayon X**

A girl of seventeen was today given a new heart in a transplant operation which lasted ten hours.

Une jeune fille de dix-sept ans a reçu une greffe du cœur au cours d'une intervention qui a duré dix heures.

Research on human embryo tissue is likely to remain highly controversial.

La possibilité de faire des recherches sur l'embryon humain tend à rester un sujet de controverse.

➤ ANIMAL WORLD 24b; MEDICAL TREATMENT 11c; AGRICULTURE 24c

23b Physical sciences

Chemistry

acid l'acide *(m)*
air l'air *(m)*
alkali l'alcali *(m)*
alkaline alcalin
alloy l'alliage *(m)*
I analyze j'analyse
Bunsen burner le bec Bunsen
I calculate je calcule
chemical chimique
compound le composé
composition la composition
it dissolves il dissoud
  (dissoudre)
    it dissolves in water il se
    dissoud dans l'eau
element l'élément *(m)*
emulsion l'émulsion *(f)*
equation l'équation *(f)*
gas le gaz
inorganic inorganique
insoluble insoluble
liquid le liquide
  liquid *(adj)* liquide
Litmus paper le papier de
  tournesol
matter la matière
metal le métal
natural gas le gaz naturel
opaque opaque
periodic table le tableau de
  classification périodique des
  élements
physical physique
pure pur
it reacts il réagit
reaction la réaction
salt le sel
solid *(adj)* solide
soluble soluble
solution la solution
stable stable
substance la substance
transparent transparent

Physics & mechanics

it accelerates il accélère
  (accélérer)
acceleration l'accélération *(f)*
acoustics l'acoustique *(f)*
analysis l'analyse *(f)*
artificial artificiel[le]
boiling-point le point d'ébullition
circuit le circuit
conservation la conservation
density la densité
distance la distance
electron microscope le
  microscope électronique
energy input l'énergie *(f)*
energy output la puissance de
  sortie
it expands il se dilate
fibre/fiber la fibre
force la force
it freezes il gèle *(geler)*
formula la formule
freezing-point le point de
  congélation
friction la friction
gravity la pesanteur
I heat je fais chauffer
it heats il chauffe
heat la chaleur
heat loss la perte calorifique
invention l'invention *(f)*
laser le laser
laser beam le rayon laser
light la lumière
light beam le rayon de lumière
magnetism le magnétisme
magneto la magnéto
mass la masse
I measure je mesure
mechanics la mécanique
metallurgy la métallurgie
microscope le microscope
microwave la micro-onde
mineral le minéral

missile   **le missile**
model   **le modèle (réduit)**
motion   **le mouvement**
observation   **l'observation** (f)
optics   **l'optique** (f)
pressure   **la pression**
property   **la propriété**
proportional   **proportionnel[le]**
ray   **le rayon**
reflection   **la réflexion**
refraction   **la réfraction**
relativity   **la relativité**
resistant   **résistant**
solid   **le solide**
I sort   **je trie, je classe**
sound   **le son**
speed   **la vitesse**
structure   **la structure**
synthetic   **synthétique**
temperature   **la température**
theory   **la théorie**
time   **le temps**
transmission   **la transmission**
vapour/vapor   **la vapeur**
it vibrates   **il vibre**
vibration   **la vibration**
wave   **l'onde** (f)
   long waves   **grandes ondes**
   medium/short waves   **ondes**
   moyennes/courtes
wavelength   **la longueur d'ondes**

Electricity

battery *(large)*   **la batterie**
   battery *(small)*   **la pile**
charge   **la charge**

I charge the battery   **je mets**
   (mettre) la batterie en charge
current   **le courant**
electrical   **électrique**
electricity   **l'électricité** (f)
electricity grid/network   **le réseau**
   électrique
electrode   **l'électrode** (f)
electron   **l'électron** (m)
electronic   **électronique**
electronics   **l'électronique** (f)
negative   **négatif [-ve]**
positive   **positif [-ve]**
pylon   **le pylône**
resistance   **la résistance**
voltage   **le voltage, la tension**

Nuclear physics

atom   **l'atome** (m)
atomic   **atomique**
electron   **l'électron** (m)
fission   **la fission**
fusion   **la fusion**
molecular   **moléculaire**
molecule   **la molécule**
neutron   **le neutron**
nuclear   **nucléaire**
nuclear energy   **l'énergie** (f)
   nucléaire
nucleus   **le noyau**
particle   **la particule**
proton   **le proton**
quantum theory   **la théorie des**
   quanta
radiation   **la radiation**
reactor   **le réacteur**

Water has a boiling point of 100 degrees centigrade. It freezes at zero degrees.

What is the voltage of this equipment?

Le point d'ébullition de l'eau est de 100 degrés Celsius. Elle gèle à zéro degré Celsius.

Quel est le voltage de cet appareil?

23c The earth & space

Geology & minerals

bauxite   **la bauxite**
carbon-dating   **la datation au carbone 14**
chalk   **la craie**
chalky   **crayeux [-se], calcaire**
clay   **l'argile** *(f)*
diamond   **le diamant**
geologist   **le géologue**
gemstone   **la pierre gemme**
granite   **le granit**
graphite   **le graphite, la mine de plomb**
layer   **la couche**
lime   **la chaux**
limestone   **le calcaire**
loam   **le terreau**
marble   **le marbre**
mine   **la mine**
I mine   **j'extrais** *(extraire)*
ore   **le minerai**
quartz   **le quartz**
quarry   **la carrière**
sand   **le sable**
sandstone   **le grès**
sediment   **le sédiment**
silica   **la silice**
slate   **l'ardoise** *(f)*
soil   **le sol**
stalactite   **la stalactite**
stalagmite   **la stalagmite**

Energy & fuels

atomic energy   **l'énergie** *(f)* **atomique**
coal   **le charbon, la houille**
concentration   **la concentration**
consumption   **la consommation**
energy   **l'énergie** *(f)*
energy conservation   **les économies** *(f)* **d'énergie**
energy consumption   **la consommation d'énergie**
energy crisis   **la crise d'énergie**

energy saving   **qui economise l'énergie**
energy source   **la source d'énergie**
fossil fuels   **le combustible fossile**
fuel   **le combustible**
fuel consumption   **la consommation de combustibles**
it generates   **il produit** *(produire)*
geothermal energy   **l'énergie** *(f)* **géothermique**
global warming   **le réchauffement de l'atmosphère**
greenhouse effect   **l'effet** *(m)* **de serre**
hydro-electric dam   **le barrage** *(m)* **hydro-électrique**
hydro-electric power   **l'énergie** *(f)* **hydro-électrique, la houille blanche**
insulation   **l'isolation** *(f)*
natural gas   **le gaz naturel**
nuclear power station   **la centrale nucléaire**
nuclear reactor   **le réacteur nucléaire**
oil   **le pétrole, l'huile** *(f)*
oil production   **la production de pétrole**
oil-producing countries   **les pays** *(m)* **producteurs de pétrole**
petrol/gasoline   **l'essence** *(f)*
petroleum   **le pétrole**
raw materials   **la matière première**
solar cell   **la pile solaire**
solar energy   **l'énergie** *(f)* **solaire**
thermal energy   **l'énergie** *(f)* **thermique**
wave power   **l'énergie** *(f)* **des vagues**
tidal power station   **l'usine** *(f)* **marémotrice**
wind energy/power   **l'énergie** *(f)* **éolienne**

Space

asteroid **l'astéroïde** *(m)*
big-bang theory **la théorie du big-bang**
eclipse **l'éclipse** *(f)*
it eclipses **il éclipse**
galactic **galactique**
galaxy **la galaxie**
gravitational pull **la gravitation**
light year **l'année-lumière** *(f)*
meteorite **le météore**
moon **la lune**
  full moon **la pleine lune**
  new moon **la nouvelle lune**
orbit **l'orbite** *(f)*
planet **la planète**
solar system **le système solaire**
solstice **le solstice**
star **l'étoile** *(f)*
sun **le soleil**
sunspot **la tache solaire**
the heavens **le ciel**
universe **l'univers** *(m)*

Space research & travel

antenna **l'antenne** *(f)*
astrologer **l'astrologue** *(m)*
astronomer **l'astronome** *(m)*
astronaut **l'astronaute** *(m)*
cosmonaut **le cosmonaute**
I launch **je lance**
launch pad **la rampe de**
lancement
lunar module **le module lunaire**
moon-buggy **la jeep lunaire**
moon-walk **la marche lunaire**
observatory **l'observatoire** *(m)*
orbit **l'orbite** *(f)*
planetarium **le planétarium**
it re-enters **il rentre (dans**
l'atmosphère)
relativity **la relativité**
rocket **la fusée (interplanétaire)**
rocket fuel **le combustible**
satellite **le satellite**
  communications **le satellite de**
  télécommunications
  spy **le satellite d'espionnage**
  weather **le satellite**
  météorologique
sky lab **le laboratoire spatial**
space **l'espace** *(m)*
space flight **le voyage spatial**
space probe **la sonde spatiale**
space shuttle **la navette spatiale**
spacecraft **le vaisseau spatial**
spacesuit **le scaphandre**
stratosphere **la stratosphère**
telescope **le télescope**
time-warp **la distorsion du temps**
touchdown on land **l'atterrissage**
(m)
  on sea **l'amerrissage** *(m)*
  on moon **l'alunissage** *(m)*
zodiac **le zodiaque**

By studying the light received from stars many millions of light years away, scientists hope to discover the origins of the universe.

The earth orbits the sun.

Les scientifiques espèrent découvrir les origines de l'univers en étudiant la lumière qui provient des étoiles distantes de plusieurs millions d'années-lumière.

La terre reste en orbite autour du soleil.

➤ PLANETS & STARS, SIGNS OF THE ZODIAC App.23c

The Environment: the natural world

24a Geography

archipelago **l'archipel** *(m)*
area **la région**
bank (river) **le bord**
bay **la baie**
beach **la plage**
bog **le marais**
bottom **le fond**
canyon **le cañon, la gorge**
clean **propre, net[te]**
cliff **la falaise, l'escarpement** *(m)*
coast **la côte**
coastline **le littoral**
continent **le continent**
coppice, copse **le taillis, le boqueteau**
country **le pays**
 in the country **à la campagne**
countryside **le paysage**
creek **le ruisseau**
dangerous **dangereux [-se]**
deep **profond**
delta **le delta**
desert **le désert**
dirty **sale**
dune **la dune**
earth tremor **la secousse sismique**
earthquake **le tremblement de terre**
equator **l'équateur** *(m)*
equatorial **équatorial**
eruption **l'éruption** *(f)*
it erupts **il entre en éruption**
escarpment **l'escarpement** *(m)*
estuary **l'estuaire** *(m)*
field **le champ**
fjord **le fjord**
flat **plat**
it flows **il coule**

foothills **les contreforts** *(m)*
forest **la forêt**
friendly **accueillant**
geographical **géographique**
geography **la géographie**
geyser **le geyser**
globe **le globe**
gradient **la pente, l'inclinaison** *(f)*
hemisphere **l'hémisphère** *(f)*
high **haut**
hill **la colline**
incline/slope **la déclivité**
it is situated **il est situé**
island **l'île** *(f)*
jungle **la jungle**
lake **le lac**
land **la terre**
it is located **il se trouve**
location **l'emplacement** *(m)*, **la situation**
map **la carte**
marsh **le marais, la marécage**
meridian **le méridien**
mountain **la montagne**
mountain range **la chaîne de montagnes**
national **national**
national park **le parc national**
nature **la nature**
nice/pleasant **agréable**
ocean **l'océan** *(m)*
ocean floor **le fond sous-marin**
peaceful **paisible**
peak **le pic, le sommet**
peninsula **la péninsule**
plateau **le plateau**
pole **le pôle**
province **la province**
reef **le récif**

region **la région**
regional **régional**
ridge **l'arête** *(f)*, **la crête**
river **la rivière**
river (major) **le fleuve**
riverbed **le lit de la rivière/du fleuve**
rockpool **la flaque d'eau (dans les rochers)**
sand **le sable**
scenery **le paysage**
sea **la mer**
seaside **le bord de la mer**
shore **le rivage, le bord**
spring **le printemps**
steep **raide**
steppe **la steppe**
stream **le ruisseau**
summit **le sommet**
tall **haut, élevé**
territory **le territoire**
top **le sommet**
the tropics **les tropiques** *(m)*
tundra **la toundra**
unfriendly **froid, hostile**
valley **la vallée**
volcano **le volcan**
water **l'eau** *(f)*
    freshwater **l'eau** *(f)* **douce**
waterfall **la chute d'eau**
wood **le bois**

woodland **la région boisée**
zenith **le zénith**
zone **la zone**

Man-made features

aqueduct **l'aqueduc** *(m)*
bridge **le pont**
canal **le canal**
capital (city) **la capitale**
city **la ville, la cité**
country road **la petite route de campagne**
dam **le barrage**
embankment **le talus, le remblai**
factory **l'usine** *(f)*, **la fabrique**
farm **la ferme**
farmland **les terres** *(f)* **cultivées**
hamlet **le hameau**
harbour **le port**
industry **l'industrie** *(f)*
marina **la marina**
nature trail **l'itinéraire** *(m)* **aménagé pour amateurs de la nature**
oasis **l'oasis** *(f)*
reclaimed land **le terrain asséché**
reservoir **le réservoir**
town **la ville**
track **la trace**
village **le village**
well **le puits**

Wallonia, in the south of Belgium, is dominated by the forest uplands of the Ardennes.

La Wallonie, dans le sud de la Belgique, est une région dominée par les collines boisées des Ardennes.

The Water Authority plans to create a new reservoir. This will involve submerging several dwellings.

Le service des eaux a un projet pour créer un nouveau réservoir. Il faudra submerger plusieurs habitations.

The area was marshy and unsuitable for development.

La région était marécageuse et inadaptée au développement.

➤ ANIMAL WORLD 24b; FARMING 24c; WEATHER 24d; POLLUTION 24e

24b The animal world

Animals

animal   l'animal *(m)*
it barks   il aboie *(aboyer)*
it bites   il mord *(mordre)*
it bounds   il bondit
it breeds   il se reproduit
  (se reproduire)
budgerigar   la perruche
burrow   le terrier
cage   la cage
carnivore   le carnivore
cat   le chat
it crawls   il rampe
den   la tanière
dog   le chien
I feed   je donne à manger à
it feeds   il se nourrit
food   la nourriture
fox   le renard
frog   la grenouille
gerbil   la gerbille
goldfish   le poisson rouge
guinea pig   le cochon d'Inde
habitat   l'habitat *(m)*
hamster   le hamster
hare   le lièvre
hedgehog   le hérisson
herbivore   l'herbivore *(m)*
it hibernates   il hiberne
it howls   il hurle
hut/hutch   le clapier
I keep a cat   j'ai un chat
kitten   le chaton
lair   le repaire
it leaps   il saute
litter   la portée
mammal   le mammifère
it miaows   il miaule
mole   la taupe
mouse   la souris
omnivore   l'omnivore *(m)*
pack   la meute
pet   l'animal *(m)* familier
predator   le prédateur
prey   la proie

puppy   le chiot
rabbit   le lapin
rabies   la rage
reptile   le reptile
it roars   il rugit
safari park   la réserve
snake   le serpent
it squeaks   il couine
squirrel   l'écureuil *(m)*
I stroke   je caresse
toad   le crapaud
tortoise   la tortue
I walk (the dog)   je promène
  (promener) (le chien)
wildlife park   la réserve naturelle
wolf   le loup
zoo   le zoo

Birds

claw   la griffe
it crows   il chante
it flies   il vole
flock   la volée
it hovers   il plane
it migrates   il migre
nest   le nid
it nests   il se niche
it pecks at   il picore

Sealife/Waterlife

alligator   l'alligator *(m)*
anemone   l'anémone *(f)*
angling   la pêche (à la ligne)
coral   le corail
crab   le crabe
crocodile   le crocodile
dolphin   le dauphin
fish   le poisson
I fish   je vais à la pêche
harpoon   le harpon
hook   l'hameçon *(m)*
marine   marin
mollusc   le mollusque
net   le filet

octopus   **la pieuvre, le poulpe**
plankton   **le plancton**
rod   **la canne (à pêche)**
seal   **le phoque**
shark   **le requin, le squale**
shoal   **le banc (de poissons)**
starfish   **l'étoile** *(f)* **de mer**
it swims   **il nage**
turtle   **la tortue marine**
whale   **la baleine**
whaling   **la pêche à la baleine**

Insects

ant   **la fourmi**
bee   **l'abeille** *(f)*
   queen bee   **la reine, la repro-**
      ductrice
   worker bee   **l'ouvrière** *(f)*
bedbug   **la punaise**
beetle   **la scarabée**
bug   **l'insecte** *(m)*, **la bestiole**
butterfly   **le papillon**
it buzzes   **il bourdonne**
caterpiller   **la chenille**
cocoon   **le cocon**
cockroach   **le cafard**
cricket   **le grillon**

dragonfly   **la libellule**
flea   **la puce**
fly   **la mouche**
grasshopper   **la sauterelle**
hive   **la ruche**
insect   **l'insecte** *(m)*
invertebrate   **l'invertébré** *(m)*
ladybird/ladybug   **la coccinelle, la**
   bête à bon Dieu
larva   **la larve**
locust   **la locuste**
it metamorphoses   **il se métamor-**
   phose
mosquito   **le moustique**
moth   **le papillon de nuit**
scorpion   **le scorpion**
silkworm   **le ver à soie**
slug   **la limace**
snail   **l'escargot** *(m)*
spider   **l'araignée** *(f)*
it spins (a web)   **il tisse la toile**
it stings   **il pique**
termite   **le termite**
tick   **la tique**
web   **la toile**
wasp   **la guêpe**
worm   **le ver**

Guinea pigs and hamsters are popular pets in Britain.	**Le cochon d'Inde et le hamster sont très populaires comme animaux familiers en Grande Bretagne.**
Don't forget to walk the dog and feed the cat!	**N'oublie pas de promener le chien et de donner à manger au chat!**
The campaign to save the whale is increasing in popularity.	**La campagne pour la sauve-garde de la baleine devient de plus en plus populaire.**
The panda is in danger of extinction in the wild.	**Le panda est en danger d'extinction à l'état sauvage.**

➤ FISH & SEA FOOD 10c; FARM ANIMALS, FARMING 24c

24c Farming & gardening

Farm animals

bull **le taureau**
cattle **le bétail**
chicken **la poule**
cock **le coq**
cow **la vache**
it crows **il chante**
dairy *(adj)* **laitier [-ère]**
duck **le canard, la cane**
it eats **il mange**
feed **la nourriture**
it feeds **il se nourrit**
foal **le poulain**
fodder **le fourrage**
food *(for animals)* **l'aliment** *(m)*
it gallops **il galope**
goat **la chèvre**
goose **l'oie** *(f)*
it grazes **il broute, il pâture**
it grunts **il grogne**
horse **le cheval**
horseshoe **le fer à cheval**
it kicks **il rue**
kid **le chevreau**
I milk **je trais** *(traire)*
it moos **il meugle, il beugle**
it neighs **il hennit**
ox **le bœuf**
pasture **le pâturage**
it pecks **il picore**
pig **le cochon**
pony **le poney**
poultry **la basse-cour**
produce **les produits** *(m)*
it quacks **il cancane**
I ride (a horse) **je monte à cheval**
rooster **le coq**
I shear **je tonds** *(tondre)*
sheep **le mouton**

sheep dog **le chien de berger**
I slaughter **j'abats** *(abattre)*
stallion **l'étalon** *(m)*
it trots **il trotte**

On the farm

agricultural **agricole**
agriculture **l'agriculture** *(f)*
arable **arable**
barn **la grange**
combine harvester **la moissonneuse-batteuse**
crop **la culture**
    crop *(amount)* **la récolte**
dairy **la laiterie**
farm **la ferme**
farmhouse **la maison de ferme**
farm labourer/laborer **l'ouvrier** *(m)* **agricole**
farmyard **la cour de ferme**
fence **la barrière, la clôture**
I groom **je panse**
harvest **la moisson**
I harvest **je moissonne, je récolte**
hay **le foin**
haystack **la meule de foin**
irrigate **j'irrigue**
milk churn **le bidon à lait**
milking machine **la trayeuse (mécanique)**
orchard **le verger**
pen **l'enclos** *(m)*
pigsty **la porcherie**
silage **le fourrage ensilé, l'ensilage** *(m)*
slaughterhouse **l'abattoir** *(m)*
stable **l'écurie** *(f)*
stud farm **le haras**

Agriculture & gardening

acorn **le gland**
allotment **le lopin de terre**
barley **l'orge** *(f)*
bloom **la fleur**
bouquet **le bouquet**
bud **le bouton**
bulb **le bulbe**
bush **le buisson**
cactus **le cactus**
compost **le compost**
corn **le blé**
   corn *(US)* **le maïs**
I cultivate **je cultive**
cutting **la bouture**
I dig **je creuse**
   I dig (with spade) **je bêche**
fir **le sapin**
flax **le lin**
flower **la fleur**
it flowers/blooms **il fleurit**
flower bed **le parterre de fleurs**
foliage **le feuillage**
garden/yard **le jardin**
gardening **le jardinage**
I gather **je cueille** *(cueillir)*
grain **la céréale**
grass **l'herbe** *(f)*
I grow **je cultive**
it grows **il pousse**
hedge **la haie**
horticulture **l'horticulture** *(f)*
lawn **la pelouse**
leaf **la feuille**
maize **le maïs**
I mow **je fauche**
   I mow *(lawn)* **je tonds** *(tondre)*
oats **l'avoine** *(f)*

patio **le patio**
petal **le pétale**
I pick **je cueille** *(cueillir)*
pine **le pin**
pine-forest **la pinède**
I plant **je plante**
plant **la plante**
pond **l'étang** *(m)*
pollen **le pollen**
I reap **je moissonne**
ripe **mûr**
it ripens **il mûrit**
rockery **la rocaille**
root **la racine**
rotten **pourri**
rye **le seigle**
sap **la sève**
seed **le grain**
shed **l'abri** *(m)*
sorghum **le sorgho**
species **l'espèce** *(f)*
stem **la tige**
sweet chestnut **le marron, la châtaigne**
thorn **l'épine** *(f)*
I transplant **je transplante**
tree **l'arbre** *(m)*
tuber **le tubercule**
undergrowth **les broussailles** *(f)*
vegetable(s) **le légume**
vegetable garden **le potager**
vegetation **la végétation**
I water **j'arrose**
weed **la mauvaise herbe**
I weed **je désherbe**
wheat **le blé**
wild flower **la fleur sauvage**
it wilts **il se flétrit**

I must mow the lawn, plant some bulbs, weed the flower bed and trim the hedge.

Il faut que je tonde la pelouse, plante quelques bulbes, désherbe le parterre de fleurs et coupe la houe.

➤ FLOWERS & WEEDS, TREES App.24c; TOOLS App.8b

24d The weather

avalanche **l'avalanche** *(f)*
average temperature **la température moyenne**
bad weather **le mauvais temps**
bright **éclairci**
bright period **l'éclaircie** *(f)*
centigrade **Celsius**
changeable **variable**
climate **le climat**
climatic **climatique**
cloud **le nuage**
clouded over **couvert**
cloudless **sans nuages**
cloudy **nuageux [-se]**
cold **le froid**
it is cold **il fait froid**
cold front **le front froid**
it is cool **il fait frais**
daily temperature **la température**
damp **humide**
degree **le degré**
    above zero **au-dessus de zéro**
    below zero **au-dessous de zéro**
depression **la dépression**
drizzle **la bruine, le crachin**

dry **sec [sèche]**
dull (weather) **(le temps) maussade**
it's fine **il fait beau**
flash **l'éclair** *(m)*
fog **le brouillard**
it is foggy **il fait du brouillard**
it's freezing **il gèle** *(geler)*
freezing fog **le brouillard givrant**
frost **le givre**
frosty **glacial**
gale **le grand vent**
gale warning **l'avis** *(m)* **de coup de vent**
it's hailing **il grêle**
hailstones **des grêlons** *(m)*
heat **la chaleur**
heatwave **la vague de chaleur, la canicule**
high pressure **la haute pression (atmosphérique)**
highest temperature **la température maximale**
it's hot **il fait chaud**
ice **la glace**
Indian summer **l'été** *(m)* **indien/de la St Martin**

It will be cold tomorrow, maximum temperatures 4-6 Celsius/39-43 Fahrenheit.

Freezing fog patches in parts of eastern Quebec should clear by midday.

The whole country will be affected by rain, turning to sleet in the mountains. Snow will fall in the west, drifting in places.

Il fera froid demain, températures maximales de 4 à 6 degrés (Celsius).

Le brouillard givrant qu'on trouvera dans l'est du Québec devrait se dissiper avant midi.

Sur tout le pays il y aura de la pluie, qui sera transformée en neige fondue en altitude. Il y aura des chutes de neige dans l'ouest, avec des amoncellements possibles.

lightning **l'éclair** *(m)*, **des éclairs**
low pressure **la basse pression**
lowest temperature **la température minimale**
mild **doux [-ce]**
mist **la brume**
misty **brumeux [-se]**
monsoon **la mousson**
moon **la lune**
occluded front **le front occlus**
rain **la pluie**
it's raining **il pleut** *(pleuvoir)*
rainy **pluvieux [-se]**
shade **l'ombre** *(f)*
it shines **il brille**
shower **l'averse** (f)
snow **la neige**
snowball **la boule de neige**
snowdrift **la congère, l'amoncelle-
ment** *(m)* **de neige**
snowfall **la chute de neige**
snowflake **le flocon de neige**
snowman **le bonhomme de neige**
snow report *(for skiing)* **le bulletin
d'enneigement**
it's snowing **il neige**
snowstorm **la tempête de neige**
star **l'étoile** *(f)*

storm **la tempête**
stormy **orageux [-se]**
sultry **lourd, étouffant**
sun/sunshine **le soleil**
sunny **ensoleillé**
thunder **le tonnerre**
it's thunder **il tonne**
thunderbolt **le coup de foudre**
thunderstorm **l'orage** *(m)*
torrent **le torrent**
torrential **torrentiel[le]**
tropical **tropical**
warm **chaud**
warm front **le front chaud**
weather **le temps qu'il fait**
weather conditions **les conditions
(f) **météorologiques**
weather forecast **la météo, les
prévisions** *(f)* **de la météo**
weather report **le bulletin
météorologique, la météo**
wet **pluvieux [-se]**
What's the weather like? **Quel
temps fait-il?**
wind **le vent**
it is windy **il fait du vent, il vente**
wonderful **merveilleux [-se]**

The northeast monsoon is now
well established over southeast
Asia.

**La mousson du nord-est est
désormais bien établie sur l'Asie
du Sud-Est.**

Heavy rain has caused several
rivers in southern Ohio to burst
their banks.

**Plusieurs rivières de l'Ohio du
sud ont rompu leurs digues à
cause des pluies abondantes.**

The south of the country may be
affected by tropical storms later
tonight.

**Sur le sud du pays, dans la
soirée, il y a une possiblité
d'orages tropicaux.**

Tomorrow's temperatures will rise
to over 40°C (104°F) in the shade.

**Demain les températures
dépasseront les 40 degrés
Celsius (104° F) à l'ombre.**

24e Pollution

On the earth

artificial fertilizer   **l'engrais** *(m)* **chimique**
balance of nature   **l'équilibre** *(m)* **de la nature**
bio-degradable   **bio-dégradable**
conservation   **la préservation, la défense de l'environnement**
conservationist   **le défenseur de l'environnement**
deforestation   **le déboisement**
disaster   **le désastre, la catastrophe**
ecology   **l'écologie** *(f)*
ecosystem   **l'écosystème** *(m)*
environment   **l'environnement** *(m)*
natural resources   **les ressources** *(f)* **naturelles**
nature reserve   **la réserve naturelle**
nitrates   **les nitrates** *(m)*
pesticide   **le pesticide**
quality of life   **la qualité de la vie**
radioactive   **radioactif [-ve]**
radioactive waste   **les déchets** *(m)* **radioactifs**
rain forest   **la forêt tropicale humide**
soil erosion   **l'érosion** *(f)* **du sol**
weedkiller   **le désherbant, l'herbicide** *(m)*

In the atmosphere

acid rain   **les pluies** *(f)* **acides**
aerosol(system)   **l'aérosol** *(m)*
aerosol can   **la bombe**
air pollution   **la pollution atmosphérique**
catalytic convertor   **le pot catalytique**
CFCs   **les CFC**
emission (of gas)   **l'émission** *(f)*
lead-free/unleaded petrol   **l'essence** *(f)* **sans-plomb**
skin cancer   **le cancer de la peau**
waste gases   **les gaz** *(m)* **d'échappement**

In the rivers & seas

detergent   **le détergent**
drought   **la sécheresse**
flooding   **l'inondation** *(f)*
ground water   **la nappe phréatique**
oil slick   **la nappe de pétrole, la marée noire**
phosphates   **les phosphates** *(m)*
sea-level   **le niveau de la mer**
water level   **le niveau de l'eau**
water pollution   **la pollution de l'eau**
water suppply system   **le réseau hydrographiqe**
water supply   **l'alimentation** *(f)* **en eau**

Recent studies suggest the hole in the ozone layer will have serious consequences in the Northern Hemisphere.

Des études récentes suggèrent que le trou dans la couche d'ozone aura de graves conséquences dans l'hémisphère nord.

The city council/municipality provides facilities for recycling glass, cans and newspapers.

Le conseil municipal offre l'opportunité de recycler verres, boîtes en métal et vieux journaux.

Problems of pollution

it becomes extinct   **il disparaît**
   (disparaître)
I conserve   **j'économise**
I consume   **je consomme**
consumption   **la consommation**
I damage   **j'abîme**
danger (to)   **le danger (pour)**
I destroy   **je détruis** *(détruire)*
disposal   **l'enlèvement** *(m)* **(des**
   ordures ménagères)
I dispose of   **je me débarrasse de**
I do without   **je me prive de**
emission   **l'émission** *(f)*
it emits   **il émet** *(émettre)*, **il dégage**
I improve   **j'améliore**
I insulate   **j'isole**
I poison   **j'empoisonne**
pollutant   **le polluant**
I pollute   **je pollue**
pollution   **la pollution**
I predict   **je prédis** *(prédire)*, **je**
   prévois *(prévoir)*
I protect   **je protège** *(protéger)*
it runs out   **il s'épuise**
I store   **je mets** *(mettre)* **en réserve**
I throw away   **je jette** *(jeter)*

Waste & recycling

corrosion   **la corrosion**
damaging   **nuisible**
drainage   **le drainage**
exhaust pipe   **le tuyau**
d'échappement
harmful   **nuisible**
incinerator   **l'incinérateur** *(m)*
industrial effluent   **l'effluent** *(m)*
   industriel
industrial waste   **les déchets** *(m)*
   industriels
litter   **les déchets** *(m)*, **les ordures**
   (f)
nuclear waste   **les déchets** *(m)*
   nucléaires
poison   **le poison**
recyclable   **recyclable**
I recycle   **je recycle**
recycled paper   **le papier recyclé**
recycling skip   **le conteneur de**
   collecte de verre/papier etc.
refuse   **les ordures** *(f)*
reprocessing   **le retraitement**
residue   **les restes** *(m)*
rubbish/garbage dump   **la**
   déchetterie, la décharge
   publique
scrap metal   **la ferraille**
sewage   **les vidanges**
treatment   **le traitement**
waste (domestic)   **les ordures** *(f)*
   (ménagères)
waste disposal   **le traitement des**
   ordures
waste disposal unit   **le broyeur**
   d'ordures
waste products   **les déchets** *(m)*

– Do you think this awful
weather is normal? Don't you
think it's because of global
warming?

– Well, I think it's a combination
of the greenhouse effect and
nuclear testing.

– **Vous croyez que c'est**
normal, ce temps affreux?
Vous ne croyez pas que ce
soit à cause du réchauffement
de l'atmosphère?
– **Eh bien, moi je pense que**
c'est le résultat de l'effet de
serre combiné avec les effets
des essais nucléaires.

Government & politics

25a Political life

I abolish **je supprime**
act (of parliament) **la loi**
administration **l'administration** *(f)*
I appoint **je nomme**
appointment **la nomination, la désignation**
asylum-seeker **le réfugié politique**
it becomes law **il devient** *(devenir)* **loi**
bill **le projet de loi**
I bring down **je fais tomber**
citizen **le citoyen, la citoyenne**
civil disobedience **la résistance passive**
civil servant **le fonctionnaire**
civil war **la guerre civile**
coalition **la coalition**
it comes into effect **il entre en vigueur**
common **commun**
constitution **la constitution**
co-operation **la coopération**
corruption **la corruption**
county **le comté**
coup **le coup d'état**
crisis **la crise**
debate **le débat**
decree **le décret**
delegate **le délégué**
I demonstrate **je manifeste**
demonstration **la manifestation**
I discuss **je discute de**
discussion **la discussion**
I dismiss **je congédie**
I dissolve **je dissouds** *(dissoudre)*
I draw up (a bill) **je rédige un projet de loi**
duty **le devoir**
I emigrate **j'émigre**

equality (in-) **l'(in)égalité** *(f)*
executive **l'exécutif** *(m)*
executive *(adj)* **exécutif [-ve]**
foreign policy **la politique extérieure**
I form a pact with **je signe un pacte avec**
freedom **la liberté**
freedom of speech **la liberté de parole**
I govern **je gouverne**
government **le gouvernement**
I immigrate **j'immigre**
immigration **l'immigration** *(f)*
I introduce (a bill) **je présente (un projet de loi)**
judiciary **le pouvoir judiciaire**
law **la loi**
I lead **je dirige**
legislation **la législation**
legislature **le législatif**
liberty **la liberté**
local affairs **les affaires** *(f)* **locales**
local government **l'administration** *(f)* **locale**
long-term **à long terme**
majority **la majorité**
meeting **le meeting, la réunion**
middle-class **la bourgeoisie, la classe moyenne**
middle-class **bourgeois**
ministry **le ministère**
minority **la minorité**
moderate **modéré**
nation **la nation**
national **national**
national flag **le drapeau national**
French national flag **le drapeau tricolore**
I nationalize **je nationalise**

I oppose **je m'oppose à**
opposition **l'opposition** *(f)*
I organize **j'organise**
I overthrow **je renverse**
pact **le pacte**
I pass (a bill) **j'adopte (un projet de loi)**
policy/politics **la politique**
political **politique**
power **le pouvoir**
I privatize **je privatise**
I protest **je proteste**
public **le public**
  public *(adj)* **public [-que]**
public opinion **l'opinion** *(f)* **publique**
I ratify **je ratifie**
reactionary **réactionnaire**
I reform **je réforme**
reform **la réforme**
I reject **je rejette** *(rejeter)*
I repeal *(a law)* **j'abroge**, **je révoque**
I represent **je représente**
I repress **je réprime**
I resign **je démissionne**
responsible **responsable**

responsiblity **la responsabilité**
reunification **la réunification**
revolt **la révolte**
I rule **je gouverne**
sanction **la sanction**
seat **le siège (parlementaire)**
short-term **à court terme**
solidarity **la solidarité**
speech **le discours**
state **l'état** *(m)*
statesman **l'homme** *(m)* **d'État**
I support **je soutiens** *(soutenir)*
I take power **je m'empare du pouvoir**
(4-year) term of office **la durée/période (de 4 ans)**
I throw out (a bill) **je rejette** *(rejeter)* **(un projet de loi)**
unconstitutional **inconstitutionnel[le]**
unilateral **unilatéral**
unity **l'unité** *(f)*
veto **le veto**
I veto **j'exerce le droit de veto**
welfare **le bien-être**
working class **la classe ouvrière**

The MP/Deputy introduced a bill to legalize the use of cannabis.

Le député a présenté un projet de loi pour légaliser l'usage du cannabis.

The Lower Chamber voted on the question of immigration controls.

La Chambre des Députés a voté sur la question des contrôles de l'immigration.

The Treasury promised to cut the proportion of national income taken in taxes to 30 per cent.

Le Ministère des Finances a promis de réduire la proportion de la taxe sur le revenu à 30 pour cent.

French Government funding for the arts is to be cut next year.

Les subventions données par le gouvernement français aux arts doivent être réduites l'année prochaine.

25b Elections & ideology

Elections

ballot	**le scrutin**
ballot box	**les urnes** *(f)*
ballot paper	**le bulletin de vote**
by-election	**l'élection** *(f)* **partielle**
I hold an election	**je procède** *(procéder)* **à une élection**
campaign	**la campagne**
candidate	**le candidat**
constituency	**la circonscription**
count	**le dépouillement (des votes d'un scrutin)**
I elect	**j'élis**
election	**l'élection** *(f)*
electorate	**l'électorat** *(m)*
enfranchised	**admis au suffrage**
entitled to vote	**qui a le droit de vote**
floating vote	**le vote flottant**
general election	**les élections** *(f)* **législatives**
I go to the polls	**je me rends** *(se rendre)* **aux urnes**
I hold (an election)	**je procède** *(procéder)* **à une élection**
opinion poll	**le sondage d'opinion**
poll	**le scrutin**
primary	**primaire**
recount	**le deuxième compte (des suffrages)**
I recount	**je compte de nouveau**
referendum	**le référendum**
right to vote	**le droit de vote**
seven-year term of office *(French presidency)*	**le septennat**
I stand for election	**je me présente aux élections**
suffrage	**le suffrage**
swing	**le revirement d'opinion**
universal suffrage	**le suffrage universel**
vote	**le vote**
I vote (for)	**je vote (pour)**
voter	**l'électeur** *(m)*

Parliamentary elections are held every 5 years. Presidential elections in the USA occur every four years.

Les élections législatives ont lieu tous les 5 ans. Les élections présidentielles aux États-Unis ont lieu tous les quatre ans.

The voters went to the polls today; it was a record turn-out.

Aujourd'hui les électeurs se sont rendus aux urnes: c'était un scrutin record.

An opinion poll taken yesterday gave the Democrats a two point lead over the Republicans.

Un sondage d'opinion effectué hier a révélé que les Démocrates ont deux points d'avance sur les Républicains.

Vote Christian Democrat!

Votez Démocrate Chrétien!

In the local elections, the Liberal Democrat Party won a majority of seats on the town council.

Aux élections municipales, le Parti Libéral-Démocrate a gagné une majorité de sièges au conseil municipal.

Political ideology

anarchist **l'anarchiste** *(m)*, **l'anar** *(m) (fam)*

anarchy **l'anarchie** *(f)*

anti-Semitism **l'antisémitisme** *(m)*

anti-Semitic **l'antisémite** *(m)*

aristocracy **l'aristocratie** *(f)*

aristocrat **l'aristocrate** *(m)*

aristocratic **aristocrate**

capitalism **la capitalisme**

capitalist **capitaliste**

centre/center ground **le centre**

communism **le communisme**

communist **communiste**

conservatism **le conservatisme**

conservative **le conservateur**

democracy **la démocratie**

democrat **le démocrate**

democratic **démocrate**

dictator **le dictateur**

dictatorship **la dictature**

duke **le duc**

empire **l'empire** *(m)*

emperor/empress **un empereur, une impératrice**

extremist **un/une extrémiste**

fascism **le fascisme**

fascist **le fasciste**

I gain independence **je gagne l'indépendance**

Green party **le parti des Écologistes/Écolos, les Verts**

ideology **l'idéologie** *(f)*

imperialism **l'impérialisme** *(f)*

imperialist **impérialiste**

independence **l'indépendance** *(f)*

independent **indépendant**

king **le roi**

Labour party **le parti Travailliste**

left **la gauche**

left-wing **de la gauche**

liberal **libéral**

Liberal Democrats **les Démocrates-Libéraux** *(m)*

liberalism **le libéralisme**

Liberals **les Libéraux** *(m)*

marxism **le marxisme**

marxist **le marxiste**

monarchy **la monarchie**

nationalism **le nationalisme**

nationalist **nationaliste**

patriotic **patriote**

patriotism **le pariotisme**

prince **le prince**

princess **la princesse**

queen **la reine**

racism **le racisme**

racist **raciste**

radicalism **le radicalisme**

radical **radical**

republic **la république**

republican **républicain**

republicanism **le républicanisme**

revolutionary **révolutionnaire**

right **la droite**

right-wing **de la droite**

royal **royal**

royalist **royaliste**

socialism **le socialisme**

socialist **socialiste**

Socialist **le/la socialiste**

French political parties

le Mouvement des radicaux de Gauche (MRG) Radical Left

le Parti communiste français (PCF) Communist Party

le Parti socialiste (PS) Socialist Party

le Rassemblement pour la République (RPR) Gaullist Republican Assembly

L'Union pour la démocratie française (UDF) Democrats

les Verts Green Party

le Front National National Front

Crime & justice

26a Crime

accomplice **le complice**

armed **armé**

assault **l'agression** *(f)*

assault and battery **coups** *(m)* **et blessures** *(f)*

battered baby **l'enfant** *(m)* **martyre**

burglar **le cambrioleur**

burglary **le cambriolage, le vol avec effraction**

I burgle/burglarize **je cambriole, je dévalise**

car theft **le vol de voiture**

theft *(from car)* **le vol à la roulotte**

child abuse **les mauvais traitements** *(m)* **infligés à un enfant**

! come to blows **j'en viens** *(venir)* **aux mains**

I commit **je commets** *(commettre)*

crime **le crime**

crime rate **le taux de la délinquance**

crime wave **la vague de criminalité**

criminal **le criminel, la criminelle**

I deceive **je trompe**

delinquency **la délinquance**

drug abuse **la toxicomanie**

drug addict **le toxicomane, le drogué**

drug barons **les gros trafiquants** *(m)*

drug dealer **le trafiquant**

drug pusher **le revendeur/la revendeuse de drogue**

drugs **la drogue**

drug-trafficking **le trafic de la drogue**

I embezzle **je détourne (de l'argent)**

embezzlement **le détournement de fonds**

extortion **l'extorsion** *(f)*

I fight **je me bats** *(se battre)*

fight **la bagarre**

firearm **une arme à feu**

I forge *(banknote)* **je contrefais** *(contrefaire)*

I forge *(signature)* **je falsifie**

forged **faux [fausse]**

forgery **la contrefaçon**

fraud **la supercherie, la fraude**

gang **la bande, le gang**

gang warfare **la guerre entre les bandes**

grievous bodily harm (GBH) **coups** *(m)* **et blessures** *(f)*

gun **le fusil**

handbag snatching **le vol à l'arraché**

handcuffs **les menottes** *(f)*

Help! **Au secours!**

hoax (call) **la mauvaise plaisanterie**

I hi-jack **je détourne un avion**

hi-jacker **le pirate de l'air**

hold-up **le hold-up**

hooker **la putain** *(fam)*, **la prostituée**

hostage **l'otage** *(m)*

I importune **j'importune**

I injure/wound **je blesse**

I joy ride **je fais une virée/une balade (dans une voiture volée)**

joy riding **la balade (dans une voiture volée)**

I kidnap **j'enlève** *(enlever)*

kidnapper **le kidnappeur, le ravisseur**

kidnapping **le kidnapping, le rapt**
I kill **je tue**
killer **le tueur**
knifing **l'agression** (f) **à coups de couteau**
legal (il-) **(il)légal**
living off immoral earnings **le proxénétisme**
mafia **la mafia**
menace to society **un danger public**
I mug **j'agresse**
mugger **l'agresseur** (m)
mugging **l'agression** (f)
murder **le meurtre**
I murder **j'assassine**
murderer **l'assassin** (m)
I offend **je commets** (commettre) **une infraction**
pickpocket **le voleur à la tire, le pickpocket**
pickpocketing **le vol à la tire**
pimp **le proxénète, le maquereau** (fam)

pimping **le proxénétisme**
poison **le poison**
I poison **j'empoisonne**
procuring **le proxénétisme**
prostitute **la prostituée**
prostitution **la prostitution**
public enemy No.1 **l'ennemi** (m) **public numéro un**
I rape **je viole**
rape **le viol**
receiver **le receleur, la receleuse**
reprisals **les représailles** (f)
shop-lifting **le vol à l'étalage**
I steal **je vole**
stolen goods **la marchandise volée**
terrorist **le terroriste**
torture **la torture**
thief **le voleur**
traffic offence/violation **la contravention**
trafficking **le trafic**
I traffick **je trafique**
underworld **le milieu**
victim **la victime**

Pablo Escobar, the world's most infamous drug baron, was killed in a shoot-out with police and the army in Medellín.

He was stopped by the police for speeding in a residential area.

Members of the public have begun to give information to the police about the rape of two teenage girls by a gang last week.

Many inner city areas have seen an increase in crimes against the person as well as break-ins.

Pablo Escobar, le narco-trafiquant le plus infâme du monde, a été tué au cours d'une fusillade contre la police et l'armée.

La police l'a arrêté pour excès de vitesse dans un quartier résidentiel.

Le public a commencé à donner des informations à la police sur le viol de deux jeunes filles commis la semaine dernière par une bande de voyous.

Beacoup de quartiers déshérités ont connu une augmentation de crimes contre la personne et des cambriolages.

➤ WEAPONS 27b; ADDICTION & VIOLENCE 12d

26b Trial

accusation **l'accusation** (f)
I accuse **j'accuse**
accused person **l'accusé** (m)
I acquit **j'acquitte**
I acquit for lack of evidence **je rends** (rendre) **une ordonnance de non-lieu**
appeal **le pourvoi, l'appel** (m)
I appeal **je fais appel**
case for the defence **les arguments** (m) **en faveur de l'accusé**
compensation **la compensation, la rénumeration**
confession **l'aveu** (m)
I confess **je passe aux aveux**
I convince **je convaincs** (convaincre), **je persuade**
costs **les dépens** (m), **les frais** (m) **judiciaires**
counsel for the defendant/defense **(l'avocat** (m) **de) la défense**
court **la cour, le tribunal**
court of appeal **la cour d'appel**
courtroom **la salle du tribunal**
criminal court **le tribunal correctionnel**
I cross-question **je fais subir un interrogatoire à**
I debate **le débat**
defence/defense **la défense**
I defend **je défends**
I defend (myself) **je me défends**
defendant **un accusé, une accusée**
diminished responsibility **la responsabilité atténuée**
I disagree **je ne suis pas d'accord**
I discuss **je discute**
district attorney (US) **le représentant du ministère public**
dock/witness-box **le banc des accusés**

I enquire **j'enquête sur**
evidence **la preuve**
examining magistrate **le juge d'instruction**
extenuating circumstances **des circonstances** (f) **atténuantes**
I extradite **j'extrade**
eye-witness **le témoin oculaire**
I find guilty **je déclare coupable**
he was found guilty **il a été déclaré coupable**
I give evidence **je témoigne**
I give evidence for the defence/ defense **je témoigne pour la défense**
guilt **la culpabilité**
guilty **coupable**
high court of appeal **la cour de cassation**
impeach **je mets** (mettre) **en accusation**
impeachment **la mise en accusation**
indictment **l'acte** (f) **d'accusation**
indictment in court **le réquisitoire**
innocence **l'innocence** (f)
innocent **innocent, non coupable**
judge **le juge**
juror **le juré**
jury **le jury**
jury-box **le banc des jurés**
justice **la justice**
lawsuit **le procès**
lawyer **l'avocat** (m)
leniency **la clémence**
life imprisonment **la peine de prison à vie, la réclusion à vie à perpétuité**
litigation **le litige**
magistrate **le magistrat**
magistrate's court **le tribunal d'instance**
mercy **la pitié, l'indulgence** (f)
minor offence **le délit mineur**

miscarriage of justice   **l'erreur** *(f)* **judiciaire**
motive   **le motif, l'intention** *(f)*
not guilty   **non coupable**
oath   **le serment**
offence   **le délit, l'infraction** *(f)*
on remand   **en détention préventive, en prévention**
I pass judgement   **je prononce, je rends** *(rendre)* **un jugement**
perjury   **le faux serment, le parjure**
plea   **la défense, l'argument** *(m)*
I plead (not) guilty   **je plaide (non) coupable**
premeditation   **la préméditation**
I prosecute   **je poursuis** *(poursuivre)* **en justice**
prosecution   **l'accusation** *(f)*
public prosecutor   **le procureur (de la République)**
public prosecutor's office   **le parquet**
I question   **je questionne**
I interrogate   **j'interroge**
retrial   **le nouveau procès**
I rescue   **je sauve**

reward   **la récompense**
speech for the defence/defense   **le plaidoyer, la plaidoirie**
I stand accused   **je suis accusé**
I stand bail for *(someone)*   **je me porte garant pour**
statement   **la déposition**
I sue/I take to court   **j'intente un procès à**
summing up   **le résumé**
summons   **la citation**
I suspect   **je soupçonne, je suspecte**
suspect   **le suspect, la suspecte**
Supreme Court   **la Cour suprême**
sustained!   **accordée!**
I swear   **je jure**
I take legal proceedings   **je poursuis** *(poursuivre)* **en justice**
I take prisoner   **je fais prisonnier**
trial   **le procès**
unanimous   **unanime**
verdict   **le verdict**
I witness   **je suis témoin de, j'assiste à**
witness   **le témoin**
writ   **l'acte** *(m)* **judiciaire**

The case against the accused was dismissed on grounds of insufficient evidence.

On a déclaré un non-lieu pour insuffisance de preuves.

The accused had strong connections in the underworld.

L'accusé avait des relations importantes dans le milieu.

The judge imposed a fine of 5,000 French francs and ordered the accused to pay costs.

Le juge a imposé une amende de 5.000 francs et a condamné l'accuséaux dépens.

A man will appear in court today charged with the attempted murder of a 14-month old baby boy.

Un homme, inculpé d'une tentative de meurtre d'un enfant de 14 mois, comparaîtra ce matin devant la Cour d'Assises.

26c Punishment & crime prevention

Punishment

confinement/imprisonment **la réclusion (criminelle)**

in solitary confinement **en isolement**

I convict **je déclare coupable**

convict **le détenu**

death penalty **la peine de mort**

I deport **je déporte**

I escape **je m'échappe, je m'évade**

fine **l'amende** *(f)*

I fine **je condamne à une amende**

I free **je libère** *(libérer)*

hard labour/labor **les travaux** *(m)* **forcés**

I imprison **j'emprisonne, je mets** *(mettre)* **en prison**

jail sentence **la peine de prison**

life sentence **la réclusion à perpétuité**

prison **la prison**

prisoner **le détenu, la détenue, le prisonnier, la prisonnière**

I punish **je punis**

punishment **la punition, le châtiment**

I release on bail **je mets** *(mettre)* **en liberté provisoire sous caution**

I reprieve a condemned prisoner **j'accorde une remise de peine au condamné**

I sentence to death **je condamne à mort**

I serve a sentence **je purge une peine**

sentence **la sentence, la peine**

severity **la sévérité**

suspended sentence **la condamnation avec sursis**

a term of 10 years **une peine de 10 ans**

Crime prevention

alarm **l'alarme** *(f)*

burglar/car alarm **la sonnerie d'alarme**

autopsy **l'autopsie** *(f)*

arrest **l'arrestation** *(f)*

I arrest **j'arrête**

baton **la matraque**

(hearing) in camera **à huis clos**

chief of police **le commissaire de police**

civil law **le code civile**

crime prevention **la lutte contre le crime**

criminal law **le droit pénal**

criminal record **le casier judiciaire**

clean *(record)* **vierge**

customs **la douane**

customs officer **le douanier**

deportation **la déportation**

– What was the verdict in the trial?

– He was sentenced to four years imprisonment.

– Will he serve that long?

– No, nothing like it. He'd already spent 8 months on remand/ awaiting trial. He'll probably be out in two years.

– Quel a été le verdict à la fin du procès?

– On l'a condamné à une peine de quatre ans.

– Et il en purgera autant?

– Pas du tout! Il avait déjà passé huit mois en détention préventive, avant le procès. Il en sortira probablement dans deux ans.

detective **le détective**
drugs raid **la rafle, la saisie de drogues**
drugs squad **la Brigade des Stupéfiants, les Stups** *(fam)*
enquiry/inquiry **l'enquête** *(f)*
error **l'erreur** *(f)*, **la bavure**
escape **la fuite, l'évasion** *(f)*
I escape (to) **j'échappe, je m'échappe (de)**
examination **l'examen** *(m)*
I examine **j'examine**
extradition **l'extradition** *(f)*
fingerprints **les empreintes** *(f)* **digitales**
fugitive **le fugitif, la fugitive**
guard dog **le chien de garde**
handcuff **les menottes** *(f)*
identikit/photofit picture **le portrait-robot**
informer **le délateur, la délatrice**
interview **l'entrevue** *(f)*
I interview **j'interroge**
I investigate **je fais une enquête**
investigation **l'enquête** *(f)*
investigator **un investigateur, une investigatrice**
private investigator **le détective privé**
key **la clé**
law **la loi**
law-breaking **l'infraction** *(f)*, **le délit**
lock **la serrure**

I lock **je ferme à clef**
padlock **le cadenas**
plain-clothes **en civil**
police **la police**
policeman/police officer **l'agent** *(m)* **de police**
policewoman **la femme agent (de police)**
police badge **la plaque**
police constable *(UK)* **l'agent** *(m)*, **le gendarme**
police record **le casier judiciaire**
clean *(record)* **vierge**
police station **le commissariat**
reward **la récompense**
riot police **les CRS (la Compagnie Républicaine de Sécurité)**
security **la sécurité**
security firm **la société de surveillance**
I set bail at $5,000 **je fixe la caution à $5.000**
speed trap **le piège de police pour contrôle de vitesse**
station **le commissariat**
traffic police **la police de la route/circulation**
traffic warden **le contractuel, la contractuelle**
truncheon **la matraque**
warrant **le mandat**
search warrant **le mandat de perquisition**

– Did he plead guilty?
– Yes, to manslaughter on grounds of diminished responsibility/insanity.

He was convicted of breaking and entering and given a suspended sentence of two years.

– Il a plaidé coupable?
– Oui, à l'homicide involontaire, pour raison de responsabilité atténuée.

Il a été déclaré coupable de vol avec effraction, et on l'a condamné à une peine de deux ans avec sursis.

➤ ADDICTION & VIOLENCE 11d

27 **War & Peace**

27a War

I abduct **j'enlève** *(enlever)*
aggression **l'agression** *(f)*
aerial bombing **le bombardement aérien**
air force **l'armée** *(f)* **de l'air**
I airlift **évacue par pont aérien**
air-raid **l'attaque** *(f)* **aérienne, le raid aérien**
air-raid shelter **l'abri** *(m)*
air-raid warning **l'alerte** *(f)* **(aérienne)**
ambush **l'embuscade** *(f)*
anti-aircraft **anti-aérien[ne]**
army **l'armée** *(f)*
I assassinate **j'assassine**
assault **l'assaut** *(m)*
atomic **atomique**
atrocity **l'atrocité** *(f)*
I attack **j'attaque**
attack **l'attaque** *(f)*
barracks **la caserne**
battle **la bataille**
battlefield **le champ de bataille**
blast **l'explosion** *(f)*, **le souffle**
I blockade **je bloque**
blockade **le blocus**
I blow up **je fais sauter**
bomb alert **l'alerte** *(f)* **à la bombe**
bombardment **le bombardement**
brave **courageux [-se]**
war breaks out **la guerre éclate**
I call up **j'appelle** *(appeler)* **sous les drapeaux**
camp **le camp**
campaign **la campagne**
I capture **je capture**
causes of war **les causes** *(f)*
I claim responsibility for **je revendique**

I commit *(an act)* **je commets** *(commettre)*
conflict **le conflit**
confrontation **l'affrontement** *(m)*
I contaminate **je contamine**
conventional *(weapon)* **classique**
court-marshal **le conseil de guerre**
cowardly **lâche**
the plane crashes **l'avion** *(m)* **s'écrase**
I crush *(opposition)* **j'écrase**
I declare (war) **je déclare (la guerre)**
defeat **la défaite**
I defeat **je bats** *(battre)*
I am defeated **je suis vaincu** *(vaincre)*
defence/defense **la défense**
I defend **je défends**
I destroy **je détruis** *(détruire)*
I detain **je détiens** *(détenir)*
I detect **je détecte, je découvre** *(découvrir)*
devastating **dévastateur [-trice]**
enemy **l'ennemi** *(m)*
espionage **l'espionnage** *(m)*
ethnic cleansing **le nettoyage/ l'épuration** *(f)* **ethnique**
I evacuate **j'évacue**
evacuation **l'évacuation** *(f)*
I fight a battle **je livre bataille**
I fight off **je repousse**
I flee **je fuis** *(fuir)*, **je m'enfuis** *(enfuir)*
front **le front**
genocide **le génocide**
guerrilla warfare **la guerrilla**
harmful **nuisible**

headquarters **le quartier général**
hostilities **les hostilités** *(f)*
I interrogate **j'interroge**
interrogation **l'interrogation** *(f)*
I intervene **j'interviens** *(intervenir)*
intervention **l'intervention** *(f)*
intimidation **l'intimidation** *(f)*
I invade **j'envahis**
invasion **l'invasion** *(f)*
I issue an ultimatum **je lance un ultimatum**
I liquidate **j'anéantis**
manoeuvres/maneuvers **les manœuvres** *(f)*
massacre **le massacre**
missing in action **porté disparu**
military service **le service militaire**
mobilization **la mobilisation**
I mobilize **je mobilise**
morale **le moral**
multilateral **multilatéral**
navy **la marine**
nuclear **nucléaire**
occupation **l'occupation** *(f)*
I occupy **j'occupe**
offensive **l'offensive** *(f)*
I patrol **je fais une patrouille**
peace **la paix**
propaganda **la propagande**
I provoke **je provoque**
battle rages **la bataille fait rage**
raid **le raid**

rank **le grade, le rang**
reinforcements **les renforts** *(m)*
reprisals **les représailles** *(f)*
I resist **je résiste à**
resistance **la résistance**
review **le revue**
I revolt **je me révolte**
revolution **la révolution**
riot **l'émeute** *(f)*
rubble **les décombres** *(f)*
shelter **l'abri** *(m)*
skirmish **l'accrochage** *(m)*
I spy **je fais de l'espionnage**
I start a war **je déclare la guerre**
strategy **la stratégie**
striking power **la force de frappe**
the vessel submerges **le vaisseau plonge/s'immerge**
the vessel surfaces **le vaisseau fait surface**
survival **la survie**
tactics **la tactique**
terrorist attack **l'attentat** *(m)* **terroriste**
I threaten **je menace**
trench **la tranchée**
underground **clandestin**
war **la guerre**
war crime **le crime de guerre**
war-mongering **belliciste**
I win **je gagne, je suis victorieux [-se]**

Hitler invaded Poland on September 1, 1939. Two days later, Britain and France declared war on Germany.

Hitler envahit la Pologne le 1er septembre 1939. Deux jours après, la Grande-Bretagne et la France déclarèrent la guerre à l'Allemagne.

The Christmas truce was broken as hostilities broke out again in Bosnia.

La trêve de Noël a été rompue, alors que des hostilités ont de nouveau éclaté en Bosnie.

Civil wars are the bloodiest of all.

Les plus ensanglantées de toutes sont les guerres civiles.

➤ PEACE, INTERNATIONAL RELATIONS 27c

27b Military personnel & weaponry

aggressor   l'agresseur *(m)*
ally   un allié, une alliée
archer   l'archer *(m)*
assassin   l'assassin *(m)*
casualty *(dead)*   le mort
   casualty *(injured)*   le blessé
cavalry   la cavalerie
civilian   le civil, la civile
commandos   les commandos *(m)*
conscientious objector   l'objecteur
   (m) de conscience
conscript   le conscrit, l'appelé *(m)*
convoy   le convoi
deserter   le déserteur
division   la division
foot soldier   le fantassin
general   le général
guard   le garde
guerrilla   le guerrillero
hostage   l'otage *(m)*
infantry   l'infanterie *(f)*
intelligence officer   l'officier *(m)* de
   renseignements
marines *(UK)*   les fusiliers marins
   (m)
marines *(US)*   les marines *(m)*
NCO   le sous-officier
orderly   le planton
parachutist   le parachutiste
prisoner of war   le prisonnier de
   guerre
rebel   le/la rebelle
recruit   la recrue
regiment   le régiment
seaman/sailor   le marin
secret agent   l'agent *(m)* secret
sentry   la sentinelle
sniper   le tireur isolé, le sniper
soldier   le soldat
spy   l'espion *(m)*
squadron   l'escadron *(m)*
staff   l'état-major *(m)*
terrorist   le terroriste
traitor   le traitre

troops   les troupes *(f)*
victor   le vainqueur
War Minister/Secretary of War   le
   Ministre de la Guerre

Weaponry & its effects

I aim (at)   je vise (sur)
aircraft carrier   le porte-avions
ammunition   les munitions *(f)*
armaments   les armements *(m)*
armoured/armored   blindé
arms   les armes *(m)*
arms manufacturer   le fabricant
   d'armes
arms race   la course aux armements
artillery   l'artillerie *(f)*
bacteriological   bactériologique
barbed wire   les barbelés *(m)*
bayonet   la baïonnette
I bomb(ard)   je bombarde
bomb   la bombe
bombardment   le bombardement
bomber *(aircraft)*   le bombardier
bullet   la balle
car bomb   la voiture piégée
crossbow   l'arbalète *(f)*
chemical   chimique
destroyer *(ship)*   le contre-
   torpilleur, le destroyer
I execute   j'exécute
I explode a bomb   je fais exploser
   une bombe
explosive   l'explosif *(m)*
fall-out   les retombées *(f)*
fighter plane   l'avion *(m)* de
   chasse, le chasseur
I fire (at)   je tire (sur)
frigate   la frégate
gas   le gaz
gas attack   l'attaque *(m)* au gaz
gun   le fusil
hand-grenade   la grenade
H-bomb   la bombe-H
it hits   il frappe, il atteint

(atteindre) le but
jet *(plane)* le réacteur
I kill je tue
knife le couteau
laser le laser
letter-bomb la lettre piégée
machine-gun la mitrailleuse
minefield le champ de mines
mine-sweeper le dragueur de mines
missile le missile
missile launcher le lance-missiles
mortar le mortier
neutron bomb la bombe à neutrons
nuclear test l'essai *(m)* nucléaire
nuclear warhead la tête *(f)* nucléaire, l'ogive *(f)* nucléaire
pistol le pistolet
poison gas le gaz toxique/asphyxiant
radar le radar
radar screen l'écran *(m)* du radar
radiation la radiation
radiation sickness le mal des rayons
radio-active radioactif [-ve]
revolver le revolver
rifle le fusil

rocket la fusée
rocket attack l'attaque *(f)* à la roquette
sabotage le sabotage
shell l'obus *(m)*
I shoot dead j'abats *(abattre)*
shotgun le fusil de chasse
shrapnel le shrapnel, les éclats *(m)* d'obus
siege le siège
I sink the ship je fais couler le navire
the ship sinks le navire coule/sombre
I stock-pile je constitue des réserves
submachine-gun la mitraillette
submarine le sous-marin
tank le char
target la cible
I test je teste, j'examine
torpedo la torpille
torpedo attack une attaque à la torpille
I torpedo je torpille
warship le vaisseau de guerre
weapon l'arme *(f)*
wound la blessure, la plaie
I wound je blesse

Yesterday a man was shot dead by a sniper.

Hier un homme a été abattu par un tireur isolé/un sniper.

The explosion was several miles away, but it knocked everyone to the ground. Then the alert sounded for chemical weapons.

L'explosion s'est produite à plusieurs kilomètres de distance, mais la force a jeté tout le monde au sol. Puis on a sonné l'alerte aux armes chimiques.

The event which has most marked the twentieth century is the Second World War.

L'événement qui a le plus marqué le vingtième siècle, c'est la deuxième guerre mondiale.

➤ CRIME 26a

27c Peace & international relations

Peace

ban the bomb campaign **la campagne contre la bombe**
cease-fire **le cessez-le-feu**
control **le contrôle**
I demobilize **je démobilise**
deterrent **la force de dissuasion**
I diminish tension **je travaille pour diminuer la tension**
disarmament **le désarmement**
exchanges of information **des échanges** *(m)* **d'informations**
free **libre**
I free **je libère** *(libérer)*
human rights **les droits** *(m)* **de l'homme**
I make peace **je conclus** *(conclure)* **la paix**
I mediate **je sers** *(servir)* **d'intermédiaire**
national service **le service national**
negotiable **négociable, à débattre**
negotiation **la négociation, les** *(m)* **pourparlers**
neutral **neutre**
neutrality **la neutralité**
pacifist **le/la pacifiste**
pacifism **le pacifisme**
peace agreement **l'accord** *(m)*
peace plan **le plan pour la paix**

peace protester **le militant pour la paix**
peace talks **les pourparlers** *(m)* **de paix**
peace-keeping force **les forces** *(f)* **de maintien de la paix**
surrender **la capitulation**
I surrender **je me rends** *(se rendre)*, **je capitule**
test ban **l'interdiction** *(f)* **des essais (nucléaires)**
treaty **le traité**
uncommitted **neutraliste**
victory **la victoire**

International relations

aid **l'aide** *(f)*
ambassador **l'ambassadeur** *(m)*
arms reduction **la réduction des armements**
attaché **un attaché, une attachée**
citizen **le citoyen, la citoyenne**
citizenship **la citoyenneté**
consul **le consul**
consulate **le consulat**
developing countries **les pays** *(m)* **en voie de développement**
diplomacy **la diplomatie**
diplomat **le/la diplomate**
diplomatic immunity **l'immunité** *(f)* **diplomatique**

Emergency food-aid was dropped on the mountains by UN Forces.

Les forces de l'ONU ont parachuté une aide alimentaire d'urgence dans les montagnes.

The French Government was in danger of being embroiled in a diplomatic row.

Le gouvernement français risquait de se laisser entraîner dans une dispute diplomatique.

Importers continue to take advantage of the lowest possible tariff rates.

Les importateurs continuent de bénéficier des droits de douane les plus bas possibles.

embassy   **l'ambassade** *(f)*
emergency   **d'urgence**
envoy   **un envoyé, une envoyée**
famine   **la famine**
foreign   **extérieur, étranger [-ère]**
foreigner   **un étranger, une étrangère**
foreign relations   **les relations** *(f)* **extérieures**
gap between rich and poor   **l'écart** *(m)* **entre les riches et les pauvres**
I impose sanctions (against)   **je prends** *(prendre)* **des sanctions** *(f)* **économiques (contre)**
international aid   **l'aide** *(f)*
I join (organization)   **je deviens** *(devenir)* **membre de**
national security   **la sécurité nationale**
non aligned   **non aligné**
overseas   **outre-mer**
partner   **le/la partenaire**
relief organization   **l'organisation** *(f)* **humanitaire**
relief supplies   **les secours** *(m)*
I represent   **je représente**
I ratify (treaty)   **je ratifie**
sanctions   **les sanctions** *(f)*
summit meeting   **la rencontre au sommet**
Third World   **le Tiers Monde**

Trade

agricultural policy   **la politique agricole**
balance of payments   **la balance des paiements**
balance of trade   **la balance commerciale**
currency   **la monnaie, la devise**
customs   **la douane**
customs union   **l'union** *(f)* **douanière**
exchange rate   **le taux de change**
exports   **les exportations** *(f)*
floating currency   **la devise flottante**
it floats   **il flotte**
foreign investment   **l'investissement** *(m)* **étranger**
free trade   **le libre-échange**
free-trade zone   **la zone franche**
import controls   **les limites** *(f)* **sur les importations**
imports   **les importations** *(f)*
tariff barriers   **la barrière douanière**
tariffs   **les tarifs** *(m)* **douaniers**
trade   **le commerce**
trade gap   **le déficit extérieur**
trade talks   **les négociations** *(f)* **commerciales**
trading partner   **la partenaire commercial**

The Secretary of State left this morning for a meeting with his opposite number in London.

Le Ministre des Affaires Étrangères est parti ce matin pour un meeting avec son homologue à Londres.

The European Commission is looking into allegations of unfair trading practices/practises.

La Commission Européenne va faire une enquête sur certaines allégations de pratiques commerciales frauduleuse.

➤ COUNTRIES App.20a; THE ECONOMY 14e

C

APPENDICES

Appendices

Appendices are numbered by the Vocabulary to which they most closely relate.

3b Clocks & watches

alarm clock **le réveil**
clock **la pendule**
cuckoo clock **le coucou**
dial **le cadran**
digital watch **la montre à affichage numérique**
egg-timer **le sablier**
grandfather clock **l'horloge** *(f)* **comtoise/de parquet**
hand (of a clock) **l'aiguille** *(f)*
 second hand **la trotteuse**
 minute hand **la grande aiguille**
 hour hand **la petite aiguille**
hour-glass **le sablier**
pendulum **le balancier**
stop-watch **le chronomètre**
sundial **le cadran solaire**
timer *(cooker/lighting)* **la minuterie**
watch **la montre**
watch strap **le bracelet de montre**
I wind up **je remonte**

4d Mathematical & geometrical terms

acute **aigu**
algebra **l'algèbre** *(f)*
algebraic **algébrique**
Arabic numerals **les nombres** *(m)* **arabes**
arithmetic **l'arithmétique** *(m)*
arithmetical **arithmétique**
average **la moyenne**
axis **l'axe** *(m)*
circumference **la circonférence**
complex **complexe**
constant **la constante**
cube **le cube**
cube root **la racine cubique**
cubed **au cube**
decimal **la décimale**
equality **l'égalité** *(f)*
factor **le facteur**
I factorize **je factorise**
fraction **la fraction**
function **la fonction**
geometry **la géométrie**
geometrical **géométrique**
imaginary **imaginaire**
integer **le nombre entier**
irrational **irrationnel**
logarithm **le logarithme**
mean **la moyenne**
median **la médiane**
multiple **le multiple**
nine is to three as ... **neuf est à trois ce que ...**
natural **naturel**
numerical **numérique**
obtuse **obtus**
prime **premier [-ère]**
product **le produit**
probability **la probabilité**
I raise to a power **j'élève à la puissance**
 to the fifth power **puissance cinq**
 to the nth power **puissance n**
radius **le rayon**
rational **rationnel**
quotient **le quotient**
real **réel**
reciprocal **réciproque**
Roman **Romain**
set **l'ensemble** *(m)*
square **le carré**
square root **la racine carrée**
symmetry **la symétrie**
symmetrical **symétrique**
table **la table**

tangent la tangente
trigonometry la trigonométrie
variable la variable
vector le vecteur

5b Parts of the body

ankle la cheville
arm le bras
back le dos
backbone la colonne vertébrale
bladder la vessie
blood le sang
blood pressure la tension
  artérielle
body le corps
bone l'os *(m)*
bowel l'intestin *(m)*
brain le cerveau
breast la poitrine, le sein
buttock les fesses *(f)*
cheek la joue
chest la poitrine
chin le menton
ear l'oreille *(f)*
elbow le coude
eye l'œil *(m)*, des yeux
eyebrow le sourcil
eyelash le cil
face le visage
finger le doigt
fingernail l'ongle *(m)*
foot le pied
forehead le front
genitalia les organes *(m)*
  génitaux
gland la glande
hair les cheveux *(m)*
hand la main
head la tête
heart le coeur
hip la hanche
hormone l'hormone *(f)*
index finger l'index *(m)*
jaw la mâchoire
kidney le rein
knee le genou

knuckle l'articulation *(f)*
leg la jambe
lid la paupière
lip la lèvre
liver le foie
lung le poumon
mouth la bouche
muscle le muscle
nape of neck la nuque
neck le cou
nose le nez
nostril la narine
organ l'organe *(m)*
part of body la partie du corps
penis le pénis
sex organs les organes *(m)*
  sexuels
shoulder l'épaule *(f)*
skin la peau
stomach l'estomac *(m)*
thigh la cuisse
throat la gorge
thumb le pouce
toe l'orteil *(m)*
tongue la langue
tooth la dent
vagina le vagin
waist la taille
womb l'utérus *(m)*
wrist le poignet

6a Human characteristics

absent-minded distrait
active actif [-ve]
adaptable capable de s'adapter
affection (-ate) l'affection *(f)*,
  affectueux [-se]
aggression l'agression *(f)*
aggressive agressif [-ve]
ambition l'ambition *(f)*
ambitious ambitieux [-se]
amusing amusant
anxious anxieux [-se]
arrogant arrogant
artistic artistique
attractive attrayant

6a Human characteristics (cont.)

bad-tempered   **qui a mauvais caractère**

bad/evil   **méchant**

boring   **ennuyeux [-se]**

brave   **brave**

care   **le soin**

careful   **soigneux [-se]**

careless   **négligent**

charm   **le charme**

charming   **charmant**

cheek   **l'insolence** *(f)*

cheeky   **insolent**

cheerful   **joyeux [-se]**

clever   **intelligent**

cold   **froid**

comic   **comique**

confidence   **la confiance**

confident   **confiant**

conscientious   **consciencieux [-se]**

courage   **le courage**

courtesy   **la courtoisie**

cowardly   **lâche**

creative   **créatif [-ve]**

critical   **critique**

cruel   **cruel[le]**

cruelty   **la cruauté**

cultured   **cultivé**

cunning   **l'habileté** *(f)*

curiosity   **la curiosité**

decisive (in-)   **(in)décisif [-ve]**

demanding   **exigeant**

dependence   **la dépendance**

dependent (in-)   **(in)dépendant**

dishonest   **malhonnête**

dishonesty   **la malhonnêteté**

disobedience   **la désobéissance**

distrustful   **méfiant**

eccentric   **excentrique**

energetic   **énergique**

envious   **envieux**

envy   **l'envie** *(f)*

extroverted   **extraverti**

faithful (un-)   **(in)fidèle**

faithfulness   **la fidélité**

friendly (un-)   **(in)amical**

frivolous   **frivole**

generosity   **la générosité**

generous   **généreux [-se]**

gentle   **gentil[le]**

gentleness   **la gentillesse**

good-tempered   **qui a bon caractère**

gluttony   **la gourmandise**

greed *(for money)*   **l'avidité** *(f)*

greedy   **gourmand**

hard-working   **travailleur**

helpful   **serviable**

honest   **honnête**

honesty   **l'honnêteté** *(f)*

honour/honor   **l'honneur** *(m)*

humane (in-)   **(in)humain**

humble   **humble**

humorous   **humoristique**

hypocritical   **hypocrite**

idealistic   **idéaliste**

imagination   **l'imagination** *(f)*

imaginative   **imaginatif [-ve]**

independence   **l'indépendance** *(f)*

individualistic   **individualiste**

innocence   **l'innocence** *(f)*

innocent   **innocent**

inquisitive   **curieux [-se]**

intelligence   **l'intelligence** *(f)*

intelligent   **intelligent**

introverted   **introverti**

ironic   **ironique**

kind   **gentil[le]**

kindness   **la gentillesse**

laziness   **la paresse**

lazy   **paresseux [-se]**

liberal   **libéral**

likeable   **sympathique**

lively   **vivant**

lonely   **seul**

loveable   **adorable**

mad   **fou [folle]**

madness   **la folie**

malicious   **méchant**

mature (im-)   **(im)mature**

mean/stingy   **avare**

modest   **modeste**

modesty **la modestie**
moody **lunatique, ténébreux [-se]**
moral (im-) **(im)moral**
naive **naïf [-ve]**
naivity **la naïveté**
natural **naturel[le]**
naughty **méchant**
nervous **nerveux [-se]**
nervousness **la nervosité**
nice **gentil[le]**
niceness **la gentillesse**
obedience **l'obéissance** *(f)*
obedient (dis-) **(dés)obéissant**
open **franc[he]**
openness **la franchise**
optimistic **optimiste**
original (-ity) **original**
originality **l'originalité** *(f)*
patience (im-) **la patience**
 (l'impatience *(f)*)
patient (im-) **(im)patient**
pessimistic **pessimiste**
pleasant **agréable**
polite (im-) **(im)poli**
politeness **la politesse**
possessive **possessif [-ve]**
prejudiced (un-) **(im)partial**
pride **la fierté**
proud **fier [-ère]**
reasonable (un-) **(ir)raisonnable**
rebellious **rebelle**
reserved **réservé**
respect **le respect**
respectable **respectable**
respectful **respectueux [-se]**
responsible (ir-) **(ir)responsable**
rude **vulgaire**
rudeness **la vulgarité**
sad **triste**
sarcastic **sarcastique**
scornful **méprisant**
self-confident **sûr de soi**
self-esteem **l'amour** *(m)* **propre**
selfish (un-) **égoïste (généreux**
 [-se])
selfishness **l'égoïsme** *(m)*

self-sufficient **autosuffisant**
sensible **sensé**
sensitive (in-) **(in)sensible**
serious **sérieux [-se]**
shy **timide**
silent **silencieux [-se]**
silly **bête**
sincerity **la sincérité**
skilful **doué**
sociable (un-) **(in)sociable**
strange **bizarre**
strict **sévère**
stubborn **têtu**
stupid(ity) **stupide (la stupidité)**
suspicious **suspect**
sweet **adorable**
sympathetic (un-) **compatissant**
 (peu compatissant)
sympathy **la compassion**
tact **le tact**
he is tactful/tactless **il est plein de**
 tact/il manque de tact
talented **talentueux [-se]**
talkative **bavard**
temperamental **capricieux [-se]**
thoughtful **attentionné**
thoughtless **étourdi**
tidy (un-) **(dés)ordonné**
tolerance (in-) **la tolérance**
 (l'intolérance *(f)*)
tolerant (in-) **(in)tolérant**
traditional (un-) **(non-)**
 traditionnel[le]
trust **la confiance**
trusting **confiant**
vain **vaniteux [-se]**
vanity **la vanité**
violent **violent**
virtuous **virtueux [-se]**
warm **chaleureux [-se]**
well-adjusted **bien adapté**
well-behaved *(child)* **sage**
wisdom **la sagesse**
wise **sage**
wit **l'esprit** *(m)*
witty **spirituel[le]**

8b Tools

axe/ax **la hache**
bit **le foret**
blade **la lame**
bolt **le boulon**
bucket **le seau**
chain saw **la tronçonneuse**
chisel **le ciseau**
crowbar **la pince-monseigneur** *(m)*
drill **le foret, la mèche**
file **la lime**
garden gloves **les gants** *(m)*
garden shears **la cisaille de jardinier**
hammer **le marteau**
hedge clippers **le sécateur à haie**
hoe **l'houe** *(f)*, **la binette**
hose **le tuyau d'arrosage**
ladder **l'échelle** *(f)*
lawn-mower **la tondeuse (à gazon)**
mallet **le maillet**
nail **le clou**
nut **l'écrou** *(m)*
paint **la peinture**
paint brush **le pinceau**
pickax(e) **la pioche**
plane **le rabot**
pliers **le pince**
rake **le râteau**
roller **le rouleau de jardin**
sandpaper **le papier de verre**
saw **la scie**
screw **la vis**
screwdriver **le tournevis**
shovel **la pelle**
spade **la bêche**
spanner/wrench (adjustable) **la clé à molette**
spirit level **le niveau à bulle**
stepladder **l'escabeau** *(m)*
toolbox **la boîte à outils**
trowel **le déplantoir**
varnish **le vernis**
vice **l'étau** *(m)*
weedkiller **le désherbant, l'herbicide** *(m)*

9a Shops, stores & services

antique shop/store **(chez) l'antiquaire** *(m)*
art shop/store **la boutique d'objets d'art**
baker's/bakery **la boulangerie**
bank **la banque**
betting shop//bookmaker's **le PMU**
bookshop/store **la librairie**
boutique **la boutique**
butcher's **la boucherie**
cakeshop/store **la patisserie**
car accesory/spares shop/store **le magasin de pièces détachées**
charity shop/store **la boutique d'une œuvre de bienfaisance**
chemist's/drugstore **la droguerie**
clothes shop/store **la boutique de prêt-à-porter**
cobbler's **la cordonnerie**
cosmetics shop/store **la parfumerie**
covered market **le marché couvert**
dairy **la crèmerie**
delicatessen **la charcuterie, le traiteur**
department store **le grand magasin**
dress shop/store **la boutique de prêt-à-porter**
drugstore **la pharmacie**
dry-cleaners **la blanchisserie**
electrical shop/store **le comptoir électrique**
fast-food shop/store **le restaurant à service rapide**
fishmonger's **la poissonnerie**
fishstall **le poissonnier (au marché)**
florist's **chez le/la fleuriste**
furniture shop/store **le magasin de meubles**
garden centre/center **la jardinerie**

greengrocer's **le magasin de fruits et légumes**

grocer's **l'épicerie** *(f)*

hairdresser **le coiffeur, la coiffeuse**

hairdresser's **le salon de coiffure**

hardware shop/store **la quincaillerie**

health-food shop/store **le magasin de diététique**

hypermarket **l'hypermarché** *(m)*

indoor market **le marché couvert**

jeweller's/jewelry store **la bijouterie**

kiosk **le kiosque**

launderette **la laverie**

lottery shop/store/kiosk **le kiosque de PMU**

mail-order house **la maison de vente par correspondance**

market **le marché**

menswear shop/store **le magasin de prêt-à-porter masculin**

model shop/store **le magasin d'aéromodélisme**

music shop/store **le magasin de musique**

newsagent's/newsstand **la maison de la presse**

newspaper kiosk **le kiosque à journaux**

open-air/outdoor market **le marché en plein air**

optician's **chez l'opticien**

petshop/pet store **le magasin pour animaux domestiques**

pharmacy **la pharmacie**

photographic shop/store **le magasin de matériel photographique**

post-office **la poste**

pottery shop/store **le magasin de poterie**

shoe repair shop/store **la cordonnerie**

shoeshop/store **le magasin de chaussures**

shop/store **le magasin**

shopping arcade **le centre commercial, la galerie marchande**

shopping centre **le centre commercial**

shopping mall **la galerie marchande**

souvenir shop/store **le magasin de souvenirs**

sports shop/store **le magasin de sport**

stationer's/stationery store **la papeterie**

store **le magasin**

superstore **la grande surface**

supermarket **le supermarché**

sweetshop/candy store **le magasin de bonbons**

take-away food shop/store **le magasin de plats à emporter**

tobacconist's/tobacco store **le bureau de tabac**

toyshop/store **le magasin de jouets**

travel agent's/store **l'agence** *(f)* **de voyage**

vendor **le vendeur, la vendeuse**

vending machine **le distributeur**

video-shop/store **le magasin de cassettes vidéo**

9a Currencies

dollar **le dollar**

escudo **l'escudo** *(m)*

franc **le franc**

lira **la lire**

mark **le mark**

pence **les pence**

penny **le penny**

peseta **la peseta**

peso **le peso**

pound sterling **la livre sterling**

rouble **le rouble**

9c Jewellery/Jewelry

bangle **le bracelet**
chain bracelet **la gourmette**
brooch **la broche**
carat **le carat**
chain **la chaînette**
charm **la breloque**
cuff links **les boutons** (m) de **manchette**
earring **les boucles** (f) **d'oreilles**
engagement ring **la bague de fiançailles**
eternity ring **la bague de fidélité**
jewel **le bijou**
jewel box **le coffret à bijoux**
jewellery/jewelry **les bijoux** (m)
medallion **le médaillon**
necklace **le collier**
pendant **le pendentif**
precious stone/gem **la pierre précieuse**
real **véritable**
ring **la bague**
semi-precious **la pierre fine/semi-précieuse**
tiara **le diadème**
tie pin **l'épingle** (f) à cravate
wedding ring **l'alliance** (f)

9c Precious stones & metals

agate **l'agate** (f)
amber **l'ambre** (m)
amethyst **l'améthyste** (f)
chrome **le chrome**
copper **le cuivre**
coral **le corail**
crystal **le cristal**
diamond **le diamant**
emerald **l'émeraude** (f)
gold **l'or** (m)
gold plate **plaqué or**
ivory **l'ivoire** (m)
mother of pearl **la nacre**
onyx **l'onyx** (m)
pearl **la perle**

pewter **l'étain** (m)
platinum **le platine**
quartz **le quartz**
ruby **le rubis**
sapphire **le saphir**
silver plate **plaqué argent**
silver **l'argent** (m)
topaz **la topaze**
turquoise **la turquoise**

10c Herbs & spices

aniseed **l'anis** (m)
basil **le basilic**
bay leaf **la feuille de laurier** (m)
caper **la câpre**
caraway **le cumin**
chivers **la ciboulette**
cinnamon **la cannelle**
clove **le clou de girofle** (m)
dill **l'aneth** (m)
garlic **l'ail** (m)
ginger **le gingembre**
marjoram **la marjolaine**
mint **la menthe**
mixed herbs **les fines herbes** (f)
mustard **la moutarde**
nutmeg **la noix (de) muscade** (f)
oregano **l'origan** (m)
parsley **le persil**
pepper **le poivre**
rosemary **le romarin**
saffron **le safran**
sage **la sauge**
tarragon **l'estragon** (m)
thyme **le thym**

10d Cooking utensils

alumin(i)um foil **le papier d'aluminium**
baking tray **la plaque à gâteaux**
carving knife **le couteau à découper**
colander **la passoire**
food processor **le robot de cuisine**

fork   la fourchette
frying pan/fry-pan   la poêle
grater   la râpe
greaseproof/wax paper   le papier
   sulfurisé
grill   le gril
kettle   la bouilloire
knife   le couteau
lid   le couvercle
pot   la marmite
rolling pin   le rouleau (à
   pâtisserie)
saucepan/casserole dish   la
   cocotte
scales   la balance
sieve   le tamis
skewer   la brochette
spatula   la spatule
spoon   la cuiller, la cuillère
tablespoon   la cuiller de service
tablespoonful   la cuillerée à soupe
teaspoon   la petite cuiller, la
   cuiller à thé/café
teaspoonful   la cuillerée à café
tenderizer   l'attendrisseur *(m)*
tin/can-opener   l'ouvre-boîtes *(m)*

___

10d Smoking

ashtray   le cendrier
box of matches   la boîte
   d'allumettes
cigar   le cigare
cigarette   la cigarette
lighter   le briquet
matches   les allumettes *(f)*
pipe   la pipe
smoke   la fumée
I smoke   je fume
smoking   fumer
tobacco   le tabac
tobacconist's   les bureaux *(m)* de
   tabac

11c Hospital departments

Admissions   l'accueil *(m)*
Casualty/Emergency   les urgences
   (f)
Consulting Room   la salle de
   consultation
Coronary Care   la cardiologie
Dialysis Unit   le service de dialyse
ENT/Ear, Nose and Throat   ORL
   (f), l'otorhynolaryngologie *(f)*
Eye Infirmary   le service
   d'ophtalmologie
Geriatrics   la gérontologie
Gynaecology Ward   le service de
   gynécologie
Infectious Diseases   les maladies
   (f) infectieuses
Intensive Care   les soins *(m)*
   intensifs
Intensive Care Ward   la salle de
   réanimation
Maternity   la maternité
Medical Ward   le service de
   médecine
Mortuary   la morgue
Oncology   l'oncologie *(f)*
Operating Theatre   le bloc
   opératoire
Orthopaedic   orthopédique
Out-Patients Department   le
   service de consultations
   externes
Paedeatrics   la pédiatrie
Pathology   la pathologie
Pharmacy   la pharmacie
Psychiatry   la psychiatrie
Reception   la réception
Recovery Room   la salle de soins
   post-opératoires
Surgery   la chirurgie
Transfusion   la transfusion
Treatment Room   la salle de soins
Ward   la salle
X-Ray   la radiographie

11c Illnesses & diseases

AIDS   le SIDA
angina   l'infection (f) pulmonaire
appendicitis   l'appendicite (f)
arthritis   l'arthrose (f)
asthma   l'asthme (m)
bacillus   le bacille
bacteria   la bactérie
bronchitis   la bronchite
bubonic plague   la peste
   bubonique
cancer   le cancer
catarrh   le catarrhe
chickenpox   la varicelle
cholera   le choléra
colic   la colique
cold   le rhume
constipation   la constipation
corn   le cor
cough   la toux
deafness   la surdité
death   la mort
depression   la dépression
dermatitis   la dermatite
diabetes   le diabète
diarrhoea   la diarrhée
diptheria   la diphtérie
disease   la maladie
dizziness   le vertige,
   l'étourdissement (m)
earache   le mal d'oreille
eczema   l'eczéma (m)
epilepsy   l'épilepsie
fever   la fièvre
flatulence   la flatulence
flu   la grippe
food-poisoning   l'intoxication (f)
   alimentaire
gall-stone   le calcul biliaire
German measles   la rubéole
gingivitis   la gingivite
gonorrhoea   la blennorragie
haemorrrhoids   les hémorroïdes
   (f)
headache   le mal de tête
heart attack   la crise cardiaque

hepatitis   l'hépatite (f)
hernia   la hernie
high blood pressure
   l'hypertension (f)
HIV   le VIH, le HIV
illness   la maladie
incontinence   l'incontinence (f)
influenza   la grippe
infection   l'infection (f)
jaundice   la jaunisse
leukaemia   la leucémie
malaria   le paludisme, la malaria
measles   la rougeole
meningitis   la méningite
mental illness   la maladie mentale
microbe   le microbe
migraine   la migraine
mumps   les oreillons
overdose   l'overdose (f)
piles   des hémorroïdes
pneumonia   la pneumonie
polio   la polio
pregnancy   la grossesse
rabies   la rage
rheumatism   le rhumatisme
salmonella   la salmonelle
scabies   la gale
seasickness   le mal de mer
sickness   la maladie
smallpox   la variole
stomach ache   le mal à l'estomac
stomach upset   l'indigestion (f)
stroke   l'attaque (f)
stye   l'orgelet (m)
syphilis   la syphilis
temperature   la température
tetanus   le tétanos
thrombosis   la thrombose
tonsillitis   l'amygdalite (f)
toothache   le mal de dents, (avoir)
   mal aux dents
tuberculosis   la tuberculose
ulcer   l'ulcère (m)
urinary infection   l'infection (f)
   urinaire
venereal disease   la maladie
   vénérienne

whooping cough   **la coqueluche**
yellow fever   **la fièvre jaune**

11d Hairdresser

bleach   **la décoloration**
blow-dry   **le brushing**
colour/color chart   **le nuancier**
colour/color rinse   **la coloration**
I cut   **je coupe**
dye   **la teinture**
fringe/bangs   **la frange**
hair   **les cheveux** (m)
   dry   **sec [sèche]**
   greasy/oily   **gras[se]**
   grey/gray   **gris**
haircut   **la coupe de cheveux**
I have my hair cut   **je me fais
   couper les cheveux**
hairdresser   **le coiffeur**
hairspray   **la laque**
hairdo   **la coiffure**
moustache   **la moustache**
perm(anent wave)   **la permanente**
setting lotion/gel   **le fixateur**
shampoo and set   **un shampooing
   et une mise en plis**
short   **court**
sideboards/sideburns   **les favoris**
   (pl)
sides (of head)   **les côtés** (m)
top (of head)   **le dessus de la tête**
trim   **la coupe d'entretien**
I trim   **je rafraîchis**
   I trim (beard)   **je taille**

13a Christian groups

Anglican Church   **l'Église** (f)
   anglicane
French Reformed Church   **l'Église**
   (f) **réformée de France**
Jehovah's Witnesses   **les Témoins**
   (m) **de Jéhovah**
Methodists   **les Méthodistes** (m)
Mormons   **les Mormons** (f)
   (l'Église (f) **de Jésus-Christ des**

   saints des derniers jours)
Old Catholic Church   **l'Église** (f)
   catholique traditionaliste
Pentecostalists   **les Églises** (f)
   pentecôtistes
Presyterians   **les Presbytériens**
   (m)
Roman Catholic Church   **l'Église**
   (f) **catholique**
Quakers/Society of Friends   **les
   Quakers, la Société religieuse
   des Amis**
Seventh Day Adventists   **les
   Adventistes** (m)
Unitarians   **les Unitariens** (m)

13b Holidays & religious festivals

All Saints (Nov 1)   **la Toussaint (le
   1er nov)**
All Souls (Nov 2)   **le jour des
   Morts (le 2 nov)**
Ascension Day   **l'Ascension** (f)
Ash Wednesday   **le mercredi des
   Cendres**
Assumption Day (Aug 15)
   l'Assomption (f) **(le 15 août)**
Bar-mitzvah   **le bar-mitzva**
Boxing Day (Dec 26)   **le lendemain
   de Noël (le 26 déc)**
Candlemass   **la Chandeleur**
Carneval   **Carnaval** (m)
Christmas   **Noël** (m)
   at Christmas   **à Noël**
Christmas Day   **le jour de Noël**
Christmas Eve   **la veille de Noël**
Corpus Christi   **la Fête-Dieu**
Divali   **le Dïpavâlî**
Easter   **Pâques** (fpl)
Easter Monday   **le lundi de
   Pâques**
Easter Sunday   **le dimanche de
   Pâques**
Eid   **l'Id** (m)
Feast of the Assumption
   l'Assomption (f)

festival   **le festival**
Good Friday   **le vendredi Saint**
Hanukkah   **Hanouka /la fête des lumières**
Hallowe'en   **la veille de la Toussaint**
Labour/Labor Day   **la fête du travail**
Lent   **le Carême**
New Year's Eve   **la Saint-Sylvestre**
New Year's Day   **le jour de l'an**
   Jewish New Year   **le Rosh Haschana**
Palm Sunday   **les Rameaux** *(m)*
Passover   **la Pâque**
Ramadan   **le Ramadan**
Sabbath   **le Chabbat, le sabbat**
Shrove Tuesday   **le Mardi gras**
Whitsuntide   **la Pentecôte**
Yom Kippur   **le Yom Kippour**

14b Professions & jobs

The arts

actor/actress   **un acteur, une actrice**
announcer   **un annonceur, une annonceuse**
architect   **un architecte**
artist   **un artiste**
book-seller   **un libraire**
cameraman   **un caméraman**
editor   **un rédacteur**
film/movie director   **un réalisateur**
film/movie star   **une star de cinéma**
journalist   **un/une journaliste**
musician   **un musicien, une musicienne**
painter (*artist*)   **un peintre**
photographer   **un photographe**
poet   **un poète**
printer   **un imprimeur**
producer (theatre)   **un metteur en scène**
publisher   **un éditeur**

reporter   **un reporter**
sculptor   **un sculpteur**
singer   **un chanteur, une chanteuse**
TV announcer   **un speaker, une speakerine**
writer   **un écrivain, un auteur**

Education & research

headteacher/principal   **un directeur, une directrice, un principal**
lecturer   **un professeur**
physicist   **un physicien, une physicienne**
primary teacher   **un instituteur, une institutrice**
researcher   **un chercheur, une chercheuse**
scientist   **un/une scientifique**
secondary teacher   **un professeur**
student   **un étudiant, une étudiante**
technician   **un technicien, une technicienne**

Food & retail

baker   **un boulanger, une boulangère**
brewer   **un brasseur**
butcher   **un boucher, une bouchère**
buyer   **un acheteur, une acheteuse**
caterer (supplying meals)   **un traiteur**
chemist/drugist   **un pharmacien, une pharmacienne**
icook   **un cuisinier, une cuisinière**
farmer   **un fermier**
fisherman   **un pêcheur**
fishmonger   **le poissonnier**
florist   **un fleuriste, une fleuriste**
greengrocer   **un marchand de fruits et légumes, un primeur**
grocer   **un épicier, une épicière**
jjeweller/jeweler   **un bijoutier, un**

bijoutière
pharmacist   un pharmacien
pork-butcher   un charcutier
representative   un représentant
shop assistant   un employé/une
   employée de magasin
shopkeeper/storekeeper   un
   commerçant, une
   commerçante
tobacconist   un marchand de
   tabac
waiter   un garçon (de café), un
   serveur
wine-grower   un viticulteur, une
   viticultrice

Government service
civil-servant   un/une fonctionnaire
clerk   un employé, une employée
customs officer   un douanier
fireman   un sapeur-pompier
judge   un juge
member of Parliament/senator   un
   député
minister   un ministre
officer   un officier
policeman   un agent de police
policewoman   une femme agent
   (de police)
politician   un homme politique
sailor   un marin
secret agent   un agent secret
serviceman   un militaire
soldier   un soldat

Health care
dentist   un/une dentiste
doctor (Dr)   un docteur, une
   femme docteur
midwife   une sage-femme
nurse   un infirmier, une infirmière
optician   un opticien, une
   opticienne
physician   un médecin
psychiatrist   un/une psychiatre
psychologist   un/une psychologue
surgeon   un chirurgien, une

femme chirurgien
vet   un/une vétérinaire

Manufacturing & construction
bricklayer   un maçon
builder   un constructeur, un
   entrepreneur
carpenter   un menuisier
engineer   un ingénieur
foreman   un contremaître
glazier   un vitrier
industrialist   un industriel, un chef
   d'industrie
labourer/laborer   un ouvrier
manufacturer   un fabricant
mechanic   un mécanicien
metalworker   un ferronnier
miner   un mineur
plasterer   un plâtrier
stonemason   un tailleur de
   pierres, un maçon

Services
accountant   un comptable
actuary   un/une actuaire
agent   un agent
bank-manager   un directeur de
   banque
business-man   un homme
   d'affaires
business-woman   une femme
   d'affaires
careers adviser   un conseiller, une
   conseillère d'orientation
caretaker   un/une concierge
cleaner   une femme de ménage,
   un agent de nettoyage
computer programmer   un
   progammeur, une
   progammeuse
counsellor   un conseiller, une
   conseillère
draughtsman   un dessinateur, une
   dessinatrice
dustman/garbageman   un éboueur
electrician   un électricien
estate/real estate agent   un agent

immobilier
furniture remover   **un déménageur**
gardener   **un jardinier**
gasman   **un employé du gaz**
guide   **un guide**
hairdresser   **un coiffeur, une coiffeuse**
insurance agent/broker   **un assureur**
interpreter   **un interprète**
lawyer   **un avocat**
librarian   **un/une bibliothécaire**
office worker   **un employé de bureau**
painter & decorator   **un peintre décorateur**
plumber   **un plombier**
postman   **un facteur**
priest   **un prêtre**
receptionist   **un/une réceptionniste**
servant   **un/une domestique, une bonne**
social worker   **un assistant/une assistante social**
solicitor   **un avocat, un notaire**
stockbroker   **un agent de change**
surveyor   **un géomètre, un expert**
tax inspector   **un percepteur**
trade-unionist   **un syndicaliste**
translator   **un traducteur, une traductrice**
travel agent   **un agent touristique**
typist   **un/une dactylo**
undertaker   **un entrepreneur de pompes funèbres**

Transport

airhostess   **une hôtesse de l'air**
busdriver   **un conducteur d'autobus**
driver   **un conducteur, une conductrice**
driving instructor   **un moniteur/une monitrice d'auto-école**
lorry-driver   **un camionneur, un routier**

pilot   **un pilote**
taxi-driver   **un chauffeur de taxi**
ticket inspector   **un contrôleur de billets**

14b Places of work

blast furnace   **le haut-fourneau**
branch office   **l'agence** *(f)* **succursale**
brewery   **la brasserie**
business park   **le complexe commercial**
construction site   **le chantier de construction**
distillery   **la distillerie**
factory   **l'usine** *(f)*, **la fabrique**
farm   **la ferme**
foundry   **la fonderie**
head office   **le siège social**
hospital   **l'hôpital** *(m)*
limited liability company   **la société à responsabilité limité**
mill   **l'usine** *(f)*
   paper mill   **l'usine** *(f)* **de papeterie, la papeterie**
   rolling mill   **la laminerie**
   sawmill   **la scierie**
   spinning mill   **la filature**
   steel mill   **l'aciérie** *(f)*
   weaving mill   **un tissage**
mine (coal)   **la mine (de charbon)**
office   **le bureau**
plant   **l'usine** *(f)*, **la fabrique**
shop/store   **le magasin**
steelworks/steel plant   **l'aciérie** *(f)*
sweatshop   **l'atelier** *(m)* (où on exploite les ouvriers)
theme park   **le parc d'attractions**
vineyard   **le vignoble**
warehouse   **l'entrepôt** *(m)*
workshop   **l'atelier** *(m)*

15c Letter-writing formulae

Dear   **Cher**
Dear Mr. and Mrs. ...   **Chers**

Monsieur et Madame ...
Dear Peter   **Cher Peter**
Dear Sir/Madam
   Monsieur/Madame
Madam   **Madame**
greetings from   **salutations de**
I am pleased   **je suis heureux**
   [-se]
I enclose   **je joins** *(joindre)*
all the best   **Meilleurs vœux**
best wishes from   **amitiés de la**
   part de
Love & kisses   **Bons baisers,**
   Grosses bises
Love from   **affectueusement**
With best wishes   **bien**
   amicalement
with kind regards   **meilleurs**
   souvenirs
Yours faithfully   **je vous prie**
   d'agréer mes salutations
   distinguées
Yours sincerely   **je vous prie**
   d'agréer l'expression de mes
   sentiments les meilleurs

15d Computer hardware

---

adaptor   **l'adaptateur** *(m)*
battery   **la pile**
battery pack   **le paquet de piles**
CD-ROM   **le CD-ROM**
CD-ROM drive   **le lecteur de**
   CD-ROM
central processing unit   **l'unité** *(f)*
   centrale
charger   **le chargeur**
chip   **la puce**
computer   **l'ordinateur** *(m)*
computer system   **le système**
   informatique
desk-top   **un PC de bureau**
disk drive   **le lecteur de disque**
diskette   **la disquette**
display   **l'affichage** *(m)*
double density (disk)   **la double**
   densité (d'un disque)

drive   **le lecteur**
electrical socket   **la prise**
   électrique
floppy disk   **la disquette**
floppy drive   **le lecteur de**
   disquette
front-end processor   **le processeur**
   frontal
function key   **la touche de**
   fonction
hard disc/disk   **le disque dur**
hard drive   **le lecteur de disque**
   dur
hardware   **le hardware, le matériel**
high density disc/disk   **la disquette**
   à haute densité
IBM clone   **le clone IBM**
IBM-compatible   **compatible avec**
   IBM
input device   **l'unité** *(f)*
   périphérique d'entrée
integrated circuit   **le circuit intégré**
interface   **l'interface** *(f)*
joystick   **la manette de jeu, le**
   joystick
keyboard   **le clavier**
lap-top   **l'ordinateur** *(m)* **portable**
liquid crystal display   **l'affichage**
   (m) **à cristaux liquides**
local area network (LAN)   **le réseau**
   local
main-frame computer   **l'ordinateur**
   (m) **central**
micro-processor   **le**
   microprocesseur
mini computer   **le mini-ordinateur**
modem   **le modem**
monitor (colour/color)   **le moniteur**
   en couleur
mouse   **la souris**
network   **le réseau,**
   l'interconnexion *(f)*
networked   **interconnecté**
on line   **en ligne**
personal computer/PC
   l'ordinateur *(m)* **individuel/PC**
plug-in drive   **le lecteur à fiche**

pocket book   **le PC de poche, un notebook**
port   **le port**
portable   **portable**
processor   **l'unité** *(f)* **centrale**
QWERTY/AZERTY keyboard   **le clavier QWERTY/AZERTY**
random access memory/RAM   **la mémoire vive/RAM**
resolution   **la résolution**
screen   **l'écran** *(m)*
scroll bar   **la barre de déplacement**
socket/port   **la prise/le port**
storage   **la mémoire**
terminal   **le terminal**
touch screen   **l'écran** *(m)* **tactile**
VDU   **la console de visualisation**
viewdata system   **le système de vidéographie interactive**
visual display unit   **la console de visualisation**
wide area network (WAN)   **le réseau régional**

15d Computer software

algebraic   **algébrique**
algorithm   **l'algorithme** *(m)*
antivirus program(me)   **le programme antivirus**
bug   **le défaut, l'erreur** *(f)*
byte   **l'octet** *(m)*
coded   **codé**
coding   **le codage**
command   **la commande**
compatibility   **la compatibilité**
compatible (in-)   **(in)compatible**
computer aided design (CAD)   **la conception assistée par ordinateur (CAO)**
computer aided learning (CAL)   **l'enseignement** *(m)* **assisté par ordinateur**
computer aided language learning (CALL)   **l'apprentissage** *(m)* **des langues assisté par**

ordinateur
computer language   **le langage de programmation**
copy   **la copie**
data capture   **la saisie des données**
data logging   **l'enregistrement** *(m)* **des données**
data   **les données** *(f)*
databank   **le stockage de données**
data processing   **le traitement des données**
database   **la base de données**
default option   **l'option** *(f)* **implicite**
double clicking   **le double clic**
escape   **(la touche d') échappement**
exit   **la touche de sortie**
file   **le fichier**
file management   **la gestion de fichiers**
flow chart   **l'organigramme** *(m)*
format   **le format**
function   **la fonction**
graphical application   **l'application** *(f)* **graphique**
graphics   **les représentations** *(f)* **graphiques**
graphical   **graphique**
graphics accelerator   **l'accélérateur** *(m)* **graphique**
help   **l'aide** *(f)*
help menu   **le menu d'aide**
language   **la langue**
logic circuit   **le circuit logique**
logic gate   **la porte logique**
macro   **macro**
memory   **la mémoire**
menu   **le menu**
operating system   **le système d'exploitation**
output   **la sortie**
output unit   **l'unité** *(f)* **de sortie**
package   **le progiciel**
peripherals   **les périphériques**
password   **le mot de passe**

program **le programme**
programmable **programmable**
programmer **le programmeur**
programming **la programmation**
pull-down menu **le menu qui défile vers le bas**
reference archive **l'archive** (f) **de référence**
return **(la touche) retour**
screensaver **le protecteur d'écran**
setup **la disposition**
storage **la mémoire**
software **le logiciel**
software package **le progiciel**
space **(la touche d')espacement**
spreadsheet **le tableur**
statistics package **le progiciel de statistiques**
user-friendly **facile à utiliser**
virus **le virus**

15d Computer printing

continuous (paper) **en continu**
daisy wheel **la marguerite**
dot matrix **la matrice**
font **la police de caractères**
hard copy **la copie sur papier**
ink cartridge **la cartouche d'encre**
inkjet **le jet d'encre**
laser printer **l'imprimante** (f) **laser**
low/high density **la basse/haute densité**
A4 paper **le papier format A4**
paper feed **le système d'alimentation de papier**
paper tray **le tiroir de papier**
printer **l'imprimante** (f)
  bubble printer **l'imprimante** (f) **à jet d'encre**
ribbon **le ruban**
roller **le rouleau**
sheet feeder **le chargeur de papier**
style **le style**
toner **le rouleau d'encre**

16a Hobbies

angling **la pêche (à la ligne)**
bee-keeping **l'apiculture** (f)
collecting antiques **faire la collection des antiquités**
archeology **l'archéologie** (f)
archery **le tir à l'arc**
ballroom dancing **la danse de salon**
birdwatching **l'ornithologie** (f)
carpentry **la menuiserie**
chess **les échecs** (m)
collecting stamps **faire la collection de timbres**
dancing **la danse**
fishing **la pêche**
gardening **le jardinage**
gambling **le jeu d'argent**
going to the cinema/movies **aller au cinéma**
listening to music **écouter de la musique**
knitting **le tricot**
photography **la photographie**
playing chess **jouer aux échecs**
reading **la lecture**
sewing **la couture**
spinning **le filage**
walking **la marche**
watching television **regarder la télévision**

16c Photography

automatic **automatique**
cable release **le déclencheur**
camera **l'appareil** (m)
camera case **l'étui** (m) **(à appareil photo)**
I develop **je développe**
developing/processing **la développement**
I enlarge **j'agrandis**
exposure **la pose**
exposure counter **le compte-poses**

film   la pellicule
   black and white   en noir et blanc
   colour/color   en couleurs
film winder   le levier d'avancement
filter   le filtre
fine grain   à grain fin
flash   le flash
flash attachment   la glissière du flash
home movie   le film d'amateur
I focus the camera   je fais la mise au point
in focus   net[te], au point
out of focus   flou, pas au point
jammed   bloqué
lens   l'objectif (m)
   telephoto lens   le téléobjectif
   wide-angle lens   le grand-angle
lens cap   le capuchon (d'objectif)
light   la lumière
   artificial   artificiel[le]
   daylight   du jour
light meter   la cellule photo-électrique
movie camera   la caméra
negative   le négatif
over-exposed   surexposé
over-exposure   la surexposition
picture   l'image (f)
photogenic   photogénique
photo(graph)   la photo(graphie)
   holiday/vacation photo   la photo de vacances
   passport photo   la photo d'identité
photograph album   l'album (m) de photos
roll of film   la bobine
shutter   l'obturateur (m)
slide   la diapo(sitive)
I take photos   je prends (prendre) des photos
video camera   la caméra vidéo
video cassette   la vidéocassette

17b Architectural features

alcove   l'alcôve (f), le renfoncement
arch   l'arche (f), la voûte
architrave   l'architrave (f)
atrium   l'atrium (m)
bas relief   le bas-relief
battlement   le créneau
buttress   le contrefort
capital   la capitale
colonnade   la colonnade
column   la colonne
   doric   dorique
   ionic   ionien[ne]
   corinthian   corinthien[ne]
concave   concave
convex   convexe
corner-stone   la pierre angulaire
cupola   la coupole
diptych   le diptyque
drawbridge   le pont-levis
eaves   l'avant-toit (m)
embrasure   l'embrasure (f)
façade   la façade
fanlight   la fenêtre en demi-lune
gable   le pignon
gargoyle   la gargouille
half-timbered   à poutres apparentes, à colombages
hanging buttress   l'arc-boutant (m)
haut-relief   le haut-relief
headstone   la clef de voûte
herringbone   à chevrons
molding   les moulures (f)
nave   le nef
ogive   l'ogive (f)
overhanging   en surplomb, en saillie
pagoda   la pagode
pilaster   le pilastre
pinnacle   le pinacle
plinth   la plinthe
porch   le porche
portico   le portique
rear arch   l'arc (m) intérieur
roof   le toit

rosette   **la rosette**
rotunda   **la rotonde**
sacristy   **la sacristie**
spire/steeple   **la flèche**
stained-glass window   **le vitrail, la verrière**
transept   **le transept**
triptych   **le triptyque**
triumphal arch   **l'arc** *(m)* **de triomphe**
vault   **la voûte**
vaulted   **voûté**
vitrail   **le vitrail**
volute   **la volute**
wainscot   **la boiserie, le lambris**

17d Musicians & instruments

accompanist   **un accompagnateur, une accompagnatrice**
accordionist   **l'accordéoniste** *(m)*
alto *(adj)*   **alto**
alto (singer)   **le contralto, (le haute-contre), l'alto** *(f)*
bagpipe   **la cornemuse**
baritone   **le baryton**
bass *(singer)*   **la basse**
bass clarinet   **la clarinette de basse**
bassoon   **le basson**
bassoonist   **le joueur de basson**
bells   **les clochettes**
bugle   **le cor de chasse**
busker   **le chanteur des rues**
castanets   **les castagnettes** *(f)*
cellist   **le/la violoncelliste**
cello   **le violoncelle**
clarinet   **la clarinette**
clarinettist   **le/la clarinettiste**
classical guitar   **la guitare classique**
clavicord   **le clavicorde**
contralto   **le contralto**
cornet   **le cornet à pistons**
counter-tenor   **le haute-contre**
cymbal   **les cymbales** *(f)*
double bass   **la contrebasse**

double bassoon   **le contrebasson**
drum   **la batterie**
electronic organ   **l'orgue** *(f)* **électronique**
euphonium   **la basse**
flautist   **le/la flûtiste**
flute   **la flûte**
French horn   **le cor**
grand piano   **le piano à queue**
guitar   **la guitare**
guitarist   **le/la guitariste**
harmonium   **l'harmonium** *(m)*
harp   **la harpe**
harpist   **le/la harpiste**
harpsichord   **le clavecin**
harpsichordist   **le/la claveciniste**
horn   **le cor anglais**
hurdy-gurdy   **l'orgue** *(m)* **de barbarie**
jews' harp   **la guimbarde**
librettist   **le librettiste**
lyre   **la lyre**
mandolin   **la mandoline**
mezzo-soprano   **mezzo-soprano**
mouth-organ   **le harmonica**
oboe player   **le joueur de hautbois**
oboe   **le hautbois**
orchestra leader   **le premier violon**
orchestra players   **les membres** *(m)* **de l'orchestre**
organ   **un orgue**
   church organ   **les grandes orgues** *(m)*
organist   **un/une organiste**
percussion   **les instruments** *(m)* **à percussion**
percussionist   **le percussioniste**
pianist   **le/la pianiste**
piano   **le piano**
pipe   **le flûtiau**
recorder   **la flûte**
saxophone   **le saxophone**
saxophonist   **le/la saxophoniste**
soprano   **le/la soprano**
squeeze-box   **l'accordéon** *(m)*
steel drum   **le tambour de fer**
string instruments   **les instruments**

(m) **à cordes**
synthesizer **le synthétiseur**
tenor **le ténor**
tin whistle **le flageolet**
triangle **le triangle**
trombone **le trombone**
trombonist **le joueur/la joueuse de trombone**
trumpet **la trompette**
tuba **le tuba**
viol **la viole**
viola player **l'altiste** *(m/f)*
viola **l'alto** *(m)*
violin **le violon**
violinist **le/la violoniste**
violoncello **le violoncelle**
vocalist **le chanteur**
Welsh harp **la harpe galloise**
wind instruments **les instruments à vent**
xylophone **le xylophone**

17d Musical forms

aria **l'aria** *(f)*
ballad **la ballade**
cantata **la cantate**
chamber music **la musique de chambre**
choral music **la musique**
concerto **le concerto**
  oboe concerto **le concerto pour hautbois**
duet **le duo**
fugue **la fugue**
madrigal **le madrigal**
music drama **le drame en musique**
musical (comedy) **la comédie musicale**
nocturne **le nocturne**
octet **l'octuor** *(m)*
opera **l'opéra** *(m)*
operetta **l'opérette** *(f)*
oratorio **l'oratorio** *(m)*
overture **l'ouverture** *(f)*
piano trio **le trio de pianos**

plainsong **le plain-chant**
prelude **le prélude**
quartet **le quartuor**
quintet **le quintette**
requiem Mass **la messe de requiem**
sacred music **la musique sacrée**
serenade **la sérénade**
sextet **le sextuor**
septet **le septuor**
sonata **la sonate**
song-cycle **le cycle de chansons**
suite **la suite**
symphony **la symphonie**
string quartet **le quartuor d'instruments à corde**
trio **le trio**

17d Musical terms

accompaniment **l'accompagnement** *(m)*
arpeggio **l'arpège** *(m)*
bar **la mesure**
beat **la mesure**
bow **l'archet** *(m)*
bowing **le coup d'archet**
cadence **la cadence**
chord **l'accord** *(m)*
clef **le ton**
  bass **basse**
  treble **soprano**
discord **la dissonance**
first violin **le premier violon**
flat (key) **bémol**
  B*b* major **Si bémol**
  flat *(out of tune)* **faux [-se]**
improvisation **l'improvisation** *(f)*
key **le ton**
  major/minor key **le ton majeur/mineur**
C minor **Do mineur**
mute **la sourdine**
note **la note**
  breve **la double rond**
  minim/half note **la blanche**
  crotchet/quarter note **la noire**

quaver/eighth note   **la croche**
semi-breve   **la ronde**
semiquaver/sixteenth note   **la double croche**
semitone   **le semiton**
principal (cello)   **le premier (violoncelle)**
rest   **la pause**
a minim rest   **la demi-pause**
scale   **la gamme**
score   **la partition, le morceau**
sharp *(key)*   **dièse** *(m)*
sharp *(out of tune)*   **aigu[ë]**
sheet (of music)   **la partition**

by ferry   **en ferry**
by helicopter   **en hélicoptère**
by hovercraft   **en aéroglisseur**
by hydrofoil   **en hydrofoil**
in a lorry   **dans un poids lourd**
by plane   **par avion**
by ship   **en bateau**
by taxi   **en taxi**
by tram   **en tramway**
by trolleybus   **en trolleybus**
in a truck   **dans un camion**
by jumbo jet   **en jumbo-jet, en gros-porteur**
by underground/subway   **en métro**

17e Film/Movie genres

adventure   **l'aventure** *(f)*
animation   **l'animation** *(f)*
black and white   **noir et blanc**
black comedy   **la comédie noire**
cartoons   **les dessins** *(m)* **animés**
comedy   **la comédie**
documentary   **le documentaire**
feature film   **le long métrage**
horror film/movie   **le film d'horreur**
low-budget   **à petit budget**
sci-fi   **de science-fiction**
short film/movie   **le court métrage**
silent cinema/movies   **le cinéma muet**
thriller   **le film à suspense**
video-clip   **le clip vidéo**
war film/movie   **le film de guerre**
western   **le western**
weepie   **le mélo**

19a Means of transport

by air   **par avion**
in an ambulance   **en ambulance**
by bicycle   **à vélo**
by bus   **en bus**
by cable-car   **en téléphérique**
by car   **en voiture**
by coach   **en car**
in a dinghy   **en canot**

19b Ships & boats

aircraft carrier   **le porte-avions**
canoe   **le canoë**
cargo boat   **le cargo**
dinghy   **le canot**
ferry   **le ferry**
hovercraft   **l'aéroglisseur** *(m)*
hydrofoil   **l'hydrofoil** *(m)*
life boat   **le canot de sauvetage**
merchant ship   **le bateau de marchandises**
ocean liner   **le paquebot**
petrol tank   **le réservoir d'essence**
rowing boat   **le canot**
sailing boat   **le voilier**
ship   **le bateau**
speed-boat   **le bateau à moteur**
submarine   **le sous-marin**
towboat   **le remorqueur**
warship   **le vaisseau de guerre**
yacht   **le yacht**

19c Parts of the car

accelerator   **l'accélérateur** *(m)*
alternator   **l'alternateur** *(m)*
automatic gear   **la boîte de vitesses automatiques**
back wheel   **la roue arrière**
battery   **la batterie**
bodywork   **la carrosserie**

bonnet/hood   **le capot**
boot/trunk   **le coffre**
brake   **le frein**
bumper   **les pare-chocs** *(m)*
carburettor   **le carburateur**
catalytic converter   **le pot**
   catalytique
choke   **le starter**
clutch   **l'embrayage** *(m)*
dashboard   **le tableau de bord**
door   **la portière**
   front door   **la portière avant**
   passenger door   **la portière du**
   passager
engine   **le moteur**
exhaust pipe   **le pot**
   d'échappement
engine   **le moteur**
front seats   **les sièges** *(m)* **avant**
front wheel   **la roue avant**
gearbox   **la boîte de vitesses**
headlights   **les phares** *(m)*
horn   **le klaxon**
hood   **la capote**
indicator   **le clignotant**
lights   **les feux** *(m)*
motor   **le moteur**
number/license plate   **la plaque**
   d'immatriculation
passenger seats   **les sièges** *(m)* **de**
   passagers
pedal   **la pédale**
   accelerator   **la pédale**
   d'accélérateur
   brake   **la pédale de frein**
   clutch   **la pédale d'embrayage**
   (m)
rear-view/rear mirror   **le**
   rétroviseur
registration number   **le numéro**
   d'immatriculation
roof   **le toit**
roof-rack   **la galerie**
safety belt   **la ceinture de**
   sécurité
spares   **les pièces** *(f)* **dét**
   achées

spare wheel   **la roue de**
secours
sparking-plug   **la bougie**
speedometer   **le compteur**
starter   **le démarreur**
steering wheel   **le volant**
tank   **le réservoir**
throttle valve   **l'accélérateur** *(m)*
tool   **l'outil** *(m)*
tool-box   **la boîte à outils**
tyre/tire   **le pneu**
   back tyre/tire   **le pneu arrière**
   front tyre/tire   **le pneu avant**
   spare tyre/tire   **le pneu de**
   rechange
tyre/tire pressure   **la pression des**
   pneus
warning triangle   **le triangle de**
   présignalisation
wheel   **la roue**
windscreen/windshield   **le pare-**
   brise
windscreen wiper/windshieldwiper
   un essuie-glace

19c Road signs

Cross now   **Traversez**
Danger!   **Attention danger!**
Diversion   **Déviation**
End of diversion   **Fin de déviation**
End of roadworks   **Fin des**
   travaux
End of motorway/expressway
   regulations   **Fin d'autoroute**
Free parking   **Stationnement**
   gratuit
Keep clear   **Interdit**
Maximum speed   **Vitesse**
   maximum
Motorway/Expressway entrance
   Entrée d'autoroute
Motorway/Expressway junction
   Sortie d'autoroute
No entry   **Entrée interdite**
No parking   **Stationnement**
   interdit

Pedestrians crossing **Passage pour piétons**
Residents only **Sauf riverains**
Road closed **Route barrée**
Roadworks **Travaux**
Stop **Stop**
Toll **Péage**

20a Tourist sights

abbey **l'abbaye** *(f)*
adventure playground **l'aire** *(f)* **de jeux**
amphitheatre/amphitheater **l'amphithéâtre** *(m)*
aquarium **l'aquarium** *(m)*
art gallery **la galerie d'art**
battle field **le champ de bataille**
battlements **les remparts** *(m)*, **les créneaux** *(m)*
boulevard **le boulevard**
castle **le château**
catacombs **les catacombes** *(f)*
cathedral **la cathédrale**
cave **la grotte**
cemetery **le cimetière**
city **la cité**
chapel **la chapelle**
church **l'église** *(f)*
concert hall **la salle de concert**
convent **le couvent**
exhibition **le quai**
folly **la folie**
fortress **le château fort**
fountain **la fontaine**
gardens **le jardin public**
harbour/harbor **le port**
library **la bibliothèque**
mansion **le manoir**
market **le marché**
monastery **le monastère**
monument **le monument**
museum **le musée**
opera **l'opéra** *(m)*
palace **le palais**
parliament building **le Parlement**
pier **le jetée**

planetarium **le planétarium**
ruins **les ruines** *(f)*
shopping area **le quartier commerçant**
square **la place**
stadium **le stade**
statue **la statue**
temple **le temple**
theatre/theater **le théâtre**
tomb **la tombe**
tower **la tour**
town centre/downtown **le centre-ville**
town hall **l'hôtel** *(m)* **de ville**
university **l'université** *(f)*
zoo **le jardin zoologique**

20a On the beach

bathing hut/cabana **la cabine**
beach **la plage**
beach ball **le ballon de plage**
bucket and spade/pail and shovel **le seau et la pelle**
deck-chair **la chaise longue**
I dive **je plonge**
diver **le plongeur, la plongeuse**
sand **le sable**
grain of sand **un grain de sable**
sandcastle **le château de sable**
sandy *(beach)* **de sable**
scuba diving **la plongée sous-marine**
sea **le mer**
sea shore **la grève**
snorkel **le tube respiratoire**
I snorkel **je nage avec un tube respiratoire**
sun-tan lotion **le lotion/lait solaire**
sunshade (umbrella) **le parasol**
I surf **je surfe, je pratique le surf**
surfboard **la planche de surf**
surfboarder **le surfeur, la surfeuse**
surfing **le surf**

I swim **je nage**
water-skiing **le ski nautique**
windsurfing/sailboarding **la planche à voile**
I go windsurfing **je fais de la planche à voile**

20a Continents & regions

Africa **l'Afrique** *(f)*
Antarctica **l'Antarctique** *(m)*
Arctic **l'Arctique** (m)
Asia **l'Asie** *(f)*
Australasia **l'Australasie** *(f)*
Balkans **les Balkans** *(m)*
Baltic States **les pays** *(m)* **baltes**
Central America **l'Amérique** *(f)* **centrale**
Eastern Europe **l'Europe** *(f)* **de l'est**
Europe **l'Europe** *(f)*
European Union **l'Union** *(f)* **européenne**
Far East **l'Extrême-Orient** *(m)*
Middle East **le Moyen-Orient**
North America **l'Amérique** *(f)* **du Nord**
Oceania **l'Océanie** *(f)*
Quebec **le Québec**
Scandinavia **la Scandinavie**
South America **l'Amérique** *(f)* **du Sud**
West Indies **les Antilles** *(f)*

20a Countries

Afghanistan **l'Afghanistan** *(m)*
Albania **l'Albanie** *(f)*
Argentina **l'Argentine** *(f)*
Austria **l'Autriche** *(f)*
Belgium **la Belgique**
Bolivia **la Bolivie**
Bosnia **la Bosnie**
Botswana **le Botswana**
Brazil **le Brésil**
Bulgaria **la Bulgarie**
Burudni **le Burundi**
Canada **le Canada**

China **la Chine**
Colombia **la Colombie**
Croatia **la Croatie**
Cuba **Cuba** *(f)*
Cyprus **Chypre** *(f)*
Czech Republic **la république Tchèque**
Denmark **le Danemark**
Ecuador **l'Équateur** *(m)*
Egypt **l'Égypte** *(f)*
England **l'Angleterre** *(f)*
Estonia **l'Estonie** *(f)*
Finland **la Finlande**
France **la France**
Germany **l'Allemagne** *(f)*
Great Britain **la Grande-Bretagne**
Greece **la Grèce**
Hungary **la Hongrie**
Iceland **l'Islande** *(f)*
India **l'Inde** *(f)*
Indonesia **l'Indonésie** *(f)*
Iran **l'Iran** *(m)*
Iraq **l'Iraq** *(m)*
Ireland **l'Irlande** *(f)*
Israel **Israël** *(m)*
Italy **l'Italie** *(f)*
Japan **le Japon**
Jordan **la Jordanie**
Kampuchea **le Kampuchéa**
Kenya **le Kenya**
Korea (North/South) **la Corée (du Nord/Sud)**
Kuwait **le Koweït**
Latvia **la Lettonie**
Lebanon **le Liban**
Libya **la Libye**
Lithuania **la Lituanie**
Luxembourg **le Luxembourg**
Malaysia **la Malaisie**
Mexico **le Mexique**
Mongolia **la Mongolie**
Morocco **le Maroc**
Netherlands **les Pays-Bas** *(m)*
New Zealand **la Nouvelle-Zélande**
Norway **la Norvège**
Pakistan **le Pakistan**
Palestine **la Palestine**

Peru **le Pérou**
Philippines **les Philippines** *(f)*
Poland **la Pologne**
Portugal **le Portugal**
Romania **la Roumanie**
Russia **la Russie**
Rwanda **le Rwanda**
Saudi Arabia **l'Arabie** *(f)* **Saoudite**
Scotland **l'Écosse** *(f)*
Serbia **la Serbie**
Slovakia **la Slovaquie**
Slovenia **la Slovénie**
South Africa **l'Afrique** *(f)* **du Sud**
former Soviet Union **l'ex-Union** *(f)*
   soviétique
Spain **l'Espagne** *(f)*
Sri Lanka **le Sri Lanka**
Sudan **le Soudan**
Sweden **la Suède**
Switzerland **la Suisse**
Syria **la Syrie**
Taiwan **Taiwan**
Tanzania **la Tanzanie**
Thailand **la Thaïlande**
Tibet **le Tibet**
Tunisia **la Tunisie**
Turkey **la Turquie**
Uganda **l'Ouganda** *(m)*
Ukraine **l'Ukraine**
United States **les États-Unis** *(m)*
Uruguay **l'Uruguay** *(m)*
Vietnam **le Vietnam**
Wales **le Pays de Galles**
former Yugoslavia **l'ex-**
   Yougoslavie *(f)*
Zaire **le Zaïre**
Zambia **la Zambie**
Zimbabwe **le Zimbabwe**

20a Oceans & seas

Adriatic Sea **l'Adriatique** *(f)*
Arctic Ocean **l'océan** *(m)* **Arctique**
Atlantic Ocean **l'Atlantique** *(m)*
Baltic Sea **la (mer) Baltique**
Bay of Biscay **le golfe de**
   Gascogne

English Channel **la Manche**
Gulf of Mexico **le golfe du**
   Mexique
Indian Ocean **l'océan** *(m)* **Indien**
Mediterranean Sea **la (mer)**
   Méditerranée
Pacific Ocean **le Pacifique**

21a Main language families

Afro-asiatic **afro-asiatique**
Altaic **altaïque**
Austronesian **austronésien[ne]**
Australian **australien[ne]**
Caucasian **caucasien[ne]**
Central and South **du Centre et**
   du Sud
Eskimo **esquimau**
Indo **indo-**
indoeuropean **indo-européen**
   Baltic **balte**
   Celtic **celte**
   Germanic **germanique**
   Hellenic **hellénique**
   Indo-iranian **indo-iranien**
   Italic **italique**
   Romance **roman**
   Slavic **slave**
independent **indépendant**
North American-Indian **indien**
   d'Amérique du Nord
Paleo-asiatic **paléo-asiatique**
Papuan **papou**
Sino-Tibetan **sino-tibétain**
Uralic **ouralien[ne]**

21a Languages

Afrikaans **l'afrikaans** *(m)*
Albanian **l'albanais** *(m)*
Arabic **l'arabe** *(m)*
Armenian **l'arménien** *(m)*
Basque **le basque**
Bengali **le bengali**
Breton **le breton**
Bulgarian **le bulgare**
Burmese **le birman**

Chinese   le chinois
Coptic   le copte
Czech   le tchèque
Danish   le danois
Dutch   le néerlandais
English   l'anglais *(m)*
Eskimo   l'esquimau *(m)*
Estonian   l'estonien *(m)*
Finnish   le finlandais
Flemish   le flamand
French   le français
German   l'allemand *(m)*
Greek   le grec
Gujarati   le goujarati
Hebrew   l'hébreu *(m)*
Hindi   le hindi
Hungarian   le hongrois
Icelandic   l'islandais *(m)*
Indonesian   l'indonésien *(m)*
Irish Gaelic   le gaélique irlandais
Italian   l'italien *(m)*
Japanese   le japonais
Korean   le coréen
Kurdish   le kurde
Latin   le latin
Mongolian   le mongolien
Norwegian   le norvégien
Persian   le perse
Polish   le polonais
Portuguese   le portugais
Punjabi   le panjabi
Rumanian   le roumain
Russian   le russe
Scottish Gaelic   le gaélique
   écossais
Slovak   le slovaque
Somali   le somali
Spanish   l'espagnol *(m)*
Swahili   le swahili
Swedish   le suèdois
Thai   le thaïlandais
Tamil   le tamoul
Tibetan   le tibétain
Turkish   le turc
Urdu   l'ourdou *(m)*
Vietnamese   le vietnamien
Welsh   le gallois

21a Nationalities*

Algerian   algérien[ne]
American   américain
American Indian   indien[ne]
   d'Amérique
Argentinian   argentin
Australian   australien[ne]
Austrian   autrichien[ne]
Belgian   belge
Brazilian   brésilien[ne]
Canadian   canadien[ne]
Egyptian   égyptien[ne]
French-Canadian   franco-
   canadien[ne]
Indian   indien[ne]
Iraqui   irakien[ne]
Iranian   iranien[ne]
Irish   irlandais
Israeli   israélien[ne]
Lebanese   libanais
Mexican   mexicain
Moroccan   marocain
New Zealander   néo-zélandais
Pakistani   pakistanais
Palestinian   palestinien[ne]
Saudi   saoudien[ne]
Scottish   écossais
South African   sud-africain
Swiss   suisse
   Swiss woman   une Suissesse
Syrian   syrien[ne]

21b Grammar

accusative   l'accusatif *(m)*
accusative *(adj)*   accusatif [-ve]
adjective   l'adjectif *(m)*
adverb   l'adverbe *(m)*
agreement   l'accord *(m)*
it agrees with   il s'accorde avec
article   l'article *(m)*
   definite   défini
   indefinite   indéfini
case   le cas
case ending   la terminaison du
   cas

* Other nationalities are as languages ➤App.21a above

clause **la proposition**
comparative **le comparatif**
conjunction **la conjonction**
dative **le datif**
definite **défini**
demonstrative **démonstratif**
direct object **l'objet** *(m)* **direct**
ending **la terminaison**
exception **l'exception** *(f)*
gender **le genre**
genitive **le génitif**
indefinite **indéfini**
indirect object **l'objet** *(m)* **indirect**
negative **négatif [-ve]**
nominative **nominatif [-ve]**
noun **le nom**
object **l'objet** *(m)*
phrase **la locution**
plural **le pluriel[le]**
  plural *(adj)* **au pluriel**
possessive **possessif [-ve]**
preposition **la préposition**
pronoun **le pronom**
  demonstrative **démonstratif**
  [-ve]
  indefinite **indéfini**
  interrogative **interrogatif [-ve]**
  personal **personnel[le]**
  relative **relatif [-ve]**
  subject **sujet**
reflexive **le réfléchi**
  reflexive *(adj)* **réfléchi**
rule **la règle**
sequence **la concordance**
singular **singulier [-ère]**
superlative **le superlatif**
  superlative *(adj)* **superlatif**
  [-ve]
word order **l'ordre** *(m)* **des mots**

Verbs

active voice **la voix active**
auxiliary **l'auxiliaire** *(m)*
compound **composé**
conditional **le conditionnel**
defective **défectif [-ve]**
formation **la formation**

future **le futur**
gerund **le nom verbal**
imperative **l'impératif** *(m)*
imperfect **l'imparfait** *(m)*
impersonal **impersonnel**
infinitive **l'infinitif** *(m)*
interrogative **l'interrogatif** *(m)*
intransitive **intransitif**
irregular **irrégulier [-ère]**
passive voice **la voix passive**
participle **le participe**
past **le passé**
  past *(adj)* **passé**
perfect **le parfait**
present **le présent**
reflexive **le réfléchi**
  reflexive *(adj)* **réfléchi**
regular **régulier [ère]**
sequence **la concordance**
simple **simple**
strong **fort**
subjunctive **le subjonctif**
system **le système**
tense **le temps**
transitive **transitif [-ve]**
use **l'emploi** *(m)*
verb **le verbe**
weak **faible**

21b Punctuation

apostrophe **l'apostrophe** *(f)*
asterisk **l'astérisque** *(m)*
bracket **la parenthèse**
colon **deux points**
comma **la virgule**
dash **le tiret**
exclamation mark **le point
  d'exclamation**
full stop/period **le point**
inverted commas **les guillemets**
  (m)
parentheses (in) **(entre)
  parenthèses** *(f)*
question mark **le point
  d'interrogation**
semicolon **le point virgule**

22b Stationery

adhesive tape   **le ruban adhésif**
board-rubber/eraser   **la brosse**
carbon paper   **le papier carbone**
card index   **le fichier**
chalk   **la craie**
clip board   **le porte-bloc à pince**
compasses, pair of   **le compas**
correction fluid   **le liquide
  correcteur**
diary/datebook   **l'agenda** *(m)*
drawing pin   **la punaise**
envelope   **l'enveloppe** *(f)*
exercise book   **le cahier
  d'exercices**
felt-tip   **le feutre**
file   **le dossier**
filing cabinet   **le classeur**
fountain pen   **le stylo (à encre)**
glue   **la colle**
guillotine   **le massicot**
highlighter   **le surligneur**
hole punch   **la perforeuse**
ink   **l'encre** *(f)*
ink refill   **la cartouche d'encre**
in-tray/out-tray   **le corbeille
  arrivée/départ**
label   **l'étiquette** *(f)*
marker   **le marqueur**
note book   **le calepin**
OHP   **le rétroprojecteur**
paper   **le papier**
paper clip   **le trombone**
paper knife   **le coupe-papier**
pen   **le stylo**
pencil   **le stylo à bille**
photocopier   **la photocopieuse**
pocket calculator   **la calculette, la
  calculatrice**
protractor   **le rapporteur**
ring binder   **le classeur à anneaux**
rubber band/elastic band   **un
  élastique**
rubber/eraser   **la gomme**
ruler   **la règle**
scalpel   **le scalpel**

scissors   **les ciseaux** *(m)*
screen   **l'écran** *(m)*
set square   **l'équerre** *(f)*
sheet of paper   **la feuille de papier**
shredder   **la déchiqueteuse**
stamp   **le timbre**
stapler   **l'agrafe** *(f)*
staple remover   **l'otagraf®** *(m)*
stationery   **la papeterie**
text-book   **le livre scolaire**
typewriter   **la machine à écrire**
typewriter ribbon   **le ruban de la
  machine à écrire**
transparency (for OHP)   **le
  transparent**
waste-paper basket   **la corbeille à
  papiers**
whiteboard   **le tableau blanc**

23a Scientific disciplines

applied sciences   **les sciences** *(f)*
  appliquées
anthropology   **l'anthropologie** *(f)*
astronomy   **l'astronomie** *(f)*
astrophysics   **l'astrophysique** *(f)*
biochemistry   **la biochimie**
biology   **la biologie**
botany   **la botanique**
chemistry   **la chimie**
geology   **la géologie**
medicine   **la médecine**
microbiology   **la microbiologie**
physics   **la physique**
physiology   **la physiologie**
psychology   **la psychologie**
social sciences   **les sciences** *(f)*
  humaines
technology   **la technologie**
zoology   **la zoologie**

23b Chemical elements

aluminium/aluminum   **l'aluminium
  *(m)***
arsenic   **l'arsenic** *(m)*
calcium   **le calcium**

carbon   **le carbone**
chlorine   **le chlore**
copper   **le cuivre**
gold   **l'or** *(m)*
hydrogen   **l'hydrogène** *(m)*
iodine   **l'iode** *(m)*
iron   **le fer**
lead   **le plomb**
magnesium   **le magnésium**
mercury   **le mercure**
nitrogen   **l'azote** *(m)*
oxygen   **l'oxygène** *(m)*
phosphorus   **le phosphore**
platinum   **le platine**
plutonium   **le plutonium**
potassium   **le potassium**
silver   **l'argent** *(m)*
sodium   **le sodium**
sulphur   **le soufre**
uranium   **l'uranium** *(m)*
zinc   **le zinc**

23b Compounds and alloys

acetic acid   **l'acide** *(m)* **acétique**
alloy   **l'alliage** *(m)*
ammonia   **l'ammoniac** *(m)*,
  l'ammoniaque *(f)*
asbestos   **l'amiante** *(f)*
brass   **le cuivre**
carbon dioxide   **le gaz carbonique**
carbon monoxide   **l'oxyde** *(m)* **de
  carbone**
copper oxide   **l'oxyde** *(m)* **de
  cuivre**
hydrochloric acid   **l'acide** *(m)*
  chlorhydrique
iron oxide   **l'oxyde** *(m)* **de fer**
lead oxide   **l'oxyde** *(m)* **de plomb**
nickel   **le nickel**
nitric acid   **l'acide** *(m)* **nitrique**
it oxidizes   **il s'oxyde**
ozone   **l'ozone** *(m)*
propane   **le propane**
silver nitrate   **le nitrate d'argent**
sodium bicarbonate   **le
  bicarbonate de soude**

sodium carbonate   **le carbonate de
  sodium**
sodium chloride   **le chlorure de
  sodium**
sulphuric acid   **l'acide** *(m)*
  sulfurique
tin   **l'étain** *(m)*

23c The Zodiac

Aries   **Bélier**
Taurus   **Taureau**
Gemini   **Gémeaux**
Cancer   **Cancer**
Leo   **Lion**
Virgo   **Vierge**
Libra   **Balance**
Scorpio   **Scorpion**
Sagittarius   **Sagittaire**
Capricorn   **Capricorne**
Aquarius   **Verseau**
Pisces   **Poisson**
Zodiac   **le zodiaque**

23c Planets and stars

Earth   **le Terre**
Venus   **Vénus** *(f)*
Mercury   **Mercure** *(f)*
Pluto   **Pluton** *(m)*
Mars   **Mars** *(f)*
Jupiter   **Jupiter** *(m)*
Saturn   **Saturne** *(f)*
Uranus   **Uranus** *(f)*
Neptune   **Neptune** *(m)*
Pole star   **l'étoile** *(f)* **polaire**
Halley's comet   **la comète de
  Halley**
Southern cross   **la croix du Sud**
Great Bear   **la grande Ourse**

24b Wild animals

baboon   **le babouin**
badger   **le blaireau**
bear   **l'ours** *(m)*

beaver   le castor
bison/buffalo   le bison
camel   le chameau
cheetah   le guépard
chimpanzee   le chimpanzé
cougar   le couguar
coyote   le coyote
deer   le cerf *(invar)*, le chevreuil
elephant   l'éléphant *(m)*
elk   l'élan *(m)*
fox   le renard
frog   la grenouille
giraffe   la girafe
gorilla   le gorille
grizzly bear   le grizzly, le grizeli
hedgehog   le hérisson
hippopotamus   l'hippopotame *(m)*
hyena   l'hyène *(f)*
jaguar   le jaguar
lion   le lion
lynx   le lynx
mink   le vison
mole   la taupe
mongoose   le mangouste
monkey   le singe
moose   l'élan *(m)*
mouse   la souris
otter   la loutre
panther   la panthère
polar bear   l'ours *(m)* polaire
puma   le puma
rat   le rat
reindeer   le renne
rhinoceros   le rhinocéros
squirrel   l'écureuil *(m)*
tiger   le tigre
vole   le campagnol
whale   la baleine
wolf   le loup
zebra   le zèbre

24b Birds

albatross   l'albatros *(m)*
blackbird   le merle
bluetit   la mésange bleue
budgerigar   la perruche

buzzard   la buse
chaffinch   le pinson
crow   la corneille, le corbeau
dove   la colombe
eagle   l'aigle *(m)*
   golden eagle   l'aigle *(m)* royal
emu   l'émeu *(m)*
hawk/falcon   le faucon
heron   le héron
hummingbird   l'oiseau-mouche
   (m), le colibri
kingfisher   le martin-pêcheur
magpie   la pie
ostrich   l'autruche *(f)*
owl   le hibou, la chouette
parrot   le perroquet
peacock/hen   le paon, la paonne
pelican   le pélican
penguin   le pingouin
pigeon   le pigeon
puffin   le macareux
robin   le rouge-gorge
seagull   la mouette
sparrow   le moineau
starling   l'étourneau *(m)*, le
   sansonnet
swallow   l'hirondelle *(m)*
swan   le cygne
swift   le martinet
thrush   la grive
woodpecker   le pic
wren   le roitelet

24b Parts of the animal body

beak   le bec
claw   la griffe
comb   la crête
feather   la plume
fin   la nageoire
fleece   la toison
fur   la fourrure
gills   les ouïes
hide   la peau
hoof   le sabot
mane   la crinière
paw   la patte

pelt **la peau**
scale **l'écaille** *(f)*
shell *(oyster, snail)* **la coquille**
  (tortoise, crab) **la carapace**
tail **la queue**
trunk **la trompe**
tusk **la défense**
udder **le pis, la mamelle**
wing **l'aile** *(f)*

24c Trees

apple tree **le pommier**
ash **le frêne**
beech **le hêtre**
cherry tree **le cerisier**
chestnut **le marronnier**
cypress **le cyprès**
eucalyptus **l'eucalyptus** *(m)*
fig tree **le figuier**
fir tree **le sapin**
fruit tree **l'arbre** *(m)* **fruitier**
holly **le houx**
maple **l'érable** *(m)*
oak **le chêne**
olive tree **l'olivier** *(m)*
palm **le palmier**
peach tree **le pêcher**
pear tree **le poirier**
pine **le pin**
plum tree **le prunier**
poplar **le peuplier**
redwood **le séquoia**
rhododendron **le rhododendron**
walnut tree **le noyer**
willow **le saule**
yew **l'if** *(m)*

24c Flowers & weeds

azalia **l'azalée** *(f)*
carnation **l'œillet** *(m)*
chrysanthemum **le chrysanthème**
clover **le trèfle**
crocus **le crocus**
daffodil **la jonquille**
dahlia **le dahlia**

daisy **la pâquerette**
dandelion **le pissenlit**
foxglove **la digitale**
geranium **le géranium**
hydrangea **l'hortensia** *(m)*
lily **le lys/lis**
nettle (stinging) **l'ortie** *(f)*
orchid **l'orchidée** *(f)*
pansy **la pensée**
poppy **le coquelicot**
primrose **la primevère**
rose **la rose**
snowdrop **le perce-neige** *(inv)*
sunflower **le tournesol**
thistle **le chardon**
tulip **la tulipe**
violet **la violette**

25a Political institutions

assembly **l'assemblée** *(f)*
association **l'association** *(f)*
cabinet **le conseil des ministres**
  shadow cabinet *(UK)* **le**
  cabinet fantôme
committee **la commission, le**
  comité
confederation **la confédération**
congress **le congrès**
council **le conseil**
federation **la fédération**
House of Representatives **la**
  Chambre des Députés,
  l'Assemblée *(f)* **nationale**
local authority **la municipalité**
Lower House/Lower Chamber **la**
  Chambre des Députés
parliament **le parlement**
party **le parti**
Senate **le Sénat**
town council **la municipalité, le**
  Conseil municipal
town hall **la mairie**
Upper House **la Chambre haute**

25a Representatives & politicians

Chancellor **le Chancelier**
congressman/woman **le député**
elected representative **l'élu** *(m)*
Foreign Minister/Secretary of State
  le Ministre des Affaires Étrangères
head of state **le chef d'État**
Home Secretary/Minister of the
  Interior **le ministre de l'Intérieur**
leader **le chef, le leader**
leader of the party/party leader **le chef du parti**
mayor **le maire**
Minister/Secretary of **le ministre**
  Arts/Culture **de la Culture**
  Defence/Defense **de la Défense**
  Education **de l'Éducation nationale**
  Employment/Labor **du Travail et de l'Emploi**
  Health **de la Santé**
  Trade/Commerce **du Commerce**
  Transport/Transportation **des Transports**
politician **l'homme** *(m)* **politique**
Prefect (Chief Executive of a
  département) **le Préfet**
President **le Président**
Prime Minister **le Premier Ministre**
representative **le député**
senator **le sénateur**
Speaker (UK) **le Président/la Présidente des communes**

27b Military ranks

admiral **l'amiral** *(m)*
airman first class (US)

marshal **le géneral de corps aérien**
brigadier **le général de brigade**
captain **le capitaine**
commodore **le contre-amiral**
corporal **le caporal-chef**
fieldmarshal **le maréchal (de France)**
general **le général**
lieutenant **le lieutenant**
major **le major**
private **le soldat (de deuxième classe), le simple sodat**
Private Smith **soldat Smith**
rear-admiral **le contre-amiral**
sergeant **le sergent**
sergeant-major **l'adjudant** *(m)*
sergeant-major *(US)* **l'adjudant-chef** *(m)*

27c International organizations

Council of Europe **le Conseil de l'Europe**
Council of Ministers **le Conseil des Ministres**
EC/European Community **la Communauté Européenne /CE**
EU/European Union **l'Union** *(f)* **Européenne/UE**
NATO/North Atlantic Treaty
  Organization **l'Organisation** *(f)* **du Traité de l'Atlantique Nord/OTAN**
OPEC/Organization of Oil Exporting
  Countries **l'Organisation** *(f)* **des Pays Exportateurs de Pétrole/OPEP**
Security Council **le Conseil de Sécurité**
UNO/United Nations Organization
  l'Organisation *(f)* **des Nations Unies /ONU**
WHO/World Health Organization
  l'Organisation *(f)* **mondiale de la Santé/OMS**
World Bank **la Banque mondiale**

D
SUBJECT INDEX

Subject index

Numbers refer to Vocabularies